REPAIRING
AMERICA

·

For Fred,
from one kindred spirit
to another,

Peace!

William Holt

april 8, 1996
Santa Barbara

REPAIRING AMERICA

AMERICA

AN ACCOUNT OF THE MOVEMENT
FOR JAPANESE-AMERICAN REDRESS

WILLIAM MINORU HOHRI

•

Foreword by John Toland

Washington State University Press
Pullman, Washington
1988

Washington State University Press, Pullman, Washington 99164-5910

92 91 90 89 88 10 9 8 7 6 5 4 3 2

Library of Congress Cataloging-in-Publication Data

Hohri, William Minoru, 1927—
        Repairing America : an account of the movement for Japanese-American redress / William Minoru
Hohri : foreword by John Toland.
            p.   cm.
        Bibliography: p.
        Includes index.
        ISBN 0-87422-033-5 (alk. paper) : $25.00. ISBN 0-87422-034-3
(pbk. alk. paper) : $15.00
        1. Japanese Americans—Evacuation and relocation. 1942-1945. 2. Japanese Americans—Civil
rights.   3. World War, 1939-1945—Claims.   4. World War, 1939-1945—Reparations.   I. Title.
D769.8.A6H64 1987
940.53' 14—dc19   88-169
                                                                                                                    CIP

ISBN 0-87422-033-5 (hardcover)
        0-87422-034-3 (paperback)

This book is printed on pH neutral, acid-free paper.

To: Michi Weglyn,
Aiko Yoshinaga-Herzig,
and Ellen Godbey Carson

CONTENTS

FOREWORD

This detailed account of the movement for Japanese-American redress is an invaluable source for anyone interested in one of the most shameful chapters in American history. A few days after Pearl Harbor, Pearl Buck wrote Eleanor Roosevelt that there was "in all the Oriental peoples a very deep sense that the white man generally is, or may be, their common enemy, and that in the final analysis it remains always a possibility that the point may come when these peoples, even such present enemies as the Chinese and Japanese, may unite as colored against white."

She warned that an underground colored solidarity was growing in the world. "We white people are for the most part ignorant or oblivious to the fact that there may develop out of all this struggle an entirely new alignment of peoples according to race and color, but the Asiatic peoples never forget the possibility, and all that they do will be done with the reservations necessary for the new alignment."

A week before the Battle of Midway Mrs. Buck voiced her concern publicly. "This Second World War has taken on a new and dangerous aspect most of all because of Japan." The main barrier between East and West, she said, was that "the white man is not willing to give up his superiority and the colored man is no longer willing to endure his inferiority. . . . The white man is still thinking in terms of colonies and colonial government. . . . The man of Asia today is not a colonial and he has made up his mind he will never be a colonial again. . . . In short if the white man does not now save himself by discovering that all men are really born free and equal, he may not be able to save himself at all. For the colored man is going to insist on that human equality and that freedom."

Unfortunately Mrs. Buck's prophetic warnings had little effect on Washington. No efforts were made to counter charges of American color prejudice by Asians. On the contrary, the government was lending weight to these charges by grossly mistreating American citizens of Japanese ancestry. Immediately after Pearl Harbor fear overran the West Coast, and demands followed that all Japanese-Americans, citizens as well as aliens, be evacuated to the interior.

Roosevelt, being a consummate politician, heeded the rising anti-Japanese sentiment. Against the advice of J. Edgar Hoover, who declared he had found not a single instance of Japanese-American disloyalty, the President ordered the War Department to implement a mass Japanese-American evacuation. The Supreme Court upheld the legality of the act. And almost all Americans heartily approved.

A similar plan to relocate German and Italian aliens aroused such widespread protest that the government canceled it, explaining that it would affect the nation's economic structure and lower morale among citizens of those nationalities. But there was no one to speak for the Nisei, who were citizens but usually referred to as "Aliens"—their skin was a different color. Some 125,000 loyal Americans, whose sole crime was their ancestry, were cruelly uprooted from their homes, which they were forced to sell for a pittance. They were interned—men, women and children—in "relocation centers" which were little better than concentration camps. Many were even deprived of their life savings and property.

Why such hysteria? The answer is simple—racism. Yet while these extreme actions are perhaps understandable under the pressure of war, the postwar attitude of our government is impossible to equate with democracy. William Hohri relates in full the long, difficult and contentious trail of redress from the first Lowry Redress Bill to the heroic efforts of the National Council for Japanese American Redress to bring justice at last to the 125,000 victims of racism. After studying the Hearings of the Commission on Wartime Relocation and Internment of Civilians held in Washington, Los Angeles, San Francisco, Seattle, Chicago and New York one could only conclude that the harrowing testimony of the Japanese victims was overwhelming, since the rebuttal of the opposition was slim and specious.

And so when the lawsuit was filed on March 16, 1983, victory seemed apparent. The government, of course, filed its motion to dismiss. This was opposed by NCJAR, and on September 30, 1983, oral arguments were held before Judge Louis Oberdorfer of the U.S. District Court for the District of Columbia. The two sides submitted memoranda. To the amazement of objective observers who had been following the case of redress for years, Judge Oberdorfer dismissed the motion *even while admitting that the victims had not been adequately compensated.*

Justice was not done, and the racism of 1941 was still with us. During the presidential campaign of 1984 all but one of the Democratic candidates for President supported the "bashing" of the Japanese, rather than looking to faults at home for America's economic decline. And in the 1986 senatorial campaign in Connecticut, the Republican candidate—emulating General DeWitt's classic remark, "A Jap's a Jap!" declared publicly, "I fought against them in World War II. I don't trust them. They lie. They cheat. They steal."

No, racism is by no means dead. It still lies just below the surface, and all those who love democracy must honor the continuing efforts of the National Council for Japanese American Redress.

John Toland
Danbury, Connecticut
December 10, 1986

PREFACE

I've done what seem like a hundred speeches, interviews, newsletters, articles, panels, and conversations on the topic of Japanese-American redress with the inevitable limitation of time or word count, never able to say it all. Hence, this book. But the limitation of time remains. This time I gave myself one year to put it all down. A year would seem sufficient to search, sift, write and rewrite. But for me it was only enough to produce an account, not a comprehensive history. I have written this account as memoir as well as history, with my self and my biases displayed. I am a Japanese-American, one of the 125,000 victims, a Christian with Taoist leanings, a participant in the civil rights and peace movements of the 1940s through the 1960s and a leader of one element of the redress movement, in short, a person who feels strongly about the issues and events described. Much of my life since 1979 has been given to the movement, so the memoir merges with the history.

History is both current and past. It is both made and reconstructed. Sometimes past history is reconstructed as current history is made. Just as the civil rights movement, in creating history, led to a reexamination of past, especially black, history, the redress movement, in its effort to find its direction and to define its reasons for its existence, has uncovered new facts about the wartime events of the mass exclusion and detention of Japanese-Americans. The culpability of leaders of government, including President Roosevelt, came into focus as we searched the archives for evidence and discussed our findings. I learned much more about the important role of resistance by Japanese-Americans, as well as the collaborative role of leaders of the Japanese American Citizens League.

But I have not attempted to write a comprehensive history of the redress movement itself. This would have entailed research beyond my financial and temperamental reach. I have not examined the files of the Japanese American Citizens League and interviewed leaders of the National Coalition for Redress/Reparations. Nor have I investigated the origins of the Washington Area Coalition on Redress. I decided there was material enough in the experiences of the National Council for Japanese American Redress for an account worthy of your reading.

In writing, I had to make decisions about terms. We Japanese-Americans continue to suffer from the deliberately misleading terminology inflicted on us and the general public by the United States, despite the unrelenting efforts by Raymond Okamura to correct us. We continue to use the official terms of "evacuation," "evacuee," and "relocation center," which were designed to obscure the reality of mass exclusion and detention. I reject these euphemisms. I also decline to use "concentration camp" as the exclusive alternative to "relocation center." I think "detention camp," "prison camp," and "concentration camp" are equally descriptive. I use "internment camp" to distinguish the camps established by the Department of Justice from those operated by the War Relocation Authority.

PREFACE

I suspect I may encounter some resistance in my reversion to the use of "Japanese-American," with its hyphen, instead of the hyphenless and largely accepted "Japanese American." While the two may function as grammatical equivalents—until one applies an adjective or attempts an adjectival use—I reject the unhyphenated form because it was deliberately designed to designate American citizens of Japanese ancestry and to exclude permanent resident aliens of Japanese ancestry. At its first convention in 1930, the Japanese American Citizens League removed the hyphen from its name to emphasize the American citizenship of its members.[1] I use the hyphenated version because I wish to designate both U.S. citizens and permanent residents of Japanese ancestry. Nor do I believe there is anything more demeaning about being a "hyphenated American" than being an Italian-American or Polish-American.

I also decided against the use of "Nikkei," a Japanese term which denotes persons of Japanese ancestry who are not citizens of Japan. "Nikkei" is not specific enough. It applies equally to Canadians, Germans, or Americans of Japanese ancestry. But I do use the terms "Issei," "Nisei," and "Sansei" even though these too are generic; they are now firmly embedded in Japanese-American language to designate the first, second, and third generation Japanese-Americans of our time. (One wonders whether these terms will persist beyond this century and be applied by the current wave of immigrants from Japan and their offspring. In America and Canada, the Japanese expression "Shin-Ijusha"—recent arrivals—is being used.)

But even as I claim this account to be my account, I am obliged to thank Jeremy Mott for his painstaking efforts in correcting an embarrassingly large number of my stylistic and grammatical flaws. His evenhandedness and objectivity mitigated the wounding of my ego. I am also indebted beyond words and repayment to Aiko and Jack Herzig for providing the primary documents that gave me substantially new insights into the history of the wartime events surrounding our exclusion and detention. I thank Ellen Godbey Carson for her patience in her repeated explanations of legal logic and constitutional intricacies. And I must thank Michi Weglyn, who served as my mentor and prodded me into writing this account. Despite all this fine assistance, if I err, the errors are mine and mine alone.

I also wish to thank for their criticism and support in this endeavor Frank Abe, Sohei Hohri, Sylvia Hohri, Yuriko Hohri, Yae Imon, Teru Kanazawa, Nelson Kitsuse, Takako Kusunoki, Phil Nash, Chiyoko Omachi, Chizuko Omori, and James Omura. Writing was half the battle. I am especially grateful to Frank Chin, Stephen Sumida and Richard Drinnon for convincing Washington State University Press to publish this work. I also thank the editor in chief of the Press, Fred Bohm, for his support, designer Sharon White, and editor Jill Whelchel for putting it all together.

William Minoru Hohri
Chicago, Illinois
1988

1. SITUATIONS
SENATE CAUCUS ROOM

Madame Chairperson and Members of the Commission:

I am William Hohri of Chicago, Illinois, Chairperson of the National Council for Japanese American Redress. I was interned at the age of fifteen. My family and I were incarcerated at Manzanar, California during the period from April 3, 1942 to August 25, 1945.[1]

In the Senate Caucus Room, the Commission on Wartime Relocation and Internment of Civilians is holding hearings in the blaze of television lights, with vidicons on their tripods arrayed along the side and still photographers squatting to avoid their line of electronic vision. The commissioners, distinguished persons all, sit a distance away behind a long green-covered table, while we witnesses sit as a group facing them behind a smaller table.

NCJAR was founded in May, 1979 for the sole purpose of obtaining monetary redress for Japanese American victims of World War II concentration camps. We seek compensation for injuries and damages suffered by the evacuees, the detainees, and the internees, or their heirs. We want reparations for the deprivation of our civil and constitutional rights; for wrongful evacuation, detention, and imprisonment and the suspension of due process; for our loss of income, property, and education; for the degradation of internment and evacuation and for the psychological, social, and cultural damage inflicted by our government.

I read my testimony into the microphone, aware of many cameras clacking and whirring, knowing that now, of that bank of vidicons, only Asahi's of Japan remains, since we are the "unimportant" witnesses of the hearings' second day. We are the victims. Network news teams worked overtime on the first day when the "important" persons, members of Congress, former government officials, white folks, testified. What could the victims possibly say that would be newsworthy? To white America we were just another minority, a minor minority, and a little slow in getting around to demanding, no, politely requesting, redress for wrongs committed against our minor selves.

In the 96th Congress, NCJAR sought enactment of legislation to provide such redress. We supported H.R.5977 sponsored by Representative Mike Lowry of Washington State and co-sponsored by twenty other members of the House of Representatives. Instead of redress legislation this Commission was established in what, in my judgment, was an act of political expediency. We believed that the further study of this matter would serve only to delay justice long overdue, justice already denied through delay to most of our parents who have died. We were opposed to the creation of this Commission because we were offended by the idea of victims of the internment having to testify in public to describe their ordeal. It seemed to us that such a procedure would impose a further humiliation—publicly forcing us to relive a cruel degradation, an exhibition which would be upsetting and distasteful. We have been exploited enough.

I am immersed in reading my statement. I do glance up occasionally at Joan Bernstein, the Commission's chairperson. She is its only woman. She had served as General Counsel to the Department of Health and Human Services. I guess that she was elected its leader in the gush of affirmative action, although apparently her main concern is to keep the hearings on schedule rather than to ask a leader's questions. On both days, members of Congress, who exercised their prerogative to speak without advance notice, ruined the schedule. After all, it is their Commission—like a kid's own football.

It is inconceivable that any other group of Americans could have had their civil and constitutional rights so massively abused by being placed under armed guard and behind barbed wire without due process. It is inconceivable that any other group of Americans, during such an ordeal, would have volunteered for military combat and engaged in legendary acts of sacrifice and heroism to prove their worth and our worth as citizens. I do not in any way denigrate the exploits of the Hawaiian 100th or the 442nd Regimental Combat Team. They had a point to prove and they did it bravely and with honor. But frankly, it is not appropriate to make continued references to their bravery as though it were necessary for our being accepted as full citizens. We are all citizens by reason of birth and by law, not by the blood sacrificed by our brothers on the battlefield.

I am aware of the full panel of commissioners. Judge William Marutani is the only Japanese-American. He looks judicially dispassionate but somehow quizzical. He is the man representing the Japanese American Citizens League. He was a member of the JACL's National Committee for Redress and writes a regular column in the weekly JACL newspaper, the *Pacific Citizen*. In his own mind, I'm sure, he believes he is judicially and judiciously disinterested. Edward Brooke, former U.S. Senator, is the only black commissioner. Father Ishmael Gromoff is the only Aleut, representing the Alaskan Native Americans from the Pribilof Islands. About 900 Aleuts were evacuated when the Japanese invaded the Aleutians, and were placed in dreadful camps on the mainland. They join their case to ours. Its inclusion allows self-conscious Japanese-Americans to say, "See! We're not just for ourselves." Representative Daniel Lungren is the only current member of Congress among the commissioners. He is a young Republican conservative. Father Robert Drinan, the lone Jesuit priest, is absent that day. He is the newly-elected president of the Americans for Democratic Action, and was a well-known member of Congress until the Pope told him to retire. His absence is disappointing. We lobbied hard for his appointment to the Commission. Former Supreme Court Justice Arthur Goldberg is the only former Supreme Court Justice among the commissioners. He is grandfatherly, voluble, freely dispensing his opinions. Hugh B. Mitchell, another former U.S. Senator, is one of two commissioners who were active in civilian government during World War II. At that time, he was on the staff of the Senator from Washington, Monrad C. Wallgren, a remarkably bigoted, anti-Japanese racist. Finally, Arthur Flemming, the other commissioner who was active in the wartime government, is the only current high level bureaucrat; he chairs the U.S. Civil Rights Commission.

The formation of this Commission was seen as merely another token, a mechanism for an official apology or for providing educational benefits. As such, it was an affront to our dignity as citizens; an affront to the terms of our freedom as spelled out in the Constitution; an affront to our great tradition of equal justice before the law. For these reasons, we were skeptical, perhaps cynical, of a Commission which is mandated to study the subject and make recommendations. The Commission in its defeat of the Lowry Redress Bill, became the answer to our legislative demand for redress.

The commissioners feel the bite of my testimony. Later, in the question period, Senator Brooke is defensive. Justice Goldberg said that he was skeptical when invited to serve as a commissioner. But now he wants me to agree with him that the Commission does have a good purpose. I have already stated my willingness to cooperate. I have been advised to present the commissioners with positive alternatives to an apology or a scholarship program.

So now, the National Council for Japanese American Redress is undertaking to institute legal proceedings to obtain redress. While we know that substantial obstacles lie in our way, we also believe that the full record of the federal government's action has not been disclosed to a court of law.

I realize that whatever the reasons which led to its creation, the Commission now has its own agenda. You are capable of making your own observations, doing your own study, and arriving at independent conclusions. We are here today to submit some proposals for your consideration. Here are three of them:

1. As you travel and listen to our Japanese American communities, please encourage testimony from the dissidents from the internment period, both Japanese and non-Japanese. Listen to the people who fought the government and its injustices, and were crushed.

Actually, it wasn't to be quite as simple as asking. Many of these men, it turned out, still regard their government with great suspicion.

2. As you listen to the victims, I think you are going to discover that by and large they have no idea what hit them. They have not read and absorbed some of the excellent books written, most notably Michi Weglyn's *Years of Infamy* and Roger Daniels's *The Decision to Relocate the Japanese Americans*. The former internees have not plowed through the documents in the files of our government and of our former officials. They are not aware of the careful premeditation that went into the construction of Executive Order 9066 which led to the government's contention that the concentration camps were not racially motivated. They only know that all the faces in their camps were Japanese.

Nor do the victims realize that their compensation for labor at six to eight cents an hour fell far below the Geneva requirement for prisoners of war. They only know that it wasn't much, that it did not allow for much improvement in their bleak, spartan existence.

And they are completely oblivious to the deeper, far more serious machinations of the War Department, which actually proposed legislation for the suspension of the writ of *habeas corpus* and legislation to cancel—if that's the proper term—our citizenship.

They only know that they were held in desolate enclaves, surrounded by barbed wire and guard towers, which no less a person than President Roosevelt called "concentration camps" in his press conferences of October 20, 1942 and November 21, 1944.

Here is an instance of the effect of NCJAR's research. We were constantly coming up with facts and documents which shed new light on disputed matters such as the propriety of the term "concentration camp." Some say this is hyperbole, an attempt to equate our camps with the death camps of the Nazi Holocaust. Roosevelt's use of the term tends to confirm its propriety.

You will not be able to do all the research necessary in the limited time you have. But you can certainly get some understanding of what still lies buried in those thousands of documents. You can consider those materials in your final report and recommendations. We will seek to provide such assistance as the Commission or its staff requests. We pledge NCJAR's cooperation in your efforts.

This was NCJAR's major contribution to the Commission. After a slow start, the Commission's staff did embark upon the task of research, and incorporated into their report much from the materials we had gathered; in addition, they did substantial research of their own.

3. The National Council for Japanese American Redress has embarked upon the task of finding a legal remedy. We are quite serious in our intent of suing the United States. But as you are aware, we face significant obstacles in court.

The question we ask you to consider is this:

Will this Commission be willing to recommend a mechanism which will enable a fair adjudication of the case for compensating the class of Japanese American internment victims? The historic fact of mass evacuation and imprisonment motivated by racial bigotry was a flagrant breach of American principles of equal justice. While the fact cannot be excised from history, remedies can be devised to compensate the victims, and help restore the democratic ideal in our society.

I am not a lawyer, so I will not attempt to enthrall you with legal arguments. But let me simply point out that, on the one hand, we have an extreme, an extraordinary deprivation of civil and constitutional rights on a massive scale. Does it not require, then, an extraordinary measure to permit the injustice to be remedied?

Ultimately, justice is due all of us, all the citizens of a democratic society. We have written and amended our own Constitution. We have enacted our own laws. By and large, we obey these laws. And when we do not, or when contentions occur, we act, often as a jury, to determine the issue on the basis of hearing the facts and applying the law.

Clearly, we Japanese Americans have not had our day in court. That, in a sentence, is the essence of this issue. Given the wisdom of our democratic system of self-government, is it not possible to find the means which will enable us to have, at long last, our day in court?

When I am done, Joan Bernstein notes that I have finished exactly on time, and I note her noting. Then Sasha Hohri and Bert Nakano testify for the National Coalition for Redress/Reparations and Min Yasui for the Japanese American Citizens League. Commissioners ask questions after hearing the panel of the three redress organizations. It is significant that there are three. In the past, only the JACL represented Japanese-American interests in Washington. Judge Marutani asked me if NCJAR would share its research. I said we would. Others asked if NCJAR would submit a proposal for enabling legislation. Of course, we would. We got positive results. So this is an important part of the story. But the real story lies in what happened to us, the Japanese-Americans, during World War II, in our memories of those years, in the origins of our redress movement during the 1940s and 1970s, and the movement's continuing history in the 1980s.

2. SITUATIONS
HISTORICAL OVERVIEW

In order to provide a historical overview, I have constructed a chronology of wartime events based upon these themes: the major events of the Pacific Theater during World War II, the decisions of the U.S. government, the actions of the domestic military command, the role of the Japanese American Citizens League (JACL), internee resistance in its various forms, the establishment and closing of the camps, and the legal and constitutional challenges that reached the Supreme Court. Each theme is identified by its own single-letter code in parentheses, in the headings and next to entries in the chronology.

World War II, Pacific Theater (W)
The big events of the war, of course, set the stage for everything else.

Government (G)
This is the dominant theme. The decisions of the civilian federal government were generally distinct from those of the military command. The civilian government controlled the course of domestic events. Its decisions at times merge with those of the military command, especially when actions of the War Department are considered. Henry L. Stimson is Secretary of War. His Assistant Secretary of War is John J. McCloy. Stimson reports to President Roosevelt. McCloy writes many memoranda for Stimson's signature and also communicates directly with the President. Tremendous power is vested in the War Department, which controls the military's Western Defense Command. It is safe to say that McCloy is the single most important decision-maker in the exclusion and detention program for Japanese-Americans.

After being built by the military command, the camps are administered by a civilian agency, the War Relocation Authority (WRA). The Department of Justice (DOJ), which includes the Federal Bureau of Investigation (FBI), is responsible for the arrest and internment of "enemy aliens" (citizens of Japan, Germany, and Italy). The DOJ also provides legal representation for the government in the legal and constitutional challenges.

Military Command (M)
The military command is the next most important theme. The Army's Western Defense Command carries out the exclusion and detention of West Coast Japanese-Americans. Initially, Lt. General John L. DeWitt heads the Western Defense Command. DeWitt's chief aide in this program is Major, briefly Lt. Colonel, then Colonel, Karl R. Bendetsen. Once President Roosevelt's Executive Order No. 9066 (EO9066) delegates authority to the Secretary of War, it is quickly redelegated to DeWitt and to other commanders. DeWitt, in turn, issues a series of public proclamations which implement exclusion and detention by defining military areas, ordering curfews, prohibiting Japanese-Americans from leaving Military Area No. 1, and finally herding Japanese-Americans into temporary and permanent detention camps through a series of orders excluding them from their communities. It is Bendetsen who designs the method of EO9066

and becomes the architect of exclusion and detention by building the camps and doing much of the detail work for DeWitt's signature.

Separate but related activities of the military command are its training of Japanese-Americans as Japanese-language interpreters for use in the Pacific Theater, and its formation of the Hawaiian 100th Infantry Battalion, a Japanese-American combat unit for the European Theater. Later, the command forms the larger 442nd Regimental Combat Team, first by enlisting Japanese-American volunteers from Hawaii and from the ten permanent detention camps and the "free zones" of the mainland, then through conscription of Japanese-Americans, detained and free.

Japanese American Citizens League (J)

The Japanese American Citizens League (JACL) was the sole voice of Japanese America. Formed in 1930 from several predecessor groups, such as the New American Citizens League, American Loyalty League, and the Seattle Progressive Citizens League, the JACL placed importance on U.S. citizenship and excluded Japanese-Americans who were not U.S. citizens. Because persons of Japanese ancestry could become citizens only through birth in the U.S., the JACL excluded many mature adults and most parents and natural community leaders. The generally youthful JACL leadership actively cooperated with government intelligence agencies, by providing criteria for official determinations of disloyalty, and by furnishing names of individuals whom the JACL leaders thought disloyal. The JACL leadership also lobbied for reinstatement of Selective Service for those interned, as well as for free citizens of Japanese ancestry. These JACL activities exacerbated tensions in the camps, whose inmates were already at odds with each other for many reasons, including the pressures of detention itself and the differing loyalties of citizens of Japan and citizens of the United States.

Resistance by Internees (R)

Many historical accounts have overlooked resistance to exclusion and detention, or have denigrated it as "troublemaking" and "lawlessness." Most histories instead emphasize the heroic exploits of the 100th Infantry Battalion and the 442nd Regimental Combat Team, some members of which volunteered from the ten camps. But the total of internee volunteers for military service throughout World War II was only 805. Later, when conscription of Japanese-Americans was reinstated, 315 internees were arrested for violation of Selective Service laws. Besides the draft resisters, there were eighty-three U.S. citizens interned at the WRA's special high security camp at Leupp, Arizona. The WRA punished these persons as "troublemakers," without hearing or trial. In addition, other "troublemakers" who were enemy aliens were sent to DOJ internment camps. These "troublemakers," both citizens and aliens, generally did nothing more than exercise their right to freedom of speech by openly criticizing the administration of the camps or the government of the United States.

Camps (C)

There were ten permanent camps established, all in states west of the Mississippi River. An eleventh camp was initially located at Moab, Utah and later moved to Leupp,

Arizona; this was the isolation camp. There were also sixteen temporary detention centers called "assembly centers," located up and down the West Coast. The government used the assembly centers while the permanent detention camps were under construction.

This chronology omits Department of Justice internment camps and other camps such as Sand Island in Hawaii.

Legal and Constitutional Challenges (L)
Several individuals were arrested for the violation of the exclusion order and Public Law 503. Other individuals attempted to challenge their internment by suing the government, using the writ of *habeas corpus*. This chronology centers on four key cases which reached the U.S. Supreme Court: Yasui, Hirabayashi, Korematsu, and Endo. The actions of the American Civil Liberties Union (ACLU) are part of this theme.

A CHRONOLOGY

1940

G According to the 1940 census, there are 126,947 Japanese-Americans in the United States and around 158,000 in the Territory of Hawaii.

G October 9 Secretary of Navy Frank Knox memorandum to President Roosevelt includes recommendation to "prepare plans for concentration camps" in order to impress the Japanese government of the seriousness of U.S. military preparedness.

1941

M November 1 Fourth Army Japanese Language School established at the Presidio of San Francisco.[1]

G November 7 Curtis B. Munson's secret report "Japanese on West Coast" to the State Dept. and the President, which states, "There is no Japanese 'problem' on the [West] Coast."[2]

M December 4 Counter Subversion Section of the Office of Naval Intelligence issues a twenty-six-page report, "Japanese Intelligence and Propaganda in the United States" for all naval districts, FBI, MID, COI, and State Dept. Report is based upon MAGIC cables and other sources and concludes:

> However, in anticipation of a possible crisis, the FBI is prepared to take into custody and detain all persons whose activities are inimical to the best interests of the United States.[3]

W December 7 The Japanese Imperial Navy attacks the United States Pacific Fleet at Pearl Harbor.

G December 7 The FBI rounds up 736 Japanese resident aliens as potential threats to national security.

J December 7 JACL's Southern California chapter forms the Anti-Axis Committee.[4]

W December 8 Japanese forces invade the Philippine Islands, then a U.S. colony.

W December 9 Japanese forces invade Malaya, then a British colony.

W December 13 Japanese forces capture Guam.

SITUATIONS

J December 19 The JACL's Anti-Axis Committee's leaders meet with the FBI's Los Angeles Field Division Office. The leaders help the FBI identify persons of Japanese ancestry, by category and individually, who they consider to be pro-Japan and dangerous.

W December 25 Japanese forces capture Wake Island.

1942

W January 11 Japanese forces invade Indonesia, then the Dutch East Indies.

M January 19 Some 317 Japanese-American members of the Hawaiian Territorial Guard were discharged without explanation on orders from Washington, D.C.[5] All during the period following Pearl Harbor Nisei soldiers were either discharged from the Army—either honorably or for the "good of the service"—or transferred to the Enlisted Reserve Corps (ERC) and sent home. On September 26, 1942, Nisei in the ERC were to be discharged.[6]

M January 26 Office of Naval Intelligence secret report "Japanese Question" recommends against the "removal and internment in concentration camps of all citizens and residents of Japanese extraction . . ."

G January 27 U.S. Attorney General Francis Biddle writes to Congressman Leland Ford and states, ". . . the decision of this department is that the program I have outlined above, together with the extensive investigations which have been carried on by the Federal Bureau of Investigation, would adequately control the problem of the Japanese population of the Pacific Coast. For this reason, and also because of the legal difficulties presently involved in attempting to intern or evacuate the thousands of American born persons of Japanese race, who are, of course, American citizens, this Department had not deemed it advisable at this time to attempt to remove all persons of the Japanese race into the interior of the country."

G February 5 Secretary of War Henry L. Stimson memorandum to Secretary of State Cordell Hull suggests "a threat of reprisals against the many Japanese nationals now enjoying negligible restrictions in the United States to insure proper treatment of our nationals in the Philippines."[7]

G February 15 The FBI roundup of Japanese resident aliens totals 2,192 on the mainland, 879 in Hawaii, and 42 in Alaska.[8]

W February 15 Japanese forces capture Singapore with 80,000 British troops and many civilians. This completed Japan's conquest of Malaya.

G February 17 At the Sand Island detention camp in Hawaii, 172 men are ordered to pack up and prepare for departure. They are to be shipped to Camp McCoy, Wisconsin.[9]

G February 19 President Roosevelt issues Executive Order No. 9066 which states:

> WHEREAS the successful prosecution of the war requires every possible protection against espionage and against sabotage to national-defense material, national-defense premises, and national-defense utilities. . . .
>
> NOW THEREFORE, by virtue of the authority vested in me as President of the United States, and Commander in Chief of the Army and Navy, I hereby authorize and direct the Secretary of War, and the Military Commanders whom he may from time to time designate, whenever he or any designated Commander deems such action necessary or desirable, to prescribe military areas in such places and of such extent as he or the appropriate Military Commander may determine, from which any or all persons may be excluded, and with respect to which, the right of any person to enter, remain in, or leave shall be subject to whatever restrictions the Secretary of War or the appropriate Military Commander may impose in his discretion. The Secretary of War is hereby authorized to provide for residents of any such area who are excluded therefrom, such transportation, food, shelter, and other accommodations as may be necessary, in the judgment of the Secretary of War or the said Military Commander, and until other arrangements are made, to accomplish the purpose of this order.

M February 25 Navy orders all Japanese-Americans to leave their homes on Terminal Island in Los Angeles harbor within forty-eight hours. These families and individuals must pack up, move, and find places to live entirely on their own, like war refugees.[10]

M March 2 Public Proclamation No. 1 from the Western Defense Command designates and establishes Military Areas Nos. 1 and 2, the first comprising a roughly 100-mile strip along the West Coast running through Washington, Oregon, California, and Arizona, and the second covering the remaining area of these states.[11]

J March 8 JACL convenes a three-day emergency National Council Meeting in San Francisco, and establishes a policy of cooperation with the government's plans for mass exclusion of Japanese-Americans.[12]

M March 9 The 172 Hawaiian Japanese arrive at the internment camp at Camp McCoy, Wisconsin.[13]

W March 9 Dutch in Indonesia surrender.

M March 11 The Army establishes the Wartime Civil Control Administration (WCCA) to implement the program of exclusion and detention and appoints Karl R. Bendetsen the WCCA's director.[14]

G March 18 Executive Order No. 9102 establishes the War Relocation Authority (WRA), Milton Eisenhower appointed its director.[15]

G March 21 Public Law 503 passed and signed into law. It provides penalties of up to a year in jail and a fine of $5,000 for civilians violating a military order in a military area.[16]

C March 21 The first camp, at Manzanar, California, opens with 2,100 "voluntary" internees. Population here reached 10,046.[17]

M March 24 Public Proclamation No. 3 from the Western Defense Command ordered a curfew "[from] and after 6:00 a.m., March 27, 1942" for all enemy aliens and "all persons of Japanese ancestry residing or being within the geographical limits of Military Area No. 1" requiring them to stay at home "between the hours of 8:00 p.m. and 6:00 a.m." and prohibiting them from "traveling more than five miles from their place of residence."[18]

M March 27 Curfew goes into effect at 6:00 a.m.[19]

M March 27 Public Proclamation No. 4 by the Western Defense Command prohibits all persons of Japanese ancestry from leaving Military Area No. 1 as of midnight March 29, 1942.[20]

L March 28 Minoru Yasui deliberately violates the curfew order in Portland, Oregon in order to test the order's constitutionality.[21]

M March 30 Prohibition of Japanese-Americans from "voluntarily" leaving the exclusion zone of Military Area No. 1 is in effect.[22] About 5,000 Japanese-Americans have already "voluntarily" relocated from Area No. 1 to Area No. 2, while 4,889 have left both areas for the interior states. Those who move to Area No. 2 in California are caught in June when the exclusion zone is expanded to cover the entire state.

M March 31 Forty-five Japanese-American families on Bainbridge Island, Washington are removed to the Manzanar detention camp. This is the first mandatory evacuation following Public Proclamation No. 4.

M April 3 General Raymond E. Lee recommends to Chief of Staff George C. Marshall that the Fourth Army Japanese Language School move to an interior command because Nisei are excluded from San Francisco. Lee also states, "It is the consensus of opinion of most officers who know the Japanese and Nisei best that the great majority of the Nisei want to be, and will be, loyal."

SITUATIONS

J April 6 JACL's National Secretary, Mike Masaoka, writes an eighteen-page letter to WRA Director, Milton Eisenhower. The letter lists the JACL's recommendations on draft status, public relations, education, religion, sports, health care, professions, business, agriculture, labor, citizenship, self-government, private resettlement, assembly centers, and permanent projects.

G April 7 Salt Lake City meeting of Western Defense Command, WRA, and other federal officials with officials of ten western states of Utah, Nevada, Idaho, New Mexico, Arizona, Washington, Oregon, Montana, Wyoming, and Colorado. WDC's Colonel Bendetsen and WRA Director Eisenhower confront bitter opposition to their program for the relocation of West Coast Japanese-Americans to the interior states.[23]

J April 7 JACL states that it "is unalterably opposed to test cases to determine the constitutionality of military regulations at this time."[24]

W April 8 Japanese forces capture Bataan, last major U.S. military base in the Philippines, with more than 35,000 U.S. and Filipino troops, who will be forced into "Death March" and brutal imprisonment.

G April 17 War Dept. proposes shift of administration of camps to WRA but with camp security remaining with the military. Proposal becomes effective June 1, 1942.[25]

W May 6 General Jonathan Wainwright surrenders Corregidor Island, last U.S. base in Philippines, with more than 11,000 troops.

C May 8 Internees begin to arrive at the camps at Poston, Arizona. Population reached 17,814.[26]

L May 16 Gordon Kiyoshi Hirabayashi deliberately violates the exclusion order in Seattle, Washington in order to test the constitutionality of exclusion.[27]

M May 19 General DeWitt requests of the Chief of Staff of the Army that "all commanding generals . . . be advised that soldiers of the Army . . . of Japanese descent be not . . . granted furloughs for the purpose of entering the states of Washington, Oregon, California, and Arizona."

G May 25 The 172 Hawaiian Japanese leave Camp McCoy, Wisconsin for Camp Forrest, Tennessee.[28]

C May 27 Internees begin to arrive at the camp at Tule Lake, California. Population reached 18,789.[29]

L May 30 Fred Toyosaburo Korematsu is arrested in San Leandro, California for violating the exclusion order.[30]

G June 1 The administration of the camp at Manzanar is changed from the Army's Wartime Civil Control Administration to the civilian War Relocation Authority. Manzanar is now a permanent detention camp, not an assembly center.[31]

M June 2 The restrictions applied to Military Area No. 1 are extended to Military Area No. 2 in California, thereby covering the entire state.

M June 5 The segregated Japanese-American Hawaiian 100th Infantry Battalion (separate) formed and shipped to Camp McCoy, Wisconsin for further training.[32]

M June 6 All Japanese-Americans in Military Area No. 1 have been removed to assembly centers or permanent detention camps. The first phase of the exclusion and detention program is completed.[33]

W June 6 End of four-day naval Battle of Midway, colossal defeat for Japanese who lost four aircraft carriers and 3,500 men. This is generally considered the turning point of the war in the Pacific.

L June 12 Yasui brought to trial in the federal courthouse in Portland, Oregon.[34]

M June 17 Selective Service discontinues induction of American citizens of Japanese ancestry and establishes their classification as 4C—"aliens ineligible for military service."[35]

G June 17 Milton Eisenhower resigns from WRA and moves to the Office of War Information (OWI). Dillon Myer becomes WRA Director.[36]

L June 22 ACLU national board, following a referendum to its national committee, instructs Roger Baldwin to inform West Coast ACLU branches that "local committees are not free to sponsor cases in which the position is taken that the government has no constitutional right to remove citizens from military areas."[37]

M June 27 Public Proclamation No. 8 designates the six camps within the Western Defense Command to be War Relocation Project Areas or exclusion zones, with penalties under Public Law 503 invoked against Japanese-Americans who disobey instructions to stay inside or outside these Areas.[38]

G June 29 The 172 Hawaiian Japanese are moved from Camp Forrest, Tennessee to Camp Livingston, Louisiana.[39]

M July 9 The removal of Japanese-Americans from Military Area No. 2 in California commences.

L July 13 Mitsuye Endo files a petition of *habeas corpus* with the Federal District Court of San Francisco.[40]

C July 20 Internees begin to arrive at the camps at Gila River, Arizona. Population reached 13,348.[41]

L July 20 Endo case heard before Judge Michael J. Roche in San Francisco. Roche to take one year for his decision of July 3, 1943.[42]

L August Nineteen Nisei of the contingent of 172 Hawaiian Japanese at Camp Livingston, Louisiana are returned to Hawaii.[43]

M August 7 All Japanese-Americans in Military Area No. 2 in California have been removed to temporary ("Assembly Center") and permanent ("Relocation Center") detention centers.[44]

C August 10 Internees begin to arrive at the camp at Minidoka, Idaho. Population reached 9,397.[45]

C August 12 Internees begin to arrive at the camp at Heart Mountain, Wyoming. Population reached 10,767.[46]

C August 13 The War Department issues proclamation WD-1 declaring the four camps outside the Western Defense Command in Arkansas, Colorado, and Wyoming to be War Relocation Project Areas, thereby providing legal sanctions for the detention of Japanese-Americans under Public Law 503.[47]

C August 20 Internees begin to arrive at the camp at Granada, Colorado. Population reached 7,318.[48]

L September 8 Korematsu case heard before Judge Adolphus F. St. Sure in San Francisco.[49]

C September 11 Internees begin to arrive at the camp at Topaz, Utah. Population reached 8,130.[50]

C September 18 Internees begin to arrive at the camp at Rohwer, Arkansas. Population reached 8,475.[51]

G October 2 All-volunteer, Nisei enlistment recommended by Elmer Davis and Milton Eisenhower of the Office of War Information (OWI) in Davis's letter to President Roosevelt: "Loyal American citizens of Japanese descent should be permitted, after individual test, to enlist in the Army and Navy. It would hardly be fair to evacuate people and then impose normal draft procedures, but voluntary enlistment would help a lot."[52]

SITUATIONS

C October 6 Internees begin to arrive at the camp at Jerome, Arkansas. Population reached 8,497.[53]

G October 12 On Columbus Day, President Roosevelt proclaims that Italian aliens are no longer to be considered as enemy aliens.[54]

L October 20 Hirabayashi case heard before Judge Lloyd D. Black in Seattle.[55]

M October 31 Second phase of exclusion and detention, the removal of Japanese-Americans from temporary "assembly centers," completed. All internees now located in ten permanent detention centers.[56]

R November 14 A physical attack on a suspected informer in Poston Camp I precipitates a chain of events including an arrest, mass protest over the arrest, and a general strike.[57]

J November 17 At Salt Lake City, the JACL convenes a special emergency session of its National Council. The JACL votes to support reinstitution of Selective Service for Japanese-American citizens.[58]

R November 19 General strike begins at Poston Camp I.[59]

R November 24 General strike ends at Poston Camp I.[60]

R December 5 At Manzanar, Fred Tayama, recently returned from the special emergency National Council meeting of the JACL in Salt Lake City as a delegate, is physically attacked by several masked assailants. Harry Ueno, president of the Kitchen Workers Union, is arrested and jailed in Independence, California. The arrest precipitates two demonstrations which result in the killing of two unarmed internees and the wounding of about eight others by the camp's military police.[61]

R December 7 Harry Ueno, Joe Kurihara, and eventually fourteen other Manzanar internees are arrested and jailed, first in Independence, later in Lone Pine, California.

1943

R January 11 Sixteen internees arrested in the aftermath of the Manzanar killings are shipped to a special, high security isolation center of the WRA at Moab, Utah. Those who are citizens of Japan are subsequently interned at the Department of Justice camp at Missoula, Montana. (It was the camp's military police who did the killing; all internees were unarmed.)

G January 28 Secretary of War announces the formation of a special, all-volunteer combat team of Japanese-Americans, hoping to recruit 1,500 from Hawaii and 3,500 from the mainland.

M February 3 WRA institutes a questionnaire containing two loyalty oaths to separate "disloyals" from "loyals" in the camps.

M February 14 A total of 9,507 Hawaiian Japanese volunteer for special combat team. They comprise one-third of all Americans of Japanese Ancestry (AJA) in Hawaii between the ages of 18 and 38. Only 1,181, or 6 per cent of the eligible males, from the mainland, volunteer.

L February 19 Yasui and Hirabayashi cases reach Court of Appeals in San Francisco.

M March 4 Public Proclamation No. 16 issued by General DeWitt to reduce Military Area No. 1 in Arizona so that the Poston and Gila River camps are no longer within the exclusion zone.

M March 15 Wartime Civil Control Administration abolished.[62]

M April Activation and training of 442nd Regimental Combat Team begins training at Camp Shelby, Mississippi.

M April 20 Exclusion of all soldiers of Japanese ancestry from the West Coast is rescinded by the Secretary of War.

G April Towards the end of April, McCloy informs Bendetsen "that there no longer existed any military necessity for the continued exclusion of all Japanese from the evacuated zone."[63]

L June 1 Supreme Court returns Korematsu case to Court of Appeals.

L June 21 Supreme Court upholds Yasui and Hirabayashi convictions for curfew violation, while avoiding the issue of exclusion in Hirabayashi.

L July 3 Judge Roche dismisses Endo *habeas corpus* petition.[64]

M July 28 War Dept. sets quota of 500 Japanese-American women for enlistment in the Women's Army Corps. One hundred thirty-nine apply.[65]

M September 2 The 100th Infantry Battalion arrives in North Africa.[66]

M September 26 The 100th Infantry Battalion goes into combat at Salerno, Italy.[67]

L December 2 Court of Appeals upholds Korematsu decision.

1944

M January 14 Selective Service for Japanese-Americans reinstated.[68]

R February 24 In the camp at Heart Mountain, Wyoming, the Fair Play Committee—"One for All—All for One"—distributes a mimeographed flyer which states:

> The Fair Play Committee was organized for the purpose of opposing all unfair practices that violate the Constitutional rights . . . and occur within our present concentration camp, state, territory or Union. It has come out strongly in recent weeks in regards to the discriminating features of the new selective service program as it applies to the Japanese Americans . . .[69]

R March 3 In Heart Mountain by this date, twelve men, of sixty-four ordered, failed to report for their preinduction physical examinations.[70]

R March During March, sixty-three men from Heart Mountain refuse to report for their preinduction physical examinations. They are arrested and incarcerated in county jails in Wyoming.[71]

R April 28 Joe Grant Masaoka and Min Yasui of the JACL interview six of the Heart Mountain draft resisters who are jailed in Cheyenne, Wyoming. In the JACL's report to the Denver office of the FBI, Masaoka and Yasui state that their purpose is ". . . to persuade any of the boys at the Cheyenne County Jail to reconsider his stand . . ."[72]

M June 2 The 442nd Regimental Combat Team lands at Naples, Italy and moves to the beaches of Anzio.[73]

R June 12 In the Cheyenne federal court, the trial of the sixty-three Heart Mountain draft resisters begins.[74]

M June 15 The 442nd and 100th join forces.[75]

R June 26 The sixty-three Heart Mountain draft resisters are found guilty and sentenced to three years in prison.[76]

C June 30 Camp at Jerome, Arkansas is closed; its internees transferred to the camp at Rohwer, Arkansas.[77]

R July James Omura, English editor of the *Rocky Shimpo*, a Denver newspaper, and seven leaders of the Heart Mountain draft resistance are arrested on draft conspiracy charges. The seven are Kiyoshi Okamoto, Paul Takeo Nakadate, Ben Wakaye, Ken Yanagi, Frank Seichi Emi, Minoru Tamesa, and Sam Horino.[78]

SITUATIONS

L October 11 Supreme Court hears Korematsu and Endo cases.[79]

W October In giant battles of Leyte, U.S. forces return to Philippines. Reconquest is completed by March, 1945.

R November A Cheyenne jury acquits James Omura of conspiracy, but convicts the seven leaders of the Heart Mountain draft resistance.[80]

R November 30 Of the total of 315 draft resisters, 263 were convicted. The 315 came from Topaz (9), Poston (112), Granada (35), Heart Mountain (88), Jerome (1), Minidoka (40), Rohwer (3), and Tule Lake (27).[81]

M December 17 Public Proclamation No. 21 rescinds mass exclusion order effective after midnight January 2, 1945.[82]

L December 18 Supreme Court upholds Korematsu conviction.

L December 18 Supreme Court frees Mitsuye Endo after a two-and-one-half-year *habeas corpus* case.[83]

1945

M January 3 Mass exclusion order rescinded. Individual exclusion applied in its stead. Individual exclusion applied to 4,963 persons, mainly at Tule Lake and to 4,810 males who had applied for expatriation.[84]

W April U.S. forces invade Okinawa. Ensuing battles last several months with enormous casualty toll.

W August 6 U.S. drops first atomic bomb on Hiroshima, ancestral home of many Japanese-Americans.

W August 8 USSR declares war on Japan.

W August 9 U.S. drops atomic bomb on Nagasaki.

W August 14 Japan surrenders unconditionally to U.S.

C October 15 Last internees leave camp at Granada, Colorado.[85]

C October 28 Last internees leave camp at Minidoka, Idaho.[86]

C October 30 Last internees leave camp at Topaz, Utah.[87]

C November 10 Last internees leave camp at Gila River, Arizona.[88]

C November 10 Last internees leave camp at Heart Mountain, Wyoming.[89]

C November 21 Last internees leave camp at Manzanar, California.[90]

C November 28 Last internees leave camp at Poston, Arizona.[91]

C November 30 Last internees leave camp at Rohwer, Arkansas.[92]

1946

C March 20 Last internees leave camp at Tule Lake, California.[93]

G June 30 War Relocation Authority terminated.

3. SITUATIONS
REMEMBERING

When asked about camp, I usually respond by saying that I was detained in April 1942 at Manzanar, California and was released after graduating from high school in June 1944. Yes, Manzanar had armed guards and barbed wire fences. Yes, we lived in tarpapered barracks, a family of seven in one bare room, twenty by twenty-five feet. These statements show that Manzanar had a school system, confirm that it was a concentration camp, and even evoke the nostalgia of the class of '44. But there is much more to be said.

Manzanar, where my family was imprisoned, like most of the other camps, cannot be found on a map. Manzanar was between Lone Pine and Independence, unknown and remote, about 200 miles due north of Los Angeles, on the way to Reno. Manzanar was east of the Sierra Nevada. During World War II gasoline rationing, Manzanar was practically inaccessible by private automobile. From a military perspective, Manzanar was four thousand feet above sea level, at the base of Mount Williamson, which rose almost perpendicularly to fourteen thousand feet—as if a two-mile-high wall separated us from the West Coast and the supposedly vulnerable bases of the United States Western Defense Command. In other words, Manzanar's geography insured that we couldn't exercise our ingrained "Jap" sneakiness against power lines, aircraft factories, naval bases, shipyards, and such—using our gardener's pruning hooks as spears and our scythes as swords. We were guilty by reason of racial perversity, but in the natural prison of Manzanar, we were harmless.

At the age of fifteen I had been aware of race. I was the youngest of six children. My two oldest brothers and my oldest sister were born in Japan and raised in America. Racist laws of that time prohibited the naturalization of Asians. Thus, these three oldest could not become citizens, although in language and culture they were Americans. Much of their high school civics lessons was of no use to them. They could never vote. They played Monopoly with a vengeance—perhaps because as "aliens ineligible for naturalization" they could not own real estate in California. All they could do was work hard at menial jobs and resign themselves to the unyielding injustices of a racist society.

A year before exclusion and detention, I had graduated from Ralph Waldo Emerson Junior High School in Westwood, California—a school with Richard Neutra architecture and beautiful children, some of whom went on to become movie stars and Olympic champions (e.g., Marilyn Monroe and Mel Patton). We Japanese-Americans, along with the Mexicans and a single black, were children of color. The school was a training ground in sex and racism. "What is 'fuck'?" the white kids asked kids from the alien world on the other side of the tracks, failing to realize how puritanical our Buddhist, Protestant, or Catholic upbringing was. I remember hearing the dirty stories about a boy and a girl fucking away, but what happened physically was alluded to, not explained in graphic detail. We enjoyed our tales of secret carnal delights despite our ignorance. But this was with boys. With girls, we sensed the emerging barrier that would separate boys of color from white girls.

Color was insurmountable. The world was friendly enough. We had our challenges in sports, and in stretching our minds to absorb knowledge and insights. But our hopes and desires were becoming irretrievably "white."

We Japanese-American boys weren't turning into Jack Armstrong, the all-American boy, a 1930s radio purveyor of Wheaties, "The Breakfast of Champions." Our hair was thick and didn't wave. Our noses were blunt. We were held on the other side of the tracks by housing covenants which prohibited us from living in all-white Westwood, through which we walked on our way to school. Our parents spoke Japanese; our fathers could hardly take part in the social amenities of a father-and-son day. We belonged to a social class of schoolboys, maids, gardeners, fruit-and-vegetable-stand clerks. It was the white knights in shining armor, not their servants, who went after white princesses. Our female images were white, silken-haired, busty, Petty Girl fantasies that made the girls from our side of the tracks seem unacceptably flat, dark, thick-haired. We abused ourselves, as they used to say, with these fantasies.

When I was a teenager, one of my friends lived in Beverly Hills where his family worked as caretakers for John Barrymore. His father was a graduate of the California Institute of Technology and was probably the most highly educated caretaker in Hollywood. My German teacher, who doted on me, was startled when in response to her question, "Willie, what would you like to be when you grow up?" I said with hand-me-down wisdom, "A postman." It was an engineer that I truly wanted to be. I had a wide-ranging curiosit⁻ ⁻bout how things worked. But in addition to clocks and airplanes, I was learning hꞈw race worked. I knew I had job opportunities in civil service but not in engineering. The source of this wisdom was my next-to-oldest brother, Takuo, who, upon graduating from high school, quickly found himself disabused of hopes for higher education and a career in photography, and hard at work pushing a lawn mower in order to help support our large family. Upon my graduation from Ralph Waldo Emerson Junior High School, we moved from West Los Angeles to North Hollywood because that's where there were lawns to be mowed. That was the summer of 1941. Six months later, the Japanese Imperial Navy launched its brilliant attack on the United States naval base and Pacific fleet at Pearl Harbor.

The sneaky, little, five-and-dime-store-junk-producing "Japs" had dared to attack the righteous, mighty America. The "Mongol barbarians" had launched an attack on Buck Rogers, Jack Armstrong, Bob Hope, and Shirley Temple. Ming had slashed Flash Gordon and was threatening to violate beautiful Dale. How dare this nation of schoolboys, gardeners, and produce clerks attack the greatest white nation on earth! The President of the United States pronounced the attack dastardly and December 7, 1941 "a date that will live in infamy." White, Christian America, so it reasoned, could be defeated only because the enemy had resorted to duplicity, fraud, treachery—a stab in the back. If there were ever a contest between good and evil, this was it. The "Japs" couldn't possibly win if they played by the rules. America had democracy, God, Jesus, Hollywood, and Ralph Waldo Emerson on its side. The "Japs" had an emperor, pagan idols, and buck-toothed, slant-eyed faces. They were a subspecies destined for servility but not yet house-broken. America had Harvard, Yale, Eli Whitney, Thomas Edison, Henry Ford, and General Motors. The "Japs" were at best quaint, ridiculously polite, and inveterate copycats, good only at producing cheap and flimsy imitations. Their technology would crumble before ours.

But being a "Jap" myself, despite my all-American convictions, I sensed contradictions in this line of reasoning. Wasn't I pretty bright? A straight-A student, only fourteen but in the tenth grade and not trying hard. "Japs" excelled in gymnastics, in which their small size was not a hindrance, and were much better than whites in art. We "Japs" seemed imbued with a sense of honor. We never got messed up with the law. And in fact, our skins were not yellow, nor were our eyes slanted. Our teeth were as straight or as crooked as the next kid's.

The outbreak of war wreaked havoc on logic as well as law. "A Jap is a Jap" was the American enunciation of the principle of the excluded middle. If the attack on Pearl Harbor revealed and confirmed a genetically based moral defect in "Yellow people," then Japanese-Americans were identically defective. On the night of December 7, 1941, before war had been declared by the United States Congress, FBI agents came to our storefront home in North Hollywood and arrested my father. My family could not understand how our father, an impoverished Christian minister, a visionary, a little scatter-brained perhaps, could be such a terrible threat to national security. He had about a dozen faithful followers who joined him in worship each Sunday at a rented American Legion hall—not enough of a congregation to sustain a family of eight. There was no trial where we could learn what the charges were—what the mistake, as it must have been, was. He was sent to a Department of Justice internment camp at Missoula, Montana. Only decades later was I to learn that hearings were held in that camp, in English. At that distance and in that language, he could hardly marshal a defense. Because his grasp of English was severely limited, he probably never understood why he was arrested. Several hundred other Japanese "enemy aliens" were rounded up that same night. Eventually, several thousand, mainly Japanese nationals, mainly male, were rounded up as threats to national security. In those days the FBI had such a wonderful public image. They had saved America from John Dillinger and Baby Face Nelson. I had a boxtop Melvin Purvis badge. The FBI was law and justice incarnate. Perhaps there was a threat? Perhaps my father was dangerous? Perhaps we were sneaky people?

The racial hatred was a warning, like a baring of fangs, or a hiss. We "Japs" were in danger. "Japs" were innately evil, and that included us. Whatever the Japanese did at Pearl Harbor, in China, or in the Philippines, we did as well. The link was racial. If the Japanese "Japs" dared to make war, didn't it stand to reason that we "Japs" in America had something up our sleeves? The ratiocinations of the media, especially the radio commentators, were persuasive. We were planning evil deeds. The FBI picked up other Issei fathers. We were subjected to a military curfew. We couldn't travel more than five miles from home, and had to be home by eight o'clock.

Then there was registration downtown. When Easter vacation for North Hollywood High School came, I told my gymnastics coach that I probably would not return after vacation. We might be taken away somewhere. He couldn't believe it. He'd leave my things in place for me so I could compete in the San Fernando Valley League tournament. By midweek, friends drove my family to a bus terminal where we boarded a caravan of buses destined for the desolate isolation of Manzanar. It meant Apple Orchard in Spanish. A nice-sounding name, even though one couldn't find it on the map. (Other camps were to have the names "Topaz," "Heart Mountain," "Granada.") It couldn't be all bad. Our bus had a young soldier guard, who looked like a high school senior. He insisted that we'd all be back home in two weeks.

The apple trees—there was a small orchard of them off in a corner of the mile-square camp—had gone wild. But the camp was mostly desert, in the middle of nowhere, in a valley that had the highest winds I've ever seen. One day I saw a small airplane flying backwards, losing ground against the wind. The wind blew dirt and sand into terrible dust storms against which the barracks, with their big cracks, were no match. We swabbed down the floors with water in a losing struggle to keep the barracks reasonably clean. When we arrived, the barracks were still under construction. Ours lacked windows. Earlier arrivals said theirs were missing roofs. The unseasoned lumber dried quickly in Manzanar's arid climate, leaving wide cracks. The tap water was not potable. We had to drink from water barrels. There was no sewage system so we had to use smelly outhouses which afforded neither privacy nor comfort. The outhouses were placed at the end of the barracks, on platforms approached by stairs. Their use was a public performance. The food was edible but awful. When Japanese-American draft resisters were sent to federal penitentiaries a few years later, they said prison food was far better than camp food. Since the camp was almost a mile above sea level, water boiled at a low temperature, so that boiled rice turned out gummy. Bathing facilities were non-existent. We used buckets for washing ourselves, our clothes, and our cubicles. No school was begun for several months. Soon boredom overwhelmed us. We played endless games of chess.

We were wards of the federal government. We received military clothes left over from World War I. We got Army khakis in summer, and Army woolens in the fall, and blue denims that were too large not only for us but for any other ordinary-sized people. The only redeeming feature of the baggy denims was the ease of converting them into the then-fashionable zoot suit. The only acceptable article of "GI" clothing was the Navy P-coat. It provided reasonable protection without outlandish style, in weather much colder than southern California's. There were jobs, but the wages were less than ten cents an hour. Since technically we were not prisoners of war, only evacuees, it didn't matter that these wages were far below the prevailing wage required by the Geneva Convention on treatment of prisoners of war.

Later, we were inoculated against typhoid and other diseases; we could drink tap water. Eventually, a sewage system was built; latrines replaced outhouses, and showers were installed. Later still, hot water was made available, at least during the day, before evening bathing began. Eventually, the volunteer cooks figured out how to cook rice at our altitude, although neither the quantity nor the quality of food ever reached the minimums stipulated by the Geneva Convention. Attacks of diarrhea persisted. They were called the "Manzanar runs." The special dietary needs of diabetics and hypertension patients were ignored with predictable, sometimes fatal, results.

We could never escape the oppressive reality of incarceration. We were prisoners. Not prisoners of war, for we were not from the enemy nation. We felt more like criminals. Our crime was genetic and cultural. It was not what we had done, but what we might be planning to do. The use of the Japanese language was forbidden in public meetings. All things Japanese were suspect. Not only were we excluded from the rest of America; we were such a feared species we were imprisoned in a concentration camp, surrounded by a barbed wire fence and guard towers.

Few of us dared to ask under what law we were imprisoned. "Normal" Americans find this hard to understand. People who have been raised within a day-to-day reality of discriminatory naturalization laws, restrictive housing covenants, job discrimination, alien land laws, and simple snooty personal bigotry are not about to question the legal basis for their confinement. Originally, Manzanar was outside the exclusion zone. After a few months, on June 2, 1942, the zone was expanded to include the entire state of California, including Manzanar. Given that, why could we not leave the camp? Only four of the ten camps were within the expanded exclusion zone. As a matter of law, each camp had its own ringed zone of military exclusion. We were confined by circles of exclusion, as in some child's game of imaginary powers. The government excluded us from broad zones of exclusion into rings of exclusion.

We didn't know what had hit us. We didn't know about the Constitution and the Bill of Rights. We knew the words, but their application escaped us. In the Minidoka camp, Henry Miyatake wrote an essay for his high school class about the unconstitutionality of the camps. Henry was an excellent student. His teacher told him that the thesis of his essay was unacceptable. Moreover, he was told, unless he withdrew the essay, he would not be allowed to graduate from high school. He did not withdraw the essay, and he did not graduate from high school. It would take years for us to understand.

4. SITUATIONS
WHY IT HAPPENED

Everyone has a theory of why World War II began. There are also numerous explanations for the exclusion and detention of Japanese-Americans, ranging from the government's giving us our just desserts for having started the whole war in the first place and somehow being responsible for the Japanese atrocities in North China and the Philippines, to the careful and now frequently quoted words of the congressional Commission on Wartime Relocation and Internment of Civilians (CWRIC): "race prejudice, war hysteria and a failure of political leadership." The Commission's reasoning is based upon recent research of both primary and secondary historical materials. It did produce a substantial report which supports its conclusions. But I believe that these conclusions fall short.

The reality of racism cannot be denied. The floodgates of racism opened wide. Anti-Japanese hatred flowed without restraint. We "Japs" were the butt of jokes. Cartoonists had a field day drawing our buck-toothed, slope-headed, stupid-looking sub-human species. "You're a Sap, Mr. Jap" became a radio hit song. Comic strips developed variations on anti-Jap plots, while comedians drew laughter from America with their "Jap" one-liners. It was a cruel time for Japanese-Americans. Victims tend to see the cause in what hurt them the worst. When the hostility of America congealed into an accusation of treachery so profound that one had to be confined behind a mountain range in a remote desert, the scar on one's soul is terrible and enduring. Racism was in evidence among governors and generals. It was Lt. General John L. DeWitt who uttered, "A Jap is a Jap." DeWitt was particularly unyielding. He had issued orders to prohibit Japanese-American soldiers from the exclusion zone, even though they were fighting and dying in the Pacific. He had to be directly instructed by his superiors to rescind such manifestly heartless and thoughtless orders.

The term "Jap" pervades official documents from within the U.S. government. The Attorney General of the United States in writing to President Roosevelt makes a point:

> You signed the Executive Order permitting exclusions so the Army could handle the Japs. It was never intended to apply to Italians and Germans.[1]

(This letter, by the way, was part of a squabble between the Department of Justice and the military over the Department's refusal to arrest persons who had received individual exclusion orders—usually persons of German or Italian ancestry—and were in violation of Public Law 503. The Department of Justice thought that PL-503 was unconstitutional.[2]) The use of a pejorative was reserved for Japanese. Moreover, its use was acceptable to the President and implies the existence of racism at the highest levels of government. But in the testimonies of former Colonel Karl R. Bendetsen and former Assistant Secretary of War John J. McCloy in November of 1981 before a federal commission, we hear that Henry Stimson and Franklin Roosevelt were honorable men, untainted by racism. The documents of history refute these latter-day protestations and confirm the racism implicit in the entire exclusion and detention program.

SITUATIONS

Christopher Thorne, in his *Allies of a Kind: the United States, Britain and the War Against Japan, 1941-45*, writes this characterization of Henry Stimson:

> . . . Stimson . . . who believed that "social equality [between white and black in the United States] . . . was basically . . . impossible . . . because of the impossibility of race mixture by marriage" and who would accept only that Negroes made "fairly good soldiers when they are officered by white men."

President Roosevelt seemed particularly unrestrained when writing to Britain's Prime Minister, Winston Churchill:

> "I have never liked the Burmese," [Roosevelt] wrote to Churchill, "and you people must have had a terrible time with them for the past fifty years. Thank the Lord you have He-Saw, We-Saw, You-Saw [i.e., U. Saw, the Prime Minister of Burma who had been in touch with the Japanese] under lock and key. I wish you could put the whole bunch of them into a frying pan with a wall around it and let them stew in their own juice."

Thorne recounts this particularly shocking insight into the President's racial beliefs:

> [Sir Ronald] Campbell, [British Minister in Washington wrote,] "[The President] said that he had set one Professor Hrdlicka of the Smithsonian Institute to work on a private study of the effect of racial crossing. A preliminary report had been given him, with all of which he by no means agreed. But it seemed to him that if we got the Japanese driven back within their islands, racial crossings might have interesting effects particularly in the Far East. For instance, Dutch-Javanese crossings were good, and Javanese-Chinese. Chinese-Malayan was a bad mixture. Hrdlicka said that the Japanese-European cross was bad, and the Chinese-European equally so. It was here he disagreed with the Professor. Experience, the President said, had shown that unlike the Japanese-European mixture, which was, he agreed, thoroughly bad, Chinese-European was not at all bad.

> "The President had asked the Professor why the Japanese were as bad as they were, and had followed up by asking about the Hairy Ainus. The Professor had said the skulls of these people were some 2,000 years less developed than ours (This sounds very little, doesn't it?). The President asked whether this might account for the nefariousness of the Japanese and had been told that it might, as they might well be the basic stock of the Japanese."

The usual arguments of the racism of ordinary citizens as a cause of the exclusion and detention program suffer from the error of misplaced power. The camps were remote and rarely visited by ordinary citizens. Ordinary citizens had only a limited understanding of events, and had little influence in the establishment of the camps. So their racism could not cause the program. But racism at the highest levels of government—a racism rarely acknowledged by historians or by leaders of government, including distinguished members of a federal commission—could effect such a program.

Still, it is debatable whether such racism alone could produce such drastic action. The reason of wartime hysteria is even less compelling. It is difficult to imagine hysteria affecting colonels and generals thousands of miles away from the action. And failed political leadership is almost a truism. Subsequent wars have demonstrated that politicians rarely have the stomach to confront their commander in chief while their troops are under fire. Yet these wars have not provided comparable acts of illegal detention, roundups of civilian Americans.

It seems unlikely that the leaders of the United States, during a desperate, total war, would destroy the productivity and loyalty of any social group, even a despised minority, without compelling reasons; Hitler and his henchmen did not rule in America. What follows is my own explanation developed through discussions, reading, and study of thousands of primary documents.

In the first six months, the war did not go well for America. The Japanese quickly overwhelmed America's imperial outposts in Guam, Wake Island, and the Philippines. General Douglas MacArthur's defeat at Manila was particularly ignominious. Manila had strong defenses, but they were designed to thwart an attack from the sea. The Japanese forces advanced overland. What happened in the Philippines had a great effect on the fate of Japanese-Americans. The Japanese had established an effective network of intelligence and subversion in the Philippines. Formosa, Japan's imperial outpost, was poised like a dagger at the Philippines. Years of preparation preceded the Japanese invasion.[3] Many tried to transfer the lesson of the Philippines to the West Coast. The similarities were strained. Everyone knew that Formosa was a Japanese military outpost. Many of the Japanese preparations there were hardly secret. A plan for imperial expansion from Formosa had been discovered years earlier and lay ignored in U.S. government files. But there was no such Japanese outpost near California. An alert and thorough intelligence community never detected any subversive activity of consequence in California. However, the Philippines campaign brought into play an ugly reality of war that few are willing to confront.

Michi Weglyn, in her book *Years of Infamy, the Untold Story of America's Concentration Camps*, revealed this dark and evil aspect of nations at war: the *quid pro quo* of reprisals against hostages. On February 5, 1942, Secretary of War Henry Stimson sent the following cable to Secretary of State Cordell Hull:

> General MacArthur has reported in a radiogram, a copy of which is enclosed, that American and British civilians in areas of the Philippines occupied by the Japanese are being subjected to extremely harsh treatment. The unnecessary harsh and rigid measures imposed, in sharp contrast to the moderate treatment of metropolitan Filipinos, are unquestionably designed to discredit the white race.

> I request that you strongly protest this unjustified treatment of civilians, and suggest that you present a threat of reprisals against the many Japanese nationals now enjoying negligible restrictions in the United States, to insure proper treatment of our nationals in the Philippines.[4]

Exactly two weeks later, on February 19, President Roosevelt issued Executive Order No. 9066, which precipitated the mass exclusion and detention of the entire West Coast population of Japanese-Americans. That order itself was deliberately nonracial in its wording, and authorized only exclusion, not detention. It applied to "any and all persons" in order to conform to the Fifth Amendment. Its terms seemed reasonable. It gave military commanders the power to remove any and all persons from military zones. One thinks of a plan to keep civilians out of combat zones or areas near sensitive military installations. But when the entire state of California, half of Oregon and Washington, and a good part of Arizona are made a military zone, we see a much different intent. And when "any and all persons" turns out to mean all persons of Japanese ancestry—and only those persons—the intent becomes clearly racial. Then, when these persons are sent to concentration camps in remote, isolated, unheard-of places, penned in by barbed wire and armed guards, the intent becomes dark and foreboding.

It is hard to imagine that in a hot war, with many lives at stake, the highest government officials would make empty threats of reprisals. If threats were to be effective, they had to be credible. In these remote camps, if the threats failed, reprisals could have been carried out with minimum public notice or opposition.

There are several established theories of the causes of detention. The War Relocation Authority (WRA) all but denied the existence of detention and sought to disguise it with official euphemisms. Terms such as "detention," "internment," and "exclusion" were officially replaced by "relocation" and "evacuation." As recently as November 1981, former Colonel Karl R. Bendetsen argued that free citizens' hostility was so great as to have required the use of barbed wire and armed guards to protect the detainees from harm. His was an outlandish form of the theory of protective detention. Nevertheless, it was widely held within the government. With the exception of Weglyn, scholars and historians state, in essence, that while the intent of the evacuation program was the eventual relocation of Japanese-Americans into ordinary communities in the interior, public hostility in the interior states prevented relocation, and thus an evacuation program became a detention program.

This theory has its source in the WRA. The WRA truly believed it was involved in relocation. It did encounter obstinate resistance, from elected officials of interior states, to the relocation of its detainees. The theory is based on historical facts. But the Army built the camps. The Army never fully relinquished control to the WRA. Armed soldiers guarded camp perimeters until the program was ended. Indeed, even when the release of detainees began, those released had first to pass the scrutiny of military intelligence as well as sign a loyalty oath devised by the military. Furthermore, the heavy hand of the military is revealed in its massive response to Miss Mitsuye Endo's filing for release under the writ of *habeas corpus* in July 1942, four months after the establishment of the WRA, four months after control presumably had passed from military to civilian authority. The military's power is also revealed by the decision of Assistant Secretary of War, John J. McCloy, in April 1943, not to announce that the military necessity for the exclusion program had ceased. The mass exclusion order was finally rescinded in January 1945. The official reason was the absence of military necessity for exclusion in the Western Defense Command. But such military necessity had ceased twenty-one months earlier by the military's own reckoning.[5] Exclusion and detention continued for these twenty-one months only because the military decided to continue them. The military's malign influence is also seen in its successful effort to suppress key evidence as the Supreme Court was deliberating its landmark decisions in the Hirabayashi, Yasui, Endo, and Korematsu cases. If the military could so effectively control the rationale for exclusion, establish criteria for detention, and fight off attempts to invoke constitutional protections and guarantees, then the military, not the WRA, established and maintained the detention program.

Even during the first year of the program, the doctrine of military necessity was contrived. The military knew from the beginning that the "facts" supporting the military necessity for exclusion were fictions. Three key "facts" were adduced. One, the presence of shore-to-ship signalings. Two, intercepted radio transmissions in the Japanese katakana code, comparable to our Morse code. And, three, the impossibility of distinguishing those Japanese-Americans who were loyal from those who were disloyal. The FBI investigated and refuted the signalings. The radio transmissions were indeed in katakana code, but originated in Japan, not the interior of California. The Federal Communications Commission meticulously checked each such report and concluded that the Army had its bearings off by 180 degrees. Military intelligence had been studying the loyalty of the Japanese-American community for years before Pearl Harbor. On December 4, 1941, three days before Pearl Harbor, the Office of Naval Intelligence, which had the specific assignment of investigating the security threat posed by the Japanese-American population, had concluded that this threat would be handled by detention of selected individuals. The FBI began implementing this selective procedure hours after the attack on Pearl Harbor, and selective detention was completed before the program of mass detention began. Thus, the U.S. government could and did, to its own satisfaction, separate disloyal from loyal Japanese-Americans.

The stated military reasons for exclusion and detention do not withstand scrutiny, yet the program was the military's program. The military went to great lengths to see that detention was not disrupted. When Mitsuye Endo sued for her release under *habeas corpus*, the War Department drafted legislation to suspend *habeas corpus*. That's a massive response. *Habeas corpus* was last suspended during the Civil War. Without *habeas corpus*, without the opportunity to defend oneself in a courtroom, all other legal rights wither away. The legislation was never submitted. Miss Endo's appeal for freedom was to take two and one-half years to decide. It took two and one-half years to implement a constitutional guarantee that should have taken a few hours, or days. These actions by the government hardly support the notion that the hostility of free citizens necessitated detention. Nor do I believe that simple racism, terrible as it is, made the highest military and government officials ignore the constraints of the Constitution that they had sworn to uphold—and waste millions of dollars on a program that harmed war production.

The need for a credible threat of reprisals, to protect lives in a desperate war, must be considered a primary cause of exclusion and detention. "Military necessity" in its most brutal and terrible form, not as a collection of fictions, overrode the normal rules of civilized behavior. If the Japanese forces were subjecting captured American and British civilians to harsh treatment, then a *quid pro quo* would be necessary. Normally, this *quid pro quo* would be harsh treatment of Japanese prisoners of war. In the first six months of the war, however, while Japan had tens of thousands of American and British civilian and military prisoners, the United States had an exceedingly small number of Japanese prisoners of war—exactly one.[6]

Ultimately, history may be understood as a set of questions rather than answers— questions whose answers lie hidden beneath memoranda, transcripts of telephone conversations, official speeches and personal diaries. Movers and shakers in our times believe not so much in divine judgment as in the judgment of history—something within their power to influence by leaving a trail of their written and spoken words. What goes on in their hearts, and their thoughts that must never be revealed, are left unstated, to be understood only as questions. Japanese troops committed atrocities. What do we call the terrible deeds committed by American troops? We know from photographs that grisly American atrocities were committed, and that these photographs were suppressed, for fear of reprisals. The extent and nature of these atrocities are only disturbing questions, with no answers. We know that lists of "dangerous" aliens were compiled before Pearl Harbor but we don't know the reasons behind the names. We know that informants for the FBI and other intelligence agencies submitted derogatory reports on individuals and leaked confidential WRA reports, but informant names are blacked out when the government releases pertinent documents. John J. McCloy, as Assistant Secretary of War and one of the mass internment program's chief decision-makers, probably comes as close as anyone to raising the critical questions. In his testimony in November 1981, before the Commission on Wartime Relocation and Internment of Civilians—a few months after my testimony—he characterized the internment program as "retribution" for the Japanese attack on Pearl Harbor.

When Judge Marutani asked, "What other Americans, Mr. McCloy, shared in the war by having their mothers, fathers, grandfathers, younger brothers and sisters incarcerated during the war?" McCloy replied:

> Lots of Americans. I saw what was done, the solicitude extended. I don't think the Japanese population was unduly subjected, considering all the exigencies to which—the amount it did share in the way of retribution for the attack that was made on Pearl Harbor.

And when asked about preventing the recurrence of a similar event in the future, he replied:

> Within 90 miles of our shores [there are] a hundred, roughly a hundred thousand people, thoroughly trained, thoroughly equipped, well trained in modern warfare, that are being set up to serve as proxies for the Soviet Union in the various strategic parts of the world. Suppose there was a raid some 10, 20, 30 years hence on [Florida], wouldn't you be apt to think about moving them, [Cuban Americans,] if there was a raid there? You can't tell.[7]

After McCloy made these statements and completed his testimony, he was warmly greeted by the distinguished members of the Commission, including former Supreme Court Justice Arthur Goldberg. To some, this display of felicitations was incongruous. But perhaps the incongruity is in one's perception of the military. For many of the victims, it was through military activity, the exploits of the famed 100th Infantry Battalion and 442nd Regimental Combat Team, that the resolution of the injustice occurred. In Bill Hosokawa's book on the JACL, McCloy is described as "a staunch friend of the Nisei."[8] McCloy has gone on to achieve the status of "The Most

Influential Private Citizen in America."[9] The title is supported by a string of achievements, both corporate and diplomatic. Victory in war brings honor and glory.

I find it strange that warriors are covered with honor and glory when war itself is so brutish. Are there rules observed when it comes to taking prisoners? Does encountering prisoners with an exhausted supply of ammunition lead to their execution? Is the gang rape of a woman by warriors on their way to the showers acceptable, for the sake of their morale? War is hell. Perhaps we Americans need the excesses of honor and glory to offset its dark, brute reality. How, then, does one protect American and British civilians from the threat of Japanese atrocities—especially when there is but a single Japanese prisoner of war in our hands?

When I first read a copy of Stimson's memorandum to Hull, I thought I'd found the smoking gun. In all of NCJAR's examination of primary documents, mainly from the National Archives, one question nagged: why were we Japanese-Americans detained? Why were we detained in remote places? If our presence on the West Coast constituted a threat to the Western Defense Command, then our removal would surely eliminate the threat. Why the concentration camps? This is where the reasons given by the CWRIC fail to withstand scrutiny. While there *was* racism and hysteria and failed political leadership, these simply do not add up to detention. They might serve to explain exclusion, but not detention. Detention was not an explicit part of President Roosevelt's Executive Order Number 9066. Nor was it part of Public Law 503, passed by Congress to enforce the executive order. Nor was it an issue in the four Supreme Court test cases. I was excited about my discovery. And was immediately deflated when I learned from Michi Weglyn that she had included the memorandum in her book, *Years of Infamy*. The documents do support the existence of a *quid pro quo*, vigorously supported by the State Department, between the American treatment of Japanese-Americans and the Japanese treatment of Americans.

Dr. David Trask, Historian of the Department of State, described the relationship in his testimony before the CWRIC in July 1981:

> [T]he Department of State had an important interest in the program [of mass exclusion and detention] because it was the agency responsible for insuring the good treatment of some 10,000 American civilians captured in the Philippines, Wake Island, Guam, China, and Japan in the early stages of the war. The Department was also interested in obtaining the early release of the prisoners. The Japanese government knew of the relocation camps and objected to the treatment of their inmates. This circumstance posed the possibility of reprisals against Americans in Japanese hands.[10]

The "possibility of reprisals" is, of course, symmetrical, equally available to both sides of a conflict. In order to be symmetrical, both sides must have comparable numbers of hostages. Trask cites 10,000 American civilians in Japanese hands. Where were the 10,000 Japanese civilians in American hands? Where but in the "relocation centers?"

(The irony and illogic of this situation challenges language. The American mistreatment of Japanese-Americans was, of course, American mistreatment of *Americans*. But this makes the State Department's fears seem nonsensical. How could the U.S. government expect that American mistreatment of Americans would affect Japanese mistreatment of Americans? The illogic becomes logic when Japanese-Americans are seen as "Japanese." Significantly, both Bendetsen and McCloy continued to say "Japanese" when referring to Japanese-Americans in their testimonies before the CWRIC in 1981.[11])

The Stimson memorandum is a disturbing document. It raises terrible questions. Did it presage the doctrine of nuclear deterrence? Was the vulnerability of Japanese-Americans to reprisals supposed to deter Japanese harsh treatment of white Americans? What if deterrence failed at this level? Would there have been escalation? What if the fortunes of war had not shifted in June 1942, with the American victory at the Battle of Midway? What if?

While my explanation of the event may lead us only to an overwhelming question, the movement to redress the event's injustices is amenable to more straightforward elucidation.

5. BEGINNINGS

EARLY STIRRINGS

The movement for redress has several beginnings. Not all lead directly to the present. The current movement goes back to 1970 and developed in a straightforward, easily understood way. Earlier stirrings stretch back to the war itself, in the acts of courageous individuals who are all but forgotten now. They were ahead of their time. Their vision, courage, and humanity were exceptional. They are kindred spirits, even if not our direct predecessors. They articulated an understanding that is worth emulation. They demonstrated a heroism that can energize our contemporary redress movement.

The First Beginning: James Omura in 1942

James Omura was among the 4,889 people who fled the exclusion zone of the Western Defense Command during a short period of "voluntary" exclusion.[1] Immediately after President Roosevelt issued Executive Order Number 9066 on February 19, 1942, enabling the exclusion of "any and all persons" from prescribed military areas, General John L. DeWitt was delegated the authority to prescribe the areas and to define who the "any" to be excluded might be.[2] The broad language of the order was quite deliberate. The original idea was to exclude everyone—thereby avoiding violation of the Fifth Amendment—and to allow all to return but the "Japs." As it turned out, they didn't have to be quite so clever. They simply excluded the "Japs."[3] On March 2, DeWitt issued Public Proclamation No. 1 which designated a broad, roughly 100-mile wide, strip along the West Coast running through Washington, Oregon, California, and Arizona as Military Area No. 1. However, he could not yet implement exclusion from this zone until Congress provided the necessary sanctions or penalties for noncooperation with the military program. The sanctions were enacted by Public Law 503, signed by the President on March 21, 1942. DeWitt wanted the violation of EO9066 to be a felony so that violators could legally be threatened with deadly force; Congress did not oblige and made it a misdemeanor. Then, on March 24, Public Proclamation No. 3 was issued, which confined Japanese-Americans to stay within a five-mile radius of their homes and required that they remain home from 8:00 p.m. to 6:00 a.m., as though they were difficult teenagers. A few days before the curfew went into effect, the first camp at Manzanar was already being built and populated by "voluntary" internees. The handwriting was on the wall. On March 27, Public Proclamation No. 4 was issued, effective midnight of the 29th, prohibiting "voluntary" movement of Japanese-Americans from Area No. 1. By the morning of March 30, the movement of Japanese-Americans was "frozen." Those who hadn't escaped from Military Area No. 1 could now expect to be interned.

James Omura lived in San Francisco and published a literary magazine called *Current Life*. Omura escaped from Military Area No. 1, the zone of "military necessity," just as the freeze descended. He moved to Denver. His wife had gone on ahead. His livelihood provided him with a degree of mobility. Farmers, fishermen, gardeners, and wage earners were less free to pull up stakes and leave. Once in Denver, Omura did more than just reestablish his own life. He helped other refugees who had escaped from the exclusion zone. He had an office for his magazine; he expanded its function by putting up a sign, "The Pacific Coast Evacuee Placement Bureau." He helped refugees find jobs and housing. He worked without fee and financed the Bureau from his own income and savings. In addition, he attempted to organize legal action against the United States, for restoration of civil and constitutional rights, and for restitution for economic losses and for violation of individual rights.

On May 1, 1942, he wrote to the Washington law firm of Colladay, Colladay and Wallace seeking their legal representation. The firm required $3,500 to begin their representation. It was more than Omura was able to raise. He later became involved in other battles to restore the demolished citizenship and constitutional rights of Japanese-Americans. These activities would be even less popular than his earlier effort to seek restitution. James Omura was the first Japanese-American to seek redress from the United States government.

The Second Beginning: Joseph Y. Kurihara in 1943

The second attempt at redress began in the camps. Actually, it took place in a camp within the camps, detention within detention. On June 1, 1943, Joseph Y. Kurihara wrote a letter from a special, high-security camp at Leupp, Arizona, to Miss Yoshiko Hosoi in block 27, barrack 13, cubicle 1, at Manzanar. It was a long letter, executed in Kurihara's well-formed script. The letter was really an essay entitled, "Niseis and the Government." Kurihara had been seized, along with fifteen other inmates of the camp at Manzanar, in the wake of an uprising on December 6, 1942, in which ten inmates were shot, two fatally, by the military police assigned to guard the camp.[4]

At the time of the shooting, Kurihara was in the Manzanar police station, trying to negotiate with the camp's administration on behalf of a group of internees. He was arrested because of his participation on the negotiating committee and also, probably, his reputation. He was considered to be the "baddest of the bad." He was a patriotic American who turned on his country in anger. Born in Hawaii, he came to California in his youth, found the racism there objectionable, and moved to Michigan, where he went to college. After the outbreak of World War I, he enlisted in the U.S. Army. He had demonstrated his loyalty. He had assumed that as a veteran he would not be interned. He had assumed that it was his right as an American to protest the violation of his constitutional rights. He had witnessed the harsh, inhumane eviction of Japanese-American families from Terminal Island on forty-eight hours' notice. His faith in America had been shaken. When exclusion was imminent, he attended a JACL-sponsored meeting in Los Angeles, intending to join in a protest. But he learned that the JACL was urging cooperation, not protest. As he said, "The goose was already cooked."[5]

The concentration camp was a particularly bitter experience for the forty-seven-year-old Nisei.[6] (The median age of American-born internees was eighteen and one-half.[7]) In his letter, Kurihara wrote:

The desert was bad enough. The mushroom barracks made it worse. The constant cyclonic storms loaded with sand and dusts made it worst. After living in a lovable, well-furnished homes with every modern conveniences, and suddenly forced to live the life of a dog is something which one cannot so readily forget. Down in our hearts we cried and cursed this government every time we were showered with sand. We slept in the dust, breathed the dust, and ate the dust. Such abominable existence one cannot forget no matter how much we tried to be patient, understand the situation, and take it bravely, however bitter it may be.

He remembered Terminal Island:

The evacuation of Terminal Island was unquestionably harsh and pitifully unjust. To command bewildered women with children suffering in mental agonies through [the] internment of their husbands [taken] by the F.B.I.'s to pack and evacuate in 48 hours was inhumanly harsh and unjust. Lost in despair, they were desperate. Automatic cooler costing $200.00 was sold for $10.00 and $500.00 Baby Grand Piano was sold for $10.00 and countless other valuable household furnitures were sold for whatever the peddlers chose to pay. Many unreplacable momentos were abandoned in tears. Children were crying, boys and girls dashing in and out to help their mothers on whose shoulders the world came crashing without mercy. Oh God, what a pitiful sight! Could this be America, the America which so blatantly preaches "Democracy?"

The question was more than rhetorical. He sought an explanation from his government and was unusually perceptive about its failed promises:

Responsible government officials further tells us to be loyal, and to enjoy our rights as American citizens. We must be ready to die for the country. We must show our loyalty. If such is the case, why are the veterans corralled like the rest of us in the camps? Have they not proven their loyalty already?

This matter of proving our loyalty to enjoy the rights of our American citizen[ship] is nothing but a hocus-pocus. Recalling the promises made to the colored boys at the outbreak of the first world war, I would like to ask you if those promises given them [for] the full liberties of American citizens were duly kept? If those promises are really being lived up to then why are they being lynched without a trial? Why are they not given the right to vote in many of the Southern States? Why are they not enjoying equal rights as citizens of the United States to attend public schools in the South without total discrimination? Every one of those rights are constitutionally guaranteed to them. Those constitutional rights were only repeated in verbal promises to the colored people as if they were something absolutely beyond the realm of their rights. To share in those coveted rights, they were told they must fight and sacrifice everything for the country and for Democracy. For the love of their progenies; for the love of their wives, mothers, and sweethearts, and for the sake of these United States of America and American Democracy, they have fought and died gloriously on the Altar of battlefield. Their rights heroically earned beyond all questions of doubt, underwritten with the blood and lives of many tens of thousands of American Negroes, are today submerged completely beneath the rights and pride of the whites. Those same promises made to the colored boys in the first world war are being repeated to the Niseis today. The colored boys refuse to be made donkies again. Shall we be fooled and be jackasses in this war?

His anger congealed and became almost palpable:

Now could America blame us for our change of mind? Could America blame us for the sympathy we extend to Japan? Could America blame us for the desire we openly express when questioned by the F.B.I. to fight for Japan against the United States?

Who in the world, with the slightest spark of manhood in him, wouldn't after 50 years of oppression, detestation, and persecution?

Have we not been orphanized, ostracized, and corralled like a bunch of prisoners in a godforsaken country?

Haven't our Constitutional rights been brazenly ignored, our economical rights completely uprooted from the Pacific Coast, and our status reduced to slavery after thousands of us have gladly fought and died for this country? Yet our loyalty was mercilessly questioned, we were called a bunch of fifth columnists, saboteurs, and spies, we who are traditionally and habitually, through hereditary instinct, loyal to the country of our birth.

In the face of what has been done to us, must we continue to submit ourselves to further insult? No! Then let us proclaim ourselves Japs! Yes, Japs! I repeat, "What is there for us to be ashamed of being a Jap?" To be born a Jap is the greatest blessing God has bestowed on us. To live as Japs is the greatest pride we can enjoy in life. And to die as Japs under the protection of the Japanese Flag which has weathered through many national storms without a defeat for 2600 years [is] the greatest honor a man can ever hope to cherish. I, [in] the name of the Niseis, proclaim ourselves Japs, 100 percent Japs, now, tomorrow, and forever.

Kurihara's statement, with its occasional lapses in pluralization and added and dropped articles, is vintage Nisei. His forthright anger and candor give away his Hawaiian origins. They express frustrations and hurts that most inmates could express only in oblique ways. Common camp expressions were "lose fight" and "stopped solid." Kurihara had been able to break through the constrictions of racial oppression. It is far more consistent with the character of an oppressed people to take a while before protesting. People who ask, "Why has it taken so long?" simply do not understand the nature of oppression. Even those oppressed have difficulty recognizing their oppression. I have a brother who has a gift for candor. Shortly after graduating from the University of Chicago in 1949, he applied for a job at the University of Chicago Press and was rejected because of his Japanese ancestry. His inner response, which he described to me, was, "Excuse me, for being a Jap." His race, which provoked his rejection, in his mind had become a disability for which he apologized as if it were *his* fault that he was rejected, not the fault of the University of Chicago Press.

Of course, Kurihara's words marked him as an incorrigible troublemaker. Kurihara was the "baddest of the bad." His transfer to the high-security camps validated his badness. Kurihara's pro-Japan sentiments became "criminal," even in the minds of other Japanese-Americans. In that time, few would dare to agree with him openly:

The only successful measure left to encourage the industrious Japanese to a permanent resettlement is to compensate them fully for the loss they were made to suffer through evacuation. No definite amount of loss can be determined readily at present. Therefore, the Government should set an approximate damage of $5,000.00 for each and every evacuee of voting age and start them on in any industry benefitting the country as a whole.[8]

His plea for reparations could not take root.

The Third Beginning: Kiyoshi Okamoto in 1946

Another early attempt at obtaining reparations grew out of another form of protest movement within the camps. The military draft, which was suspended for Japanese-Americans on June 17, 1942, was reinstated on January 14, 1944. This was not a popular decision. The injustice was too obvious. By 1944, the hard reality of detention had made a deep impression on the minds of those detained. For many, the notion of their being conscripted to fight and die to protect precious freedoms only others enjoyed was incongruous and revolting. Although more than 30,000 Japanese-Americans served in the Army, only 805 were inducted as volunteers from within the camps. (By contrast, in Hawaii, where mass exclusion and detention did not occur, almost 10,000 Americans of Japanese ancestry volunteered.) In comparison, 315 Japanese-Americans resisted the draft from within the camps. While the volunteers from the camps have been made to appear larger than life, the resisters have been almost forgotten. From the ranks of the draft resisters, another movement for reparations began. Kiyoshi Okamoto, another Hawaiian, was a leader of the Heart Mountain draft resistance movement. This movement was supported by James Omura, mentioned earlier as the first Japanese-American to demand reparations. Omura became editor of the *Rocky Shimpo*, a Japanese-American newspaper published in Denver. The Heart Mountain draft resistance leaders called themselves "The Fair Play Committee." Their principal point was simply, "Free us before you draft us."

In June 1944, the same month that the 442nd Regimental Combat Team landed in Italy, sixty-three inmates from Heart Mountain were tried, convicted, and sentenced to three years in prison for refusing to report for induction. In the following month, eight men, Kiyoshi Okamoto and six others of the Fair Play Committee, and James Omura, were arrested on charges of conspiracy to encourage draft resistance. Omura was arrested for writing editorials in the *Rocky Shimpo*. Of course, Omura and the Fair Play Committee leaders were not guilty of "conspiracy" in the everyday sense of secret, subversive plotting. On March 4 the Fair Play Committee published the following words:

> We, the members of the FPC, are not afraid to go to war—we are not afraid to risk our lives for our country. We would gladly sacrifice our lives to protect and uphold the principles and ideals of our country as set forth in the Constitution and the Bill of Rights ...

> [BUT] WITHOUT RECTIFICATION OF THE INJUSTICES COMMITTED AGAINST US [AND] WITHOUT RESTORATION OF OUR RIGHTS AS GUARANTEED BY THE CONSTITUTION, WE ARE ORDERED TO JOIN THE ARMY THROUGH DISCRIMINATORY PROCEDURES INTO A SEGREGATED COMBAT UNIT!

> ... therefore, WE MEMBERS OF THE FAIR PLAY COMMITTEE HEREBY REFUSE TO GO TO THE PHYSICAL EXAMINATION OR TO THE INDUCTION IF OR WHEN WE ARE CALLED IN ORDER TO CONTEST THE ISSUE.

> We are not being disloyal. We are not evading the draft. We are all loyal Americans fighting for JUSTICE AND DEMOCRACY RIGHT HERE AT HOME.[9]

Since when has it been "conspiracy" to invoke the United States Constitution and the Bill of Rights to protest a manifestly unjust action of the U.S. government? The Fair Play Committee had only spelled out the obvious principle implied in the observation of Elmer Davis, head of the Office of War Information, in his letter of October 2, 1942 to President Roosevelt:

> It would hardly be fair to evacuate people and then impose normal draft procedures [on them.][10]

The Heart Mountain draft resistance movement was unique because it was an organized group seeking redress and not simply courageous individuals, like Omura and Kurihara. When Okamoto was taken away, another took his place. Efforts were made to break up the movement. While the Heart Mountain resisters were languishing in the Cheyenne County Jail, two members of the Japanese American Citizens League came to the jail to try to change the resisters' minds. After interviewing six of them without success, the JACL members recommended solitary confinement:

> It seems too that the incarceration of these boys in one group bolsters and inspirits each other. Anyone in the group who might be inclined to doubt the wisdom of their conduct would be quashed by the arguments expressed to us: "We're in this far; we might as well see this through." Those who might want to change their minds, convinced of the error of their ways, would probably not be tolerated. For these reasons, separate and individual cells would allow considerable introspection and self-analysis. It would supplant individual decision for group pressure.[11]

The WRA had already tried to dissuade the young men from disobeying their induction orders. The JACL, in its quasi-official role, was not successful either. The Heart Mountain resistance held firm. Accordingly, the government responded by arresting its leaders for conspiracy.

In November 1944, seven were found guilty, and Omura was acquitted.[12] Draft resistance was not popular during World War II. Though acquitted, Omura was wiped out financially and thereby silenced. No one was defending with dollars, much less to the death, his inalienable right of free speech and his constitutional guarantee to freedom of the press. Kiyoshi Okamoto and the six others were convicted and sent to a federal penitentiary. The conviction, however, failed to withstand the scrutiny of an appeal. On December 27, 1945, the seven were freed by an appeals court's reversal of their conviction.

Okamoto kept up the fight. In 1946, he changed the committee's name to "The Fair Rights Committee" and incorporated in the state of California for the purpose of seeking restitution for the victims. His persistence was remarkable. His effort, however, did not survive the 1948 Evacuation Claims Act. The Act was supposed to provide restitution but, in fact, failed miserably, paying only for property losses, yielding on average a mere $340 per victim. Even my pushing a lawn mower at prewar rates for three months was worth more. More significantly, the Act required that compensation be contingent upon the recipient's waiving of his or her right to sue for all other injuries. One is reminded of the biblical tale of an exhausted and hungry Esau trading his birthright to Jacob for a bowl of red soup.

These three early petitioners for redress were all isolated from, and ostracized by, mainstream Japanese America. Kurihara renounced his American citizenship in anger, and transferred his allegiance to Japan. Okamoto, quite the opposite, embraced America and demanded that he be treated as an American before he would fight as one. But draft resistance was extremely unpopular during World War II. And Omura's editorial support, however carefully expressed, brought the wrath of the establishment upon him. The FBI's John Edgar Hoover tenaciously wrote orders, in the margins of field reports from his special agents, to have "Justice see if we can get him on sedition." To the Japanese American Citizens League, any action seeking redress was an anathema. It would be decades before the redress would once again be proposed and a redress movement would finally take root.

6. BEGINNINGS
BEGINNING AGAIN

Edison Uno in 1970

My first encounter with public support for redress took place at the 1970 national convention of the Japanese American Citizens League, which was held in Chicago. At the time, I was a delegate to the convention from the newly formed Chicago Liberation Chapter. This chapter was part of a broader attempt to reform the JACL, to bring the organization into step with the 1960s which had just ended. A group of convention delegates and observers came together as the National Liberation Caucus.

Most of us in the Caucus were associated with the then-current movement to repeal Title II of the Internal Security Act of 1950. Title II provided for "establishing concentration camps into which people might be put without benefit of trial."[1] The JACL's involvement in this movement was peripheral, as the name of the movement's working committee suggests: "National Ad Hoc Committee for Repeal of the Emergency Detention Act." In its Chicago activities, in which my wife, Yuriko, and I were participants, the movement was ad hoc to the point of involving mainly non-JACL support. Most of our Chicago support came from the Chicago Committee to Defend the Bill of Rights.[2]

The emergence of the Caucus was a phenomenon. The JACL had largely stayed away from the civil rights movement. During my limited participation in the civil rights movement, I rarely saw another Japanese-American face. In 1970, the JACL had yet to take a stand on the war in Vietnam. The Caucus wanted the JACL to understand that the civil rights movement was for Japanese-Americans as well as blacks; that the Vietnam war came, in part, from a racism that was anti-Asian; that our concentration camp experience had set an ugly precedent Japanese-Americans could address with the authority of firsthand experience. The Caucus also served as the link between the JACL convention and a counter-convention of radical, mainly Sansei (third generation) Japanese-Americans at Christian Fellowship Church on Chicago's North Side. If we wanted to prod the JACL, they wanted to push. The JACL felt threatened. The JACL's leaders were fearful of any public demonstrations, such as picketing, especially at their social events. So they made an effort to neutralize the perceived threat by inviting staged "radical" presentations within their convention. The Sansei radicals showed a film on the atomic bombing of Hiroshima and Nagasaki; they then used the exclamation "Hiroshima!" to vilify elements of American society that they deemed evil, such as corporations, the military, and the Vietnam war. Their strong statement drew words of outrage, directed towards the radicals, from the mostly conservative JACL members.

Our Caucus presentation, not quite so harsh, was a set of speeches. Edison Uno, one of our speakers, presented the case for reparations for our unlawful incarceration during

BEGINNINGS

World War II. He spoke in support of a resolution submitted to the convention by the Northern California-Western Nevada District Council of the JACL. This resolution called upon the JACL to seek congressional legislation to compensate all victims for wrongful incarceration; compensation was to be made on a per diem basis to individuals, estates, or heirs. To me, this was a novel, appealing idea. But the JACL hardly seemed ready to accept Uno's appeal for reparations.

The movement to repeal Title II succeeded in 1971, when President Nixon signed the repeal bill into law on September 25. Edison Uno persisted in pressing for redress within the JACL. The JACL adopted resolutions in support of redress in 1970, 1972, and 1974, largely through Uno's efforts. There is a gradualism in these resolutions; they state a position but lead to no specific action. In a January 1975 issue of the *Pacific Citizen*, Uno was reported as declaring:

> [The issue of evacuee reparations] embodies several important concepts which will have historic consequences, and its economic, social, political, and psychological impact may be significant to our children and our grandchildren.
>
> If Congress passes an evacuation reparations bill, it will accomplish several key points:
>
> 1. It would admit liability for false imprisonment, wrongful detention, loss or denial of civil rights;
>
> 2. It would pay monetary damages for mental anguish, loss of gainful employment, hardships and suffering, etc.;
>
> 3. It would admit legal liability, thereby affirming legislatively the illegal, unjust, and wrongful interpretation of the Evacuation episode;
>
> 4. If successful, it has the potential to provide our communities of many hundreds of million dollars for community needs;
>
> 5. It would vindicate the entire question of the loyalty and patriotism of all persons of Japanese ancestry;
>
> 6. It may prevent the government from taking future actions which violate the integrity and dignity of American citizens;
>
> 7. It would be an important educational vehicle to educate millions of Americans as to this American tragedy;
>
> 8. The funds would provide us the security to insure our future well-being and of future generations.

The *Pacific Citizen* story continued with this description of reparations benefitting the JACL:

> Uno envisioned construction of multi-purpose community centers, national headquarters and regional offices with reparation funds. He was of the belief the government should be paying for building the JACL Headquarters, that it should be a community center facility, and ventured he would probably be one of the first to seek space in the JACL Headquarters Building for community-based groups.

Substantial opposition to this use of reparations would emerge from Japanese-Americans in Seattle.

The Seattle Evacuation Redress Committee

Henry Miyatake, a systems engineer at the Boeing aircraft plant in Seattle, began thinking about redress in 1970 and 1971. He began a serious study of the issue during Christmas vacation in 1972. In early 1973, he was asked by Frank Matsumoto of the JACL to write a paper on the topic. The paper was the beginning of the "Seattle Plan." The "Seattle Plan" uniquely identified a method of payment in which Japanese-Americans would be permitted to designate their federal tax dollars to accumulate in a special trust fund of the Internal Revenue Service; the dollars accumulated would then be paid as redress to Japanese-American victims over a period of approximately ten years until all the victims had been redressed. The plan was to pay the oldest victims first. The plan was formally described in a document titled "An Appeal for Action to Obtain Redress for the World War II Evacuation and Imprisonment of Japanese Americans." It was dated November 19, 1975 and signed by Shosuke Sasaki, Mike Nakata, and Henry Miyatake for the Seattle Evacuation Redress Committee of the Seattle Chapter of the JACL. The imprint of Shosuke Sasaki's ascerbic, yet cautious, style is evident throughout. The writers begin with a statement of principle:

> Among the documents which form the philosophical and legal foundations of our nation, . . . no idea is more basic . . . than the principle of equality of all persons before the law. . . .[T]rue Americanism meant an unbending insistence by each individual that any government accord him equality of treatment before its laws. . . .

After describing the catastrophic events of World War II and their effects on the victims, they state:

> The fact that even after a lapse of thirty years, no real attempt has been made by Japanese Americans to obtain redress for the wrongs, humiliations and loss of income suffered by them during their totally unwarranted imprisonment indicates that the older Nisei, at least, have been so psychologically crippled by their pre-war and wartime experience that they have been unable to act as Americans should.

Although the writers exercise restraint, they clearly criticize the JACL for its past accommodationist stance. But at first they only allude to the organization:

> Passive submission or self-abasement when confronted by government tyranny or injustice was alien to the beliefs held by the founders of this nation. If, in the face of British government tyranny, they had acted like the Nisei have in the face of American government tyranny, there would be no 200th Anniversary of the founding of our country to celebrate. In commemorating the birth of our nation, therefore, it is time that Americans of Japanese ancestry repudiate the pseudo-American doctrine, promoted by white racists and apparently believed in by some former Nisei leaders, that there is one kind of Americanism for whites and another kind for non-whites.

Then they make explicit the object of their criticism:

> If Japanese Americans are as American as the J.A.C.L. has often claimed, then they should act like Americans and make every effort to seek redress through legislation and the courts for the rape of almost all their "unalienable rights" by the United States Government over thirty years ago.

They argue forcefully for legal action:

> By custom and tradition, any American who has been injured as a result of false accusa-
> tions is expected to bring those responsible into court and obtain a judgment clearing
> his name and awarding him monetary damages from the offending parties. *Failure by*
> *the slandered or libeled person to take legal action against his accusers is often regarded*
> *by the public as an indication that the charges are true* (emphasis added).

They argue that past protestations of loyalty by Nisei to white America do not remove
the stigma resulting from false accusations:

> No amount of docile submission to white officials or "demonstrations of loyalty" to the
> United States by the Nisei can ever "disprove" the false accusations in the minds of
> most white Americans. That can only be done when the Government of the United States
> either through Congress or through its courts publicly declares that the wartime uprooting
> and imprisonment of Japanese Americans was totally without justification and awards
> the victims of its wartime outrage proper and reasonable redress.

Their statements stand in sharp contrast to "The Japanese American Creed" written
by Mike Masaoka, adopted by the JACL before Pearl Harbor, and recorded in the
Congressional Record on May 9, 1941, which continues to this day to be an affirmation of the JACL:

> I am proud that I am an American citizen of Japanese ancestry, for my very background
> makes me appreciate more fully the wonderful advantages of this Nation. I believe in
> her institutions, ideals, and traditions; I glory in her heritage; I boast of her history;
> I trust in her future. She has granted me liberties and opportunities such as no individual
> enjoys in this world today. She has given me an education befitting kings. She has en-
> trusted me with the responsibilities of the franchise. She has permitted me to build a
> home, to earn a livelihood, to worship, think, speak, and act as I please—as a free man
> equal to every other man.
>
> Although some individuals may discriminate against me, I shall never become bitter or
> lose faith, for I know that such persons are not representative of the majority of the
> American people. True, I shall do all in my power to discourage such practices, but I
> shall do it in the American way—above board, in the open, through courts of law, by
> education, by proving myself to be worthy of equal treatment and consideration. I am
> firm in my belief that American sportsmanship and attitude of fair play will judge citizen-
> ship and patriotism on the basis of action and achievement, and not on the basis of physical
> characteristics.
>
> Because I believe in America, and I trust she believes in me, and because I have received
> innumerable benefits from her, I pledge myself to do honor to her at all times and in
> all places; to support her constitution; to obey her laws; to respect her flag; to defend
> her against all enemies, foreign or domestic; to actively assume my duties and obliga-
> tions as a citizen, cheerfully and without any reservations whatsoever, in the hope that
> I may become a better American in a greater America.[3]

The Creed obsequiously yields everything to government; it fails to recognize the protections and guarantees against governmental abuse and tyranny that are needed to
secure the freedom of individuals. Fortunately, the framers of the United States Constitution were not so sanguine about governments, including their own, and so added
protections of the Bill of Rights into their structure for self-government. The Seattle
Evacuation Redress Committee, taking their cue from the Constitution rather than
the Japanese American Creed, recognized the need for asserting individual rights.

Their recommendations for redress include both the so-called voluntary evacuees, those excluded but not interned, and those excluded and interned. They accomplish this by providing a fixed sum of $5,000 for all persons excluded plus a variable rate of $10 a day for those excluded and interned for each day of internment. (The Seattle movement's $5,000 is coincidentally identical to the sum recommended by Joe Kurihara in 1943. It is probable that the people in Seattle were unaware of Kurihara's earlier proposal.) These recommendations would eventually come into conflict with proposals by the national JACL.

Finally, in 1976 the JACL did pass a resolution which led to action; the JACL created a National Committee for Redress (NCR). The NCR produced a booklet on the issue of redress and formulated legislation for the 1978 convention to consider. Their proposed legislation also stimulated controversy.

In March 1977, the Seattle Evacuation Redress Committee issued a paper, "Case for Individual Reparations Payments," which argued against payments in the form of block grants to Japanese-American organizations and groups, a concept promoted by Edison Uno a few years earlier. It argued that reparations should repair the injury suffered by the individuals. Block grants to organizations would miss many individuals outside the organizations and would probably lead to contentions and legal battles on the use or misuse of such grants.

Just prior to the 1978 convention, on June 12, 1978, the Seattle Evacuation Redress Committee issued another paper, "Common Sense and Reparations." It discussed several of the Committee's disagreements with the JACL's treatment of redress.

In addition to block grants, the national JACL proposed a fixed sum of $25,000 to all Japanese-Americans who were residing within the Western Defense Command at the start of World War II. The inclusion of the entire Western Defense Command was undoubtedly an error. The Western Defense Command included the entire states of Washington, Oregon, California, and Arizona as well as the interior states of Nevada, Utah, Idaho, and Montana, whereas the exclusion zone covered only California entirely and the other states either partially or not at all. In addition to being too inclusive, the Western Defense Command excluded Japanese-Americans who had been interned from the Hawaiian Defense Command, as well as Eastern, Alaskan, and other Defense Commands.

Moreover, the fixed sum would treat all injuries suffered equally. While a completely precise treatment of the injuries of over 125,000 persons is infeasible, there does exist the broad distinction between those who were only excluded and those excluded and interned. The failure to make this broad distinction could lead to the eventual disqualification of those who suffered from exclusion only.

But the biggest issue arose over the JACL's intent to establish a trust fund administered by Japanese-Americans. The Seattle Committee was seriously concerned about the selection of such persons and the potential for the mismanagement of funds:

Moreover, we are both puzzled and alarmed by the National Committee's intention to first put all redress funds appropriated by Congress into a trust to be controlled by a Japanese American Commission. In view of the demonstrated inability of the J.A.C.L. to manage or handle its own funds, it is questionable whether a trust fund controlled by *any* casually selected Japanese American group could show any better results. Directing the management and disbursement of up to three billion dollars requires persons of a very high level of experience, ability, and integrity. Such a sum in the hands of a randomly chosen group of inexperienced Japanese Americans would become an almost irresistably tempting money depot for looting by clever knaves and crooks.

The Seattle Evacuation Redress Committee firmly believes that any funds appropriated by Congress should remain in the hands of the United States Government at least until all claims by individuals have been paid.

Fiscal opportunism and pragmatism seem to be endemic to American life. Certainly, the Japanese-American community had no special immunity to the seduction of large sums of money. But the warnings of the Committee, with their criticism of past fiscal practices by the JACL, would not be well-received by the JACL.

From its beginnings, the movement for Japanese-American redress was immersed in dissent. Its emergence as the National Council for Japanese American Redress in 1979 would not be different.

7. BEGINNINGS
FORMING NCJAR

Nelson Kitsuse, to my mind, embodies the Japanese trait of *enryo,* which can be seen as shyness, reticence, and self-effacement almost to the point of self-denigration. Nelson is an older Nisei. (I characterize Nisei who graduated from high school before World War II as older Nisei.) Older Nisei tend to be culturally more Japanese than younger ones. But in his own way Nelson can also be pushy. He managed to push me into the redress movement by saying, "I want to do something about it." Coming from him, this was almost a confrontation. This happened in January 1979.

A few years earlier, he and I had joined in an effort to seek a presidential pardon for Iva Toguri, who had been accused, tried, and convicted of treason and served a ten-year sentence for being "Tokyo Rose." The evidence clearly pointed to a gross miscarriage of justice, which had been prompted by the news media's vindictive hatred of Japan. The effort for a pardon was nationwide, led by a committee of the JACL. Nelson introduced me to Iva, who lived and worked on Chicago's North Side. Soon she became my friend and one of my heroines of Japanese-American history. In her years of trial and imprisonment, she had received little support from the Japanese-American community. Indeed, she had become a pariah among us Japanese-Americans, the realization of our worst fears: a convicted traitor. Some Japanese-American newspapers even urged her execution. I was impressed by her strength of character and integrity which, while she was in Japan during the war, allowed her to withstand the pressure from the Japanese secret police to renounce her American citizenship; which gave her the courage to return voluntarily to America to stand trial in the face of a hostile press; and which sustained her in her years of imprisonment. I found it remarkable that she survived those awful years with her integrity, graciousness, and a lively sense of humor intact.

In the 1974-77 movement for her pardon, our role had been supportive of the efforts of the JACL. Our work was confined mainly to the United Methodist churches of the Northern Illinois Conference. We dubbed our campaign "Pardon me, Iva." We felt we needed her pardon for our long years of silence as much as she needed the President's. She was finally pardoned in 1977 by President Ford, on his last day in office. I hoped that we could do something similar in the redress movement. But history is not always so accommodatingly repetitive. Two critical events would alter our course.

Nelson and I are somewhat anachronistic; we are serious Christians. We take our faith seriously. This means that each Sunday we confess, we sing, we ponder the meaning of the Scripture lessons and listen attentively to our pastor's exposition and exegesis of the Bible, agreeing or disagreeing; we allow the Word as presented to penetrate, infiltrate, and rearrange the pathways of our minds and to nurture the humankindness of our hearts. But beware, lest you think this makes us morally upright and socially sanctimonious. Nelson's characterization of original sin would probably come out as "being full of shit." (This characterization has yet to insinuate itself into our corporate affirmation of faith.) And though I love the church, I am aware of the horrors that the church has inflicted and continues to inflict on humankind in the fervor of unthought-out Christian faith, including its sexism, anti-Semitism and homophobia and its participation in imperial conquests around the earth by flag, cross, and cannon. (If this seems to be contradictory, even crazy, consider the human condition itself. Isn't the acceptance of this deep contradiction an acceptance of our humanness?)

Our faith did compel us to think through and to spell out what we meant by our decision to support the redress movement. I drafted a resolution. It included our desire to support the redress initiative of the JACL. It would be submitted first to our local church, Parish of the Holy Covenant, then to our Northern Illinois Annual Conference, a regional gathering of about 400 churches. It was passed by our church on February 6, 1979. Linda Groetzinger, another member of the Parish, suggested that we submit the resolution to our conference Board of Church and Society, which dealt with social issues, in order to receive that Board's substantial lobbying support at the next Annual Conference. So, on March 10, 1979, our resolution was presented and was passed overwhelmingly and was sent on its way to the June gathering of the Annual Conference. The Board added an amendment: our resolution was also to be submitted to the quadrennial gathering of United Methodism's supreme governing body, the General Conference, scheduled to convene in April 1980. The amendment was welcomed. It was intended as a means of strengthening support for redress. The United Methodist Church is the second largest Protestant denomination in the United States. Our voice would be enlarged considerably. The amendment, by extending our local church's commitment beyond the confines of our regional Northern Illinois Conference, was the first critical event. It was also linked to an event that had already occurred in San Francisco earlier in the month, but would not become known to us until an account was published in the *Pacific Citizen* newspaper a few days later.

The second critical event was the decision by the JACL's National Committee for Redress on March 3 to alter its program from support of redress legislation to support of legislation for a study commission. The reasons given were the national mood of fiscal conservatism, as manifested by the successful passage of California's Proposition 13, which drastically cut that state's tax revenue, and the vocal attacks on redress by Senator Samuel Ichiye Hayakawa, a conservative Republican from California. During World War II, Hayakawa was comfortably teaching English at the Illinois Institute of Technology in Chicago. He was a Canadian-Japanese immigrant, then ineligible for U.S. citizenship because of his Japanese ancestry. One's attitude towards the internment of Japanese-Americans does seem to be affected by one's experience. Few in Hayakawa's audience were aware that he'd never been interned. When they saw his Japanese face or read his Japanese name, they assumed he spoke as a victim. Hayakawa said what many white Americans wanted to hear from a Japanese-American, that the camps were a pleasant experience, which is why we had camp reunions; the camps enabled us to improve our lot in life by freeing us for higher education; and the camps allowed us to escape from our ethnic enclaves.

In JACL circles, fiscal conservatism and Hayakawa's opposition were called "political reality." To some of us, this sounded hauntingly similar to "military necessity," the rationale for the JACL's collaboration with the government's program of exclusion and detention.[1] Were we being sold down the river again? The JACL, of course, vigorously denied this—even as they continued to deny their former role as informants. Karl Nobuyuki, JACL national director, cited a *Harvard Business Review* article to explain the distinction between goals and methods. The goal of redress had not been altered, he explained. We were only deciding on the method by which we would reach that goal.[2] John Tateishi, the NCR chair, was more blunt: "any direct approach . . . would not stand the chance of seeing the light of day. Any type of legislation other than the commission . . . would never get beyond some sub-committee or committee of Congress."[3] But to Nelson and me, this sounded like a cop-out. We were both members of the JACL. We were familiar with its inability to support the civil rights movement and the protest against the war in Vietnam. We knew that when the JACL did support the repeal of Title II and the pardon for Iva Toguri, its support was limited.[4]

We were also aware of the problem of parliamentary democracy, or lack of it, within JACL. Had not the JACL's highest legislative body passed a resolution stating that the JACL would press for redress legislation? A committee may not contravene the resolution which created it and instructs it. Its task is to implement the resolution.

I had the strong feeling that history was giving us a second chance. It was *deja vu* to '42. During World War II, the JACL took its accommodationist stance for reasons of pragmatism and the preservation of an acceptable public image. In March 1942, it adopted the policy, "The Greatest Good for the Greatest Number," a remarkable policy for a racially oppressed minority. In April 1942, it expressed strong opposition to the legal test case of Minoru Yasui, by arguing that it "did not intend to create any unnecessary excuses for denouncing the Japanese as disloyal and dangerous."[5] Two years later, in April 1944, Joe Grant Masaoka and Minoru Yasui, acting as representatives of the JACL, interviewed six of the Heart Mountain draft resisters in the county jail at Cheyenne, Wyoming. In their report to the FBI, they expressed part of their reason for the interviews: "Any action which lowers public regard for Americans of Japanese ancestry compels the interest and concern of all those engaged in furthering the public acceptance of Japanese residents in the nation."[6] During this period, the JACL bowed to the inevitability of exclusion and detention, sought desperately for public acceptance, and vigorously fought any action that challenged their own course of action—even when such action included the affirmation of constitutional rights. In 1979, the JACL once again seemed to be yielding to the inevitability of legislative defeat for a redress proposal, to be seeking the commission as a more publicly palatable alternative, and to be opposed to efforts at a direct challenge to the nation for restitution under the Constitution. In the earlier period, most Japanese-Americans were unaware of decisions being made on their behalf. We hardly knew about the constitutional test cases, the substantial draft resistance, and the implications of JACL's opposition to these actions. But in 1979, we were better informed.

BEGINNINGS

Nelson and I had learned lessons from the civil rights and the peace movements. We were not about to repeat the mistakes of World War II. The question for us was not one of gaining public acceptance or enhancing our image, but of expressing ourselves unambiguously and making our case clearly heard. If we had our way, and if the effort to redress our grievances failed, we would at least have set the standard by which success and failure would be measured. We would have asserted ourselves as free citizens.

We wondered how a governmental commission, born of equivocation, could possibly become an instrument for justice. Moreover, regardless of how the JACL felt about its parliamentary procedures, and its distinction between goals and methods, its new direction clearly violated our own convictions. We had said what we meant in our resolution, and that resolution was on its way to our United Methodist Annual Conference.

We and the rest of our small United Methodist congregation faced a difficult decision. We knew we could not support the commission. Should we continue with the reparations movement? This is what we wanted to do, but we could not do so and limit ourselves to a supportive role. There was nothing to support. We'd have to become the main act; we'd have to start our own movement. A small handful of persons would have to organize a national effort. We'd already begun this task with the amendment to refer our petition to the world United Methodist General Conference. Perhaps we were being led towards our decision. For our congregation of forty-odd, this was a moment of truth.

The decision was made in April 1979. We would not withdraw our petition. Instead, we would amend it to replace support for the JACL with something more appropriate. We would find the wording in something that had yet to be written by a group we had yet to meet. I wrote a memorandum to friends in Los Angeles, Seattle, and New York. We knew of almost no other potential sources of support outside Chicago. We were almost seeking support blindly. Going ahead was an act of faith.

There were several instances in the movement which possessed the tenuous inevitability of faith. We proceeded without a clear vision of how we were to achieve the next step, while at the same time we had the clear understanding that we should proceed. This was the first instance. In retrospect, the decisions seem rational because our actions succeeded. But as we were deciding our course, we had only the vaguest notion of whether it would prove correct.

I had just been fired from a job as a computer programmer. I decided I would stay unemployed for a few months to work full-time on getting our movement started. I quickly lost many preconceptions. I thought, for example, that many JACL members and chapters would see the parliamentary problem as we had. I thought there would be a flood of letters to the *Pacific Citizen*. I thought we would get responses from our memorandum. There was almost complete silence on all fronts. Only Seattle responded to the memorandum.

I received a call late one Saturday evening from Shosuke Sasaki in Seattle. We had never met. He said something about his having a poor copy of a memorandum I'd written and wanting to ask me some questions. He wanted to know what my position was on redress. He explained to me how Seattle's interested Japanese-Americans had switched from the term "reparations" to "redress" because it was a more acceptable term. At the time, I wanted to support anything other than the study commission. I must have given the right answers. A relationship soon blossomed.

The people in Seattle had organized a number of imaginative and effective publicity events. They had held "Days of Remembrance" in which entire communities reenacted their removal from their homes to an assembly center, the first phase of detention. The most striking "Day of Remembrance" was the first. It was staged on Thanksgiving weekend in 1978. Residents of Seattle were taken to the Puyallup Fairgrounds, known in 1942 as Camp Harmony, a euphemism for a place where families lived in livestock stalls. Literally thousands turned out and made the trek in Army trucks and cars and had a great day remembering, socializing, and listening to speeches. Other "Days of Remembrance" were held. People had not forgotten. And the concept of redress was being publicized. The Seattle people were then in the midst of organizing a Washington Post advertisement which was to be a Japanese-American rebuttal of the anti-redress statements of Senator Hayakawa. They were fighting. The ad was scheduled for early May. They planned to hold press conferences simultaneous to its publication in major cities. They asked if I would organize one in Chicago. I agreed, but I had to confess to my complete lack of experience.

The press conferences were well-organized. I received a press packet, sample press release, detailed instructions on the distribution of the releases and the timing of the conference. We had a choice site. In Chicago of the 1960s and 1970s, there appeared a group of young artists who painted murals of social statement on the sides of buildings. The first one I remember was the depiction of people trying to protect their homes from the demolition machine of urban renewal. The muralists made their murals a community act by inviting ordinary people from the streets and local community to participate in the preparation of the wall and in the painting. Jim Yanagisawa had organized a mural on the parking lot wall of the Japanese American Service Committee building. It depicted the history of Japanese-Americans from immigration and settlement to exclusion and detention—the main theme—to eventual freedom and resettlement. We held our press conference in the parking lot in front of this mural. We worried whether anyone would show up. As the appointed hour arrived, so did the reporters and the television crews. It was a notable success, even though the local media was not much interested in our battle with Hayakawa. They picked up on the theme of the camps and the movement for redress.

The ad and press conferences, like the "Days of Remembrance," were products of a fertile mind: Frank Chin, playwright, creator of "Chickencoop Chinaman" (I

47

remembered reading its review in the *New Yorker)* and "Year of the Dragon" (I had seen it on PBS television). I had been receiving intimations in letters from Michi Weglyn that Frank wanted me to do something.

Michi Weglyn wrote *Years of Infamy, the Untold Story of America's Concentration Camps* in 1976. A few months before I read *Years of Infamy*, I had read Brendan Gill's *Here at the New Yorker* in which I was surprised and dismayed to learn that often writers for the *New Yorker* received no fan mail. This reticence from those reading the best writing in America, I felt, needed repair. So I decided to write to Brendan Gill. His book was head and shoulders above most of his contemporaries in its mastery of the English language. And when I read *Years of Infamy*, I wrote to Michi Weglyn. Her book was a revelation. She had performed the monumental task of using primary documents to reconstruct the history of our exclusion and detention. She placed responsibility directly on the highest leaders of U.S. government. She integrated into Japanese-American history the horrors of "segregation" and the Tule Lake Segregation Center as well as the gross injustices suffered by Peruvian Japanese, and by Japanese-Americans who were induced to renounce U.S. citizenship. The book brought new understanding of the events. Besides, she was a lay person, not an academic, a sister Japanese-American internee (Gila River), like me a teenager in camp, and an attractive woman. Gill responded six months later. Weglyn didn't take quite so long and was, to my good fortune, friendly. By 1979, we'd been exchanging letters regularly. In the movement for redress, she became an important mentor of mine.

She urged Frank Chin to contact me directly. He finally did; he urged me to assume the leadership of the movement for redress. I protested. The movement's center seemed to be in Seattle. Why not someone from Seattle? I remained noncommittal.

On Friday of the week following the press conferences, I flew to Seattle to meet the redress group there. I was met at the airport by the core of the Seattle Redress Committee: Chuck Kato, Shosuke Sasaki, and Henry Miyatake. It was an exciting weekend. They took me to a Japanese restaurant for dinner where we got acquainted. Chuck Kato was a brother United Methodist. Shosuke Sasaki was the first person I met who knew of Chu Hsi, the great neo-Confucian philosopher. And Henry Miyatake, as he drove me to my weekend's host, shared some of his pain of grief and divorce. I was asked again to assume the leadership role. Again I balked on the grounds that the movement was clearly centered in Seattle and that someone from Seattle should lead it. At the time, we still thought of ourselves as part of the JACL. They pointed out that the Seattle chapter was not well-liked by the rest of the JACL. I was unaware of such feelings, but then I was relatively isolated from the national organization. My contact was limited to the Chicago chapter. But I could see the point. A number of JACL national presidents had been elected from Chicago. Chicagoans had always been in leadership positions in the national body. They persisted. I demurred. I needed time.

I spent Saturday in an all-day meeting in the International District of Seattle, in the law office of attorney Ron Mamiya. The group there was larger than the trio who first met me. Both Mamiya and Henry Miyatake had been on the JACL's National Committee for Redress. Mamiya had been "fired" from the Committee for his attempt to forestall the decision for a study commission. He had been given the task of drafting a proposal for the legislation establishing the commission. Instead, he drafted a letter that questioned the propriety of the committee's decision. On March 12 he wrote, "It is my belief that the positions taken by the Redress Committee at our last meeting violated that mandate [of the JACL national convention]." He continued with an allusion to the source of the Committee's decision, ". . . our vote was dictated solely by the ill-reasoned interpretation of the off-the-cuff statements of our Nikkei[7] in Congress." Here he refers to a meeting of four members of the Committee with four Democratic Japanese-American members of Congress, Senators Inouye and Matsunaga and Representatives Mineta and Matsui, held in January 1979. (The reason for only four from the six-man Committee, I was to learn, was to avoid intimidating the four members of Congress.)

The idea of the commission came from this meeting with members of Congress. It came from Inouye. Inouye had been attempting to establish a commission to study the question of claims of Hawaiians who had suffered losses during the war. The JACL's National Committee for Redress was divided on the method of funding redress payments. Inouye proposed a commission to resolve this conflict. The commission could find an appropriate way of funding redress. The other members of Congress had their own thoughts. Matsunaga thought that a monument would be a fitting method of expressing redress to Japanese-Americans. Mineta opposed the establishment of a commission to do something a committee of Congress could do. Freshman Congressman Matsui favored redress but was advised that his open advocacy for redress would insure his defeat for reelection.[8]

I also met Frank Abe, who had been my main contact in preparing for the Hayakawa ad press conference, and his friend Kathy Wong, and other leaders of Seattle's Nikkei community such as Mitch Matsudaira and Tomio Moriguchi. Moriguchi would later become a major financial supporter of NCJAR. Karen Seriguchi arrived from San Francisco from where she had done much of the organizing for the *Washington Post* ad and press conferences. She would later join the staff of the JACL and run the JACL's Pacific Northwest District Office. Still later, she would become editor of the JACL's newspaper, *Pacific Citizen.*

It was in Seattle that our name, "National Council for Japanese American Redress," was coined. Later, we would adopt the symbol used for the "Days of Remembrance." Also, the new wording for the United Methodist resolution would come from a legislative proposal written here by Shosuke Sasaki. It would read, ". . . support for the World War II Japanese-American Human Rights Violation Redress Act."

I didn't realize until 1984 that the search for a leader originated in Seattle from among these people. Frank Chin had served as their contact man. Sasaki, Kato, Miyatake, Emi Somekawa, Abe, and Seriguchi had made the decision, not Chin. They wanted

8. LEGISLATIONS
FIRST LOWRY REDRESS BILL

If I would say anything profound about American democracy it would be that most Americans, while placing democracy among their articles of faith, rarely have the opportunity to practice democracy by directing their national government, except on election day. Of course, by then there aren't many choices. In Chicago, an admittedly extreme case, in voting in the Democratic primary, one used to be faced with a complete slate of offices, each having only one candidate. In national elections, there are usually two choices, which seems odd since America is a large nation. Surely there are more than two persons qualified to lead the nation as its president; there must be dozens who could legislate as representatives of a district or a state. Worse yet, the heavy hype of media polls imposes a sense of Calvinistic predestination (rooted in the "Supreme Random Number") to the outcome, making each of us akin to one of twenty million monkeys typing away for twenty million years in a statistical milieu to arrive at the people's choice, if not the complete works of the British Museum. The practice of democracy is even more limited when it comes to an ordinary citizen initiating legislative changes to the law of the land.

When NCJAR decided to separate from the JACL, one of the first questions raised was, "How are you going to introduce legislation?" What the question implied was that we couldn't petition Congress for legislation without the lobbying facilities of a national organization. My rebuttal was the bravado, "All we have to do is find a member of Congress who's willing to introduce a bill." Of course, I'd never done it.

There was one other prerequisite: formalizing our demands as a proposed bill. I was, therefore, pleased to learn in Seattle that both requirements had been met. Shosuke Sasaki had written a proposed bill. The Seattle Redress Committee had secured a promise from then freshman Representative Mike Lowry to sponsor a redress bill.

Shosuke Sasaki is tough as well as fair-minded. He was born in Japan and therefore would be considered an Issei. (There is another term, "Hansei," which may be applied to those who are peers to the Nisei but Japan-born. It is rarely used. "Issei" has the limitation of denoting, in addition to being Japan-born, the parents of the Nisei. In fact, both Nisei and Hansei have Issei as their parents.) Shosuke is unusual in being literate in both Japanese and English. He was one of the few people who read Michi Weglyn's *Years of Infamy* in both languages. (He found the Japanese version stronger than the English version.) His legislative proposal was forthright and precise. It began with ten "Whereas" clauses which spelled out the injuries suffered and the failures of the government.

WHEREAS, on February 19, 1942, President Franklin D. Roosevelt signed Executive Order 9066 which authorized the wholesale uprooting, exile and imprisonment of 120,313 persons of Japanese ancestry from the Pacific Coast areas, two thirds of whom were United States citizens; and

LEGISLATIONS

WHEREAS, the carrying out of Executive Order 9066 resulted in gross violations of seven of the ten Articles of the Bill of Rights; and

WHEREAS, such persons of Japanese ancestry in the United States were, with no evidence of misconduct and not even a pretense of a trial, deprived of their freedom, jobs, and homes, and subjected to psychological and mental suffering unlike any other body of American citizens during World War II; and

WHEREAS, it was the policy of the United States Government during and after World War II to suppress the cultural and ethnic identity of Japanese Americans; and

WHEREAS, records of the United States Government show not even one case of espionage, sabotage, or treason occurring among residents of Japanese ancestry prior to and during World War II; and

WHEREAS, martial law was never invoked in the United States; and

WHEREAS, citizens of Japanese ancestry contributed substantially to the war effort, served heroically in the United States armed forces and suffered the loss of life and limb despite the wartime denial to them of the benefits of such citizenship; and

WHEREAS, as a nation which presumes to hold itself forth to other nations as an example of the proper treatment of their minorities, continued failure by our Government to provide redress to the Japanese American victims of its own violations of human rights can only undermine America's credibility and prestige among other nations; and

WHEREAS, the Evacuation Claims Act of 1948 can in no way be regarded as an adequate or even sincere attempt to make restitution because it (1) provided for *provable* losses of *tangible* property only, (2) was carried out in such a hostile and tight-fisted manner that payments made under it amounted to *less than 10 %* of total tangible property losses estimated in 1942 by the Federal Reserve Bank of San Francisco, and (3) forced all who received payments made under it to renounce all other claims against the Government; and

WHEREAS, mass exile and imprisonment of Japanese American residents of Pacific Coast areas during World War II solely on the basis of race were contrary to the long established laws and traditions of our nation and appropriate recognition of redress for the victims of that outrage by the United States Government is long overdue.

None of these survived in the bill finally introduced. This seems to be one of the limitations of legislative redress; the recitation of injuries is disallowed. (A lawsuit, by contrast and as I would discover, requires the explication of injuries.) Sasaki's proposal then spelled out in detail the amounts to be paid for redressing the injuries, the criteria for eligibility, the method of funding and disbursement of compensation, and the immunity of compensation payments from taxes and from reductions to public assistance, and other matters. Much of this survived in the bill introduced.

I concurred on most major points, but I was confused by the method of funding proposed. It involved a rather tricky method of having the potential recipients, the victims, indicate with a check-off box on their income tax forms their desire to have their taxes allocated towards payment of redress to themselves. It seemed as though they would pay themselves.

An Internal Revenue Service Special Trust Fund shall be created for the purpose of receiving Federal Income Taxes paid by persons of Japanese descent who elect to allocate said taxes for the purposes of this Act. Such election shall be entirely voluntary; however, any persons who shall not elect to have their Federal Income Taxes put into said Trust Fund shall not be eligible to receive any redress payments pursuant to this Act. Any eligible person or next of kin of any deceased eligible person whose income is such that no Federal Income Taxes are required on it shall not be ineligible for the receipt of payments hereunder. Said Special Trust Fund shall not terminate until such time as sufficient funds are received to pay all claims and all redress payments are disbursed.

This was, of course, the Seattle Plan. Contention over this funding proposal had arisen earlier, in the JACL's National Committee for Redress. Later, a dispute flared up between me and Seattle over this issue. But I found the rest of Sasaki's ideas quite acceptable. The draft bill proposed $10,000 for each person affected by EO9066 plus $15 a day for each day of internment. Reasons for the per diem payment were that not all those affected by exclusion were interned and of those interned, the stay varied from less than a year to over four years. There were 4,889 persons who were excluded but not detained; they had "voluntarily" moved from the exclusion zone. (The total of 120,313 persons interned by EO9066 does not include the 4,889 "voluntary" excludees. The WRA had in its custody 120,313. The 4,889 were not in WRA custody, but the mass exclusion order of EO9066 clearly violated their constitutional rights.)

True to his promise, on November 28, 1979, Representative Lowry introduced a bill containing the substance of the Seattle proposal. (When the redress movement has finally subsided into history, Mike Lowry will surely be considered the one member of Congress who demonstrated leadership and courage in representing his Japanese-American constituents and championing the principles embodied in our Constitution. The movement could have easily disintegrated into acrimonious factions had not the Lowry Redress Bill provided a worthwhile goal to pursue and to organize around.) NCJAR immediately began to rally support for redress legislation in Congress and among organizations. Our first step was our United Methodist Annual Conference.

The United Methodist Church is about as old as the United States. It was formed in 1784, a year after the Treaty of Paris and the British recognition of the independence of the United States of America. Annual Conferences began as deliberative assemblies for Methodist clergy, so they could conduct the business of the church. The 1866 General Conference enacted legislation enabling lay men to be seated at annual and general conferences.[1] However, lay women were not seated until the 1904 General Conference.

The Northern Illinois Annual Conference convened in the first full week of June 1979 at Northern Illinois University in De Kalb, Illinois. There were about 1,200 members, evenly divided between laity and clergy. (Clergy are, as part of their orders, included as members of the Annual Conference; laity are elected by their local churches as members of this regional body.) They deliberated on corporate, budgetary, program, and social and theological issues. Some sophistication had developed over the dozen years of my attendance. Noncontroversial issues were placed on a consent calendar, so they could be decided in a block by a single vote of the plenary session. This device saved the plenary session the time of hearing, perhaps debating, and voting upon each such issue. Reports of various boards and agencies, for example, had to be adopted in order to become part of the record, but they rarely generated controversy; they were placed on the consent calendar. The remaining issues were divided among twelve sections, each with about 100 members. These sections, meeting concurrently, would deliberate their assigned issues in detail. The sections voted to concur or not to concur with each proposal assigned to them. Originally, the sections were limited to the expression of concurrence or nonconcurrence. Later, they were made deliberative, so they could amend proposals. Final decisions rested with the plenary session, but it was heavily influenced by votes in the sections. In fact, overwhelming concurrence or nonconcurrence, by 90 per cent or greater vote in a section, placed proposals on a second plenary-session consent calendar, for a block vote of acceptance or rejection, respectively. Only contentious issues came before the entire body for debate. Our proposal did not make it to the second consent calendar. That wasn't all bad. The section vote was strongly favorable. Now we could present the proposal to the main body so that everyone could learn about the issue and express their opinion. The proposal was well-received; the plenary session voted overwhelmingly in its favor. The support of the Northern Illinois Conference was followed by similar support in the Pacific Northwest and Oregon-Idaho Annual Conferences.

Following the Conference, the pastor of my church, Reverend Marilyn Robb, and I flew to Washington to visit several representatives and the two Illinois senators. Her representative, Abner Mikva, had recently been appointed as a judge in the U.S. Court of Appeals for District of Columbia Circuit. While expressing his support for redress, he declined to sponsor any legislation in his remaining weeks as a representative. The congregation's representative, Sidney Yates, was at first hesitant but did express support. He said that most members of the House would look to their Japanese-American colleagues for leadership. This was bad news, since we knew that both Japanese-American members, Norman Mineta and Robert Matsui, supported the JACL's study commission. We argued that this issue was one for all Americans and should not be decided by Japanese-Americans alone. Eventually, Yates, in response to persuasion from Norman Mineta, would reconsider and put his support behind the study commission. We also approached Representative Cardiss Collins, a Chicagoan and chairperson of the Congressional Black Caucus. Our scheduled meeting with her was preempted by an invitation to her from the White House. Although her staff was friendly, she, too, would eventually support the commission. But at least our presence was made known. Meeting with senators is almost impossible. We did meet with the staffs of Senator Percy and Senator Stevenson. Percy's staff categorically rejected the IRS method of funding, while Stevenson's found it intriguing. Percy's staff also declared that redress legislation would never be passed without the support of the JACL. But Marilyn Robb and I were not about to let limitations of the past deter us from making our own future.

Still, ours was a shoestring lobbying effort. For the first time, Congress felt a Japanese-American presence other than the JACL on a major issue affecting Japanese-Americans. But ours was a difficult, unequal battle. We were the new kid on the block. We knew this, and had few illusions.

Identical bills for the study commission were introduced in the Senate on August 2, 1979 (S.1647) and in the House on September 28, 1979 (H.R.5499). Lowry introduced his genuine redress bill (H.R.5977) on November 28, 1979. By the time it was introduced, the Lowry Redress Bill was considerably changed from the original Seattle proposal. The WHEREAS clauses had been removed. The base amount had been increased from $10,000 to $15,000 per person. The $15 per day of internment remained. The contentious trust-fund method of funding had been superseded by a simple appropriation. This change came in response to advice from House Speaker Thomas P. O'Neill, Jr. Amendments to the internal revenue laws, he said, would delay the bill's consideration by committees; it would have to go through the House Ways and Means Committee which had a large backlog of bills on its agenda.

Meanwhile, on September 25, 1979, I wrote my first NCJAR newsletter. It was like a common letter from me to a growing list of supporters. It was written to keep them informed of current developments and my own thoughts about the redress movement. Earlier the Seattle branch of NCJAR had published an official NCJAR newsletter, the first in a projected series of four seasonal newsletters. Theirs was more objective and anonymous than mine. My letter was mainly intended for our Chicago-area supporters. But the projected series of Seattle newsletters never materialized beyond its initial Summer 1979 edition. So my letters, published at imprecise intervals of one to two months, became the NCJAR newsletter. For many months, these newsletters were a two-man affair. I wrote, edited, printed, and mailed them. Harry Nagaoka maintained and provided the mailing labels. Later, Harry Nagaoka did the mailing as well. Gradually, more people became involved. The newsletters quickly became our link to our supporters and an important vehicle for dialogue.

In my November 1979 NCJAR newsletter, I got into a dispute with my Seattle friends over the trust-fund method of funding when I expressed my misgivings over the requirement for victims to check off their willingness to have their taxes assigned to the redress fund. My reasons were explained in an accompanying letter from Ira Glasser of the American Civil Liberties Union:

> ... we have concluded that the ACLU should not at this time endorse any of the current legislative proposals. There are many aspects of the current legislative proposals that disturb us. For example, the JACL-backed congressional commission proposal is predicated on the idea that there is need to study the question of whether the rights of Japanese-Americans were violated and, therefore, whether financial redress is justified. Given the historical background of the World War II episode, that question seems to us gratuitous and unnecessary. Any commission appointed should assume the violation and study ways of implementing the principle of financial redress.

While we and our supporters were aware of this weighty criticism of the JACL's proposal, it is doubtful if anyone in the JACL leadership was informed. Certainly, the JACL leaders never informed their rank-and-file.

> The NCJAR-supported bill, also contains a number of questionable points, such as the method of funding payments through an IRS Special Trust Fund made up of income taxes paid "by persons of Japanese descent" who elect to have their taxes used for this

purpose. People who don't contribute are not eligible for redress. This seems to us entirely unfair. There is also the problem of redress payments being exempt from all federal, state and local taxes. This may raise equal protection questions since other government benefits may not be similarly treated.[2]

Seattle's rationale for the trust-fund method was pragmatism. The income-tax check off would fund redress payments over a period of time, in a manner which would appear self-funding. The general, tax-paying public would think that *their* taxes weren't going towards these payments. Of course, this was an illusion. If the victims' taxes were going towards this end, then they would not go towards the general, federal budget. Hence, others' taxes would have to be higher, to cover this deficiency. Others would be paying for redress, as well as the victims. This was clever, perhaps, too clever. The trust-fund plan tried to avoid an issue which should not be avoided: the liability of citizens for the actions of their government. If the government did commit serious wrongs, then the citizenry should make amends. But my disagreement was not only with this deceptive cleverness; I also agreed with Ira Glasser's point about the requirement for victims to assign their taxes to the redress fund. Victims should not have to do any such thing to receive their just due.

At least, we in NCJAR listened to criticism and responded. It would be interesting to speculate about what might have happened had the JACL been required to discuss the ACLU official's criticism of its study commission proposal. The ACLU's own "hands off" policy was not without its problems. It did not enter into any significant discussion of the issues involved with the various redress groups, except with NCJAR. When we altered our position in response to ACLU criticism, the Union continued to withhold its support for the Lowry Redress Bill. Yet later, in public statements before the Commission on Wartime Relocation and Internment of Civilians, the Union would assert its support of compensatory redress.

Although the dispute over funding can be described neatly on paper, it took place between individuals and did create a breach between redress supporters in Seattle and those in Chicago. However, one friendly relationship did persist: my contact with Karen Seriguchi. Through her good spirit, she remained a strong NCJAR supporter and my trusted friend. Personal estrangement over political disputes is one of the more costly aspects of participation in a movement. I continued to cherish the other friends I'd made. The separations caused by political disagreements were painful and should not have been necessary.

While NCJAR faltered because of the dispute between Seattle and Chicago redress supporters, the Lowry Redress Bill was on its way and became a vehicle for organizing support. Mike Lowry, of course, did receive the strong support of his Japanese-American constituents in Seattle, quite independently of NCJAR. So even though the organization may have suffered, the issue and the movement thrived.

No one expected the Lowry Redress Bill to be enacted as law on the first attempt. We did want the bill to become an expression of the will of Japanese-Americans and other concerned citizens. We had to express our impatience with the temporizing study commission notion. Notably, the commission bill failed to mention either Japanese-Americans or redress. It seemed ludicrous to form a commission formed to determine "whether any wrong was committed."[3] The commission was to hold hearings in major cities containing large numbers of Japanese-Americans. Clearly, this was intended to result in having the victims tell their tales of woe while ignoring the actions of the perpetrators. Instead of victimless crime, we'd be treated to a spectacle of victims without victimizers. By contrast, the Lowry Redress Bill went straight to the point. And it was an expression of the will of Lowry's Japanese-American constituency. Polls taken subsequently have shown that it was the will of most Japanese-Americans.[4]

9. LEGISLATIONS
SENATE HEARINGS

I learned of the first congressional hearings quite by accident. On a Sunday night, March 9, 1980, I was talking by telephone to Karen Seriguchi. She told me that hearings were to be held in about a week in the United States Senate. I had already written to the chairperson of the Committee on Governmental Affairs, Senator Abraham Ribicoff, asking for an opportunity to testify. Obviously, I was not going to be invited, at least not just on the strength of my letter. So the next day I telephoned Washington to ask to testify. I reached Marilyn Harris who said that I was late, but that she would see what she could do. She called back. It was all right; I could testify. She filled me in on the particulars, such as the number of advance copies of my testimony I had to have ready for committee members by Friday, March 14, the number required for the press on Tuesday, March 18, the date of the hearings, and the person to contact for reimbursement of travel expenses.

An intense ten days followed. I had to write a statement quickly enough to have the requisite copies made and express-mailed to Washington. NCJAR people in Seattle and Chicago had to be consulted about what I would say. I sought the support of the Methodist Federation for Social Action, which had agreed to place the issue on their agenda for next month's General Conference of the United Methodist Church. And I had agreed to attend a conference of the Asian American Law Students Association at New York University on the Saturday before the hearings. That required its own speech.

The law students' conference in New York may have been more important than the hearings in Washington. I had been to New York a year earlier. Phil Nash, a law-school student, had organized an informal, Chinese dinner meeting, where I ate almost nothing. It followed an all-day conference. The people who joined us were tired and the restaurant was noisy. I had not been able to set forth our position in any coherent fashion. In 1979, I had failed to convince New Yorkers to support NCJAR. In 1980, I coveted the opportunity to try again in the more formal setting of a conference.

However, I had not been scheduled on the day's program. I arrived early and talked with Phil Nash, once again the organizer. I needed to convince him that I deserved a chance to speak. "I've come all the way from Chicago," I pleaded. Phil was afraid of an ill-tempered dispute between JACL, who had also been invited, and NCJAR. But the JACL representatives failed to show. No doubt they were busy preparing for the hearings for Tuesday. Phil squeezed me in before the lunch break. "Not more than ten minutes," he admonished.

My speech, in part, took out after the JACL. Nash's concern over our dispute was well-founded. Several prominent JACL leaders had begun proposing a foundation for good works as an alternative to redress. They seemed to imply it was improper for

Japanese-Americans to press for individual compensation; that, therefore, the JACL should seek a selfless "restitution" in the form of a foundation which would distribute money to the needy and those fighting for civil rights. While all this altruism seemed high-minded and exceedingly respectable, it confused the fundamental issues. Justice requires individual compensation when individual rights are violated. I said:

> There is an alternative redress proposal which is surfacing and which is supported by distinguished leaders of Japanese America.

> The most public of these are counselor Min Yasui and Judge William Marutani. This proposal is for a foundation for good works. This should not be called a redress proposal. It should be called an instead-of-redress proposal.

> Min Yasui's proposal is the most recent. It appeared in the JACL's newspaper, the *Pacific Citizen*, dated March 7, 1980. The counselor proposes that 400 million dollars be set aside as an endowment fund. The interest from the 400 million would be used to help internment camp victims who are in need, to support community programs, and to protect the civil rights of any person in America. These are all very noble purposes. But what have they to do with a massive violation to the Constitution and the fundamental human right to compensation for a miscarriage of justice? How do they serve to redress a very grievous wrong committed against individuals?

> It seems to me that we would be better served if the counselor and the judge stopped fiddling around with their liberal mish-mash of welfare, community organizations, civil rights altruism, and, instead, provided some legal leadership on the rationale for redress.

I described how I had gone about trying to understand the legal principles undergirding the concept of redress. I read Article I, Section 9 of the United States Constitution which states:

> The Privilege of the Writ of Habeas Corpus shall not be suspended unless when in cases of Rebellion or Invasion the public safety may require it.

I looked up the meaning of *habeas corpus* in the *Columbia Encyclopedia*. Then I found the principle of compensation for the miscarriage of justice stated in the American Convention on Human Rights, which was adopted by the Organization of American States in 1969, signed for the United States in 1977, and introduced by President Carter in the U.S. Senate in 1978. Article 10 of the Convention is entitled "The Right to Compensation" and states:

> Every person has the right to be compensated in accordance with the law in the event he has been sentenced by a final judgment through a miscarriage of justice.

This was obviously do-it-yourself legal theory. I felt that persons in the legal profession had a responsibility to help us understand what our rights were under the law. I wanted law students to understand this, especially as the Japanese-American community was then struggling with the concept of compensatory redress.

I don't know what effect this speech had. It seemed to go over well. I do think my prepared speech had the advantage of following speakers who talked extempore and rambled. And I did meet some important people and solidified earlier acquaintances. I met Gordon Hirabayashi, one of four Japanese-Americans who tested the constitutionality of their exclusion and internment during World War II and had their names made famous by Supreme Court decisions. I met Amy Uno Ishii, the sister of Edison Uno who had begun public discussion of Japanese-American redress in 1970. Amy was from Los Angeles and had helped NCJAR there. She had come with a slide presentation. I also met Mine Okubo, author of the first published book on the camps, *Citizen 13660*. She is an artist as well. I had the unusual opportunity of viewing her work at her apartment that day. I felt overwhelmed by the beauty and good feeling of her paintings. I felt it truly unfortunate for her and for the world that her work had yet to be exhibited and appreciated. I also renewed acquaintances with Michi Weglyn, the writer, Takako Kusunoki, editor of the *New York Nichibei* newspaper, and others.

New York, America's cultural capital, is also a Japanese-American cultural center. Artists and writers seem to flourish there; political thinkers and activists seemed to be better informed and developed. If Okubo was still unrecognized, Isamu Noguchi was well-established. There were writers and journalists like Michi Weglyn, Michiko Kakutani, and Takako Kusunoki; actors and dancers like Yuriko; even celebrities like Yoko Ono. The Japanese-American newspaper, the *New York Nichibei*, was well-edited, informative, and critical. New York also had a network of Nisei women who worked in various boards and agencies at church denominational headquarters, who knew each other and exchanged information and influence.

Aiko Yoshinaga Herzig was one of these. She had recently moved to Falls Church, Virginia just outside of Washington. She was an unusual creature: a Nisei activist. We met at the law students' conference so she could size me up. We had talked over the phone. She was Jack Herzig's wife. Jack had been helping NCJAR for several months now. I'd talked to Aiko and she seemed interested in joining her husband in this work. We met in the company of her old friends, and we had a good time.

When my wife, Yuriko, and I arrived in Washington on Tuesday, March 18, 1980, Aiko met us at the airport and escorted us around the Capitol. We did a little lobbying before the hearings. Aiko was interested in lobbying for us but had no experience. I had had a little experience, and didn't think lobbying was terribly difficult. I showed her what little I knew as we made the rounds of congressional offices.

The Senate hearings were held in room 3302 of the Dirksen building. It was my first experience with congressional hearings, and I was pleased with the openness of the procedures. I wondered if my tape recorder and camera were to be allowed. They were. There was little formality. We were to be heard by Senator Henry Jackson and Senator Carl Levin. Senator Charles McC. Mathias, Jr. showed up also for a few minutes, for the testimony of Clarence Mitchell of the Leadership Conference on Civil Rights.

The pecking order of political power became clear to me. First to speak were the senators on the Committee, Jackson and Levin. Next were the senators presenting testimony, Inouye and Matsunaga. But Inouye was ill and not present, while Matsunaga was late. Then the members of the House of Representatives, Wright, Mineta, and Matsui, took their turn. Then civil rights leader Clarence Mitchell spoke. Historian Roger Daniels followed. By this time, only Senator Jackson remained to hear witnesses. Finally, the one-man committee was ready to hear from ordinary citizens: Jerry Enomoto (JACL), Diane Wong (Commission on Asian American Affairs, State of Washington), myself (National Council for Japanese American Redress and Methodist Federation for Social Action), and Mike Masaoka (Nisei Lobby).

As the members of Congress spoke, I began to suspect that Senator Hayakawa, notably absent, might have been telling the truth to Dwight Chuman, English editor of the *Rafu Shimpo*, when he said, "The only condition I made the other four members of Congress to agree to was that no monetary reparations would ever be asked. If they had not agreed to that, I would not have endorsed that bill."[1]

Jim Wright, House Majority Leader, said,

> There is no way in which we can ever repay those proud and loyal Americans for having questioned their patriotism. We cannot give them back the months of their lives nor redress the shame to which we subjected them. . . . The best we can do, therefore, is to take official notice that what we did under the severe pressure of that wrenching emergency was completely out of character for us—to apologize to those on whom we inflicted the insulting assumption of their disloyalty and to avow that never again will any group of Americans be subjected to such humiliation on grounds no more valid than the blood that runs in their veins.[2]

That theme was developed by Senator Matsunaga, who was late and thus had to speak after the representatives. He said:

> Some members of the Japanese-American community do believe that the federal government should provide some form of monetary compensation to "redress" them for the injustices they suffered. However, members of this committee ought to know that an almost equal number maintain that no amount of money can ever compensate them for the loss of their "inalienable" right to life, liberty and the pursuit of happiness, or the loss of their constitutional rights.

He concluded:

> Whether or not redress is provided, the study . . . will be valuable in and of itself, not only for Japanese-Americans, but for all Americans. Passage of S.1647 will be just one more piece of evidence that ours is a Nation great enough to recognize and rectify its past mistakes.

The representatives went on in this vein. Mineta said:

> It would provide an important framework for a factual discussion of this sad chapter in our not-so-distant past. . . . In addition, the work of the Commission will educate or remind people about an event they may not remember or know much about. . . . Our greatest hope is that the knowledge gained from the proposed commission will guarantee that this tragic abuse of civil rights will never occur again.

Matsui said:

> . . . passage of this legislation will allow for the first time Federal examination of the serious economic, social, and psychological implications of the incarceration of loyal Americans during the early stages of World War II. However, equally important, passage of this bill would signal the Federal government's willingness to constructively examine errors of the past, and to define clearly its role and responsibility in the future.

I found this oblique approach to the redress issue, the ambivalence of Matsunaga's "an almost equal number maintain that no amount of money can ever compensate them" and the obligatory rhetoric of Mineta's "tragic abuse of civil rights" disconcerting. Didn't Japanese-American members of Congress have a duty to state forthrightly that the redress of grievances is required for the sake of justice and that the redress of violations of legal rights is fundamental to our form of government? Had Senator Hayakawa let the cat out of the bag? Had a deal been struck?

The Civil Rights Leader and the Historian were there to establish credibility. I was taken aback when Clarence Mitchell said that the JACL had been very helpful to the civil rights movement. When had that been? Perhaps it had happened within the inner sanctum of the Leadership Conference which Mitchell chaired. It certainly had not happened in JACL's national conventions. But the really interesting testimony came from ordinary citizens.

Jerry Enomoto was not the current president of the JACL. Nor was he the immediate past president. I remembered him from his JACL presidency in 1970, ten years earlier. I was mystified by his presence now. Why was he the spokesperson for JACL? He was the first member of the final panel to speak, the panel that included him, Diane Wong, me, and Mike Masaoka. Each of us was limited to ten minutes. We were allowed to introduce substantially more written testimony for the published record. JACL submitted about one hundred pages as their written contribution. Senator Jackson called it a "book." Later, it turned out, this "book" was actually a collection of unattributed quotations, mostly borrowed from several published writings. It was similar to the term paper of a high school student who filched material from books and passed it off as his or her own.

Many persons supporting the JACL were present in the audience. I felt like one of the few friends of the groom at a wedding, where across the aisle sat a crowd of well-wishers for the bride. Enomoto appeared to be speaking extemporaneously. So when Senator Jackson asked him what the JACL wanted to have the commission propose after their study, I expected a quick, clear, simple answer like money for victims and a trust fund for Nikkei community organizations. But Enomoto seemed to be at loss for ideas. He said:

> Mr. Chairman, I am sure my colleague, Mr. Masaoka, definitely has some opinions in that light. My feeling is the Japanese American Citizens League has a committee. They have looked into this question. They, I believe, have some thoughts in that regard. I believe that a Commission of this kind, representing a cross section of American citizens from all States and throughout the country—if they held hearings throughout the

country in various places, where everybody will then have an opportunity to tell their story and also share with the Commission their feelings as to what constitutes redress in their minds . . .

Senator Jackson interrupted and answered his own question:

> In other words, the Commission should be free, obviously, to make whatever recommendations they deem appropriate.

Enomoto replied:

> Yes, Mr. Chairman.

Diane Wong expressed the position of a state bureaucracy and straddled the fence between the commission and redress. She felt the commission should be supported for its educational value and that redress was nevertheless required. That seemed sensible. But since the Committee was not discussing alternatives to the commission, that statement was taken as support of the commission.

My statement was the only one to oppose a commission. I described the history of the redress movement and how the JACL leadership contravened its own governing assembly to arrive at the commission concept. I concluded:

> The people are not asking for a study commission. We know it was wrong. We do not need Congress or anyone else, at this late date, to undertake a study to determine whether a wrong was committed. We understand the wrong. What we need now is the opportunity to redress the wrong.
>
> We Americans of Japanese ancestry need to know that we are entitled to equal treatment under the law; that the writ of *habeas corpus* shall not be suspended because of our race; that the right to compensation for a miscarriage of justice involving years of internment shall apply to us as well as to all other human beings.
>
> Justice has already been delayed too long for our parents, the first generation of Japanese Americans, for most are now gone. Justice delayed for them is now justice denied. I pray that you do not repeat the same error for those of us who still carry the memory of those camps. S.1647 is beneath our dignity. Dismiss this sorry excuse for justice. Let us, instead, resolve to redress the victims and repair the Constitution.

It was a single voice against the Japanese-American establishment. At least there was one voice to say these things.

Mike Masaoka gave a remarkable speech. "Mr. JACL," as he was called, came out of the closet. He was joining Min Yasui and William Marutani. He announced his preference for a public trust fund that would perform good works, such as a "civil rights defense fund for all Americans, not just Japanese Americans, . . . an educational and cultural center, . . . a national resources pool to help disadvantaged and denied Americans, . . . an international operation to help the refugees of political persecution and/or natural calamities."

"My God!" I thought, "What is he saying?" I was shaking my head. "What has all this to do with redressing the victims?" I thought. "Were we to supersede the American

Civil Liberties Union and the International Red Cross? Is the JACL reaching for divinity?'' I was puzzled. I had not before heard Masaoka speak before a congressional committee. Had I reflected, I would have remembered that this same Masaoka had proposed a Nisei suicide battalion and had stood "unalterably opposed" to the constitutional test case of Minoru Yasui. I would have remembered that he is given to extremes. The statement was vintage Masaoka hyperbole. He had been an instructor in speech. His preaching was the practice of his oratorical trade.

After it was over, everyone had a good time congratulating everyone. Some folks even shook my hand; I don't know why. Perhaps because of the excitement of being at a Senate hearing. Perhaps they felt the moment was a historic occasion. I knew that our side was defeated. I also knew it was much too early for victory.

In retrospect, I was naive. I assumed the senators and representatives spoke the truth. There, at the center of the American process of self-government, I assumed that all spoke what was on their minds. There is such an air of high moral purpose about Congress and the Capitol. Three years later, in 1983, when the Commission finally finished its work, a redress bill would be introduced with the support of the JACL and the Japanese-American members of Congress. By then, Senator Hayakawa would not be in the Senate. In 1980, everyone was simply doing "a job" in order to get the commission bill passed.

Innocence has its rewards, too. A few days later, Aiko Yoshinaga Herzig agreed to become NCJAR's Washington representative, or lobbyist. Little did I realize how important her efforts would become. All I wanted, I informed her, was an early warning of the forthcoming House hearings. This she did provide. But her ultimate contribution would be far more important.

The Senate hearings gave me an education in American democracy and in life. There were more lessons to come.

10. LEGISLATIONS
GENERAL CONFERENCE OF THE UNITED METHODIST CHURCH

Fast on the heels of the New York meeting and the Senate hearings in March 1980 came the quadrennial gathering of the General Conference of the United Methodist Church, the supreme governing body of a nine-million-member denomination. It took place in Indianapolis in April. In his book, *Organizing to Beat the Devil*, Charles W. Ferguson states, "Methodism is America in microcosm. You find in its story our history—vivid, convenient, and condensed, with all the glories, violence, prejudice, and aspirations that make us a peculiar people." I had certainly found this true in my time of involvement in United Methodist politics. (Although the United Methodist Church is now a global church, its membership remains predominantly American.) During the Vietnam war, I presented resolutions calling on the Northern Illinois Conference to oppose the war. I remember razor sharp divisions of opinion, requiring standing-vote counts that resulted in decisions by ten-vote margins, once by only a single vote. The divided Northern Illinois Conference mirrored the divided public sentiment in the state of Illinois. At the 1980 General Conference, two burning issues were Iran and homosexuality. Japanese-American redress was a minor issue, but it had its moments nonetheless.

Like regional Annual Conferences, the quadrennial world General Conference of United Methodists is a splendidly democratic institution. In 1980, it received about 20,000 petitions, among them the redress petition of the Northern Illinois Conference. These came from individuals, local churches, annual conferences, organizations, boards, and agencies. The number of issues represented was considerably smaller. A process of consolidation merges many petitions for one issue into a single proposed resolution. Like the Annual Conference, the General Conference divides itself into committees. But for the General Conference the committees are topical, with concerns such as Church and Society, Pensions, and Missions. They deliberate simultaneously. The committees, in turn, divide into subcommittees, and the subcommittees may divide into sub-subcommittees, for more simultaneous deliberations.

This process is quite open, and is "political," in the sense of involving extra-deliberative influences upon the delegates. One of these influences is the selection of General Conference delegates by the immediately preceding Annual Conferences—for 1980, by the ones held in 1979. We were fortunate in the election of Reverend Martin Deppe as a delegate from the Northern Illinois Conference, after several quadrennia of failed efforts. Martin and I had become good friends during the Vietnam war period. He was a tireless and skilled organizer. I came to know and respect him as the convenor of the Renewal Caucus, a group of clergy and laity who tried to make the annual conference more open and democratic and lobbied for civil rights, against the war in Vietnam, and for equity in clergy compensation, among other things. I remember, for example, that in 1967, in the first conference I attended, only once or twice did women stand for recognition in the plenary sessions. Twelve years later, many women were actively involved in these sessions. We scandalized the 1967 Annual Conference by publishing a slate of nominees for delegates to 1968 General Conference. Delegate selection, we were told by the presiding bishop, was to be done prayerfully. We did not reject the efficacy of prayer; we simply recognized the influence a published slate might have on prayerful decisions. Each election of a delegate required a majority vote. It took many ballots to elect all the delegates. There were covert slates. With an alternative slate, the popular candidates would find it harder to win majorities. As the results of each balloting were announced, opportunities for negotiations appeared. Without published slates, delegates were selected because of their popularity or prestige, irrespective of their stand on issues. In succeeding quadrennia, other slates appeared. The process gradually opened up so that by 1979, Martin was able to run on a platform ranging from feminism to world peace.

At General Conference in 1980, Martin managed to be assigned to the sub-subcommittee of the subcommittee of the committee to which the redress petition had been assigned.

The Conference also had a National Federation of Asian American United Methodists which caucused on issues concerning Asian Americans. This group's endorsement was essential. June Shimokawa, another of the New York network of Nisei women, brought our proposed resolution before the Federation, and the group did support it. In the course of the two weeks of deliberations, the Federation would feel the long arm of Capitol Hill in Washington reaching to Indianapolis. Both Senator Inouye and Representative Mineta are United Methodists. Both attempted to block our petition because of its reference to the Lowry Redress Bill. The Federation caucused and resisted this pressure.

Our petition passed through sub-subcommittee and through subcommittee and through the full committee, receiving at each step a little more resistance, but still surviving with a strong vote in its favor. The General Conference was scheduled to adjourn on Friday evening at six o'clock. But it had not completed its agenda, so it kept on. Many delegates had checked out of their hotels. Airline traffic began to diminish as the night deepened. Accordingly, legislating had to be completed. By eleven o'clock, only one minute was allowed for discussion of each item of business, and only one amendment per main motion. That was when our petition reached the floor. The presenter's speech was cut off at sixty seconds. A delegate stood to be recognized. The presiding Bishop recognized Reverend Perry Saito of the Wisconsin Conference. Saito made an amendment which gutted our proposed resolution, converting it from support for redress legislation to support for a study. Everyone was caught off guard. Besides, there was no time for debate. The amendment passed. The main resolution passed. Shortly thereafter, Martin called me in Chicago. He tried to put the action in the best possible light, as he must do when he has a death to announce.

This news was devastating. I had spent several days at the General Conference. Our pastor, Marilyn Robb, spent a few more days. They were long, full days. In the evenings I caucused with the Methodist Federation for Social Action. Our persistence seemed to be paying off. We had taken care of all the details, and there were no signs of organized opposition. Nay votes were to be expected in a representative body. Saito had had many points along the deliberative path to propose his amendment, to argue for it, to seek support for it. Votes were taken in the Asian Federation, to which he belonged. Votes were also taken in all three committee levels. These gatherings were open to him. His amendment at the eleventh hour, without the possibility of debate, was suspect, despite his subsequent protestations of innocence. He tried to explain that the study to which he had referred was not the study commission but a study by United Methodists. He also explained that his amendment was completely proper—as if one could properly confound the parliamentary process of the General Conference of the United Methodist Church.

A few weeks later, the JACL circulated an internal memorandum which crowed about its success at the General Conference and the effectiveness of a single person there. Two months later, in the House hearings, the General Conference would go on record in support of the study commission.

11. LEGISLATIONS
HOUSE HEARINGS

By the time the House Judiciary Committee held hearings on June 2, 1980, the Japanese-American community was fully aware of what was happening and its importance. Many individuals and groups sought to be heard by the House Committee. The Senate hearings had taken almost everyone by surprise; they had missed them; now they wanted to be heard by the House. I had received ten days' notice of the Senate hearings in March. That had been brutally short, the pressure had been intense. With Aiko Herzig monitoring the House for its hearing date, I expected substantially more notice. But Aiko called on May 28, just five days in advance, to inform me of the House hearings. The pressure was doubled. This was bad enough. What was unforgiveable, in my judgment, was the Committee's callous disregard of the many requests to testify that it had received. The House Judiciary Committee arbitrarily decided that Japanese America was to be represented by three organizations: JACL, NCJAR, and the Nisei Lobby.

The JACL, of course, had a large constituency and was well-established in Washington. NCJAR had its own, much smaller, constituency. Together we represented less than four per cent of Japanese America. NCJAR was identified with the Lowry Redress Bill. The Committee decided that NCJAR was to represent all the other individuals and organizations which it chose not to hear. That was inappropriate, since NCJAR could not speak for them; we did not know what they wanted to say. Finally, the Nisei Lobby had an even more limited constituency: one man, Mike Masaoka, the lobbyist. Despite repeated efforts, we never identified anyone else who was represented by the Nisei Lobby. We concluded that it was simply Masaoka's creation, enabling him to testify as a spokesperson for Japanese America. Masaoka had been lobbying in Washington for four decades, longer than the tenure of most members of Congress. He had become an institution. Although he remained highly regarded by the JACL, neither he nor the JACL had kept pace with the Japanese-American community.

George Danielson, who represented one of the largest Japanese-American constituencies (in Monterey Park, California), chaired the hearings of the House Judiciary Committee's Subcommittee on Administrative Law and Governmental Relations. He was white-haired but vigorous. He explained the situation of the three bills before the Subcommittee. The two Commission bills, S.1647 from the Senate and H.R.5499 from the House, plus the Lowry Redress Bill, H.R.5977, would go through a process called "markup" whereby the Subcommittee uses a single bill as a vehicle and amends the vehicle as its members see fit. The full Judiciary Committee goes through a comparable process, where it is influenced but not bound by the recommendations of the Subcommittee. The product of the full committee, the "marked up" bill, then goes before the House of Representatives for its process of amendment and acceptance or rejection. Danielson announced that the vehicle for markup would be H.R.5499. At this point, S.1647 had already been amended in the Senate, to add the wartime experiences of the Aleuts to the study and the power of subpoena to the powers of the commission.

These amendments would be carried forward in H.R.5499. The Lowry Bill, H.R.5977, could be used to amend H.R.5499. But that was unlikely to occur.[1]

Seated next to Danielson were two other subcommittee members, Romano L. Mazzoli of Kentucky and Robert McClory of Illinois. Danielson, in his opening remarks, used "interred" instead of "interned"; McClory quickly corrected him. There was nervous laughter. Neither the error nor its correction appeared in the official record. Mazzoli remained relatively quiet during the hearings. Danielson and McClory dominated; both had disturbingly sentimental views about the issue under discussion, and about the democratic process.

McClory remembered aloud:

> I do have a very distinct recollection of the period, because [I] received into my home one of the young men who was interned in Poston, Arizona. He came to us and lived as a member of our family, and I regard him as a sort of stepson. He has always regarded himself as part of our family as well.

He then said simply, "Tyler Tanaka," as if the name was to be immediately and generally recognized by his largely Japanese-American audience. It was not. As though presenting his credentials, he said:

> So, I approach this subject with some firsthand knowledge. I want to indicate that I do have a special interest in this subject, almost a family interest in the subject.

That sounded pleasant enough. But it did get in the way later when he equated mass exclusion and detention of Japanese-Americans with the unofficial social discrimination suffered by German- and Irish-Americans in earlier years. There is, of course, a qualitative difference between unofficial social discrimination and governmental racial discrimination and injustice, backed by federal law.

Later in the hearings, Lowry saw this problem and was quick to identify it. He said:

> I would like to point out the basis of our bill is that this was a Government action, not discrimination that came within the society. . . . It is an action by the Government of the United States. And that action placed people into internment camps. . . .

But Danielson disagreed. He said:

> In the United States, the Government is the people of the United States.

You almost feel as though you're back in high school civics class. He explained:

> I have been here for only 10 years, but I have never observed a Government policy put into effect and remaining in effect for very long, which did not have the support of at least the vocal majority or the majority of the vocal Americans.

Does familiarity breed contempt? Or is it self-recognition that intimacy nourishes? Here at the center of American democracy, I came expecting demonstrations of elemental, gritty democratic and constitutional principles. Instead, I found McClory's sweetly sentimental, "almost family interest" invoked to deal with redress for a harsh injustice perpetrated by the government against 125,000 citizens and residents. Instead, I was to hear Danielson's pronouncement, as though he were punctuating a high school valediction, and was oblivious to the government's betrayals of public trust in Vietnam and Watergate.

> We are the Government. No policy can be enacted and stay in effect very long without the support of the majority of the people.

The House hearings reflected the inferior status of the House to the Senate. No senators testified. There was no Civil Rights Leader or Historian. Danielson introduced the "Honorable Jim Wright, our distinguished majority leader from Texas," as the first to testify. Wright said:

> Thank you very much, Mr. Chairman. It might be useful, if it would be pleasing to the committee, for my colleagues, Norm Mineta and Bob Matsui, to join me.

Danielson replied:

> I would simply be delighted if they would come forward.

Then Wright remembered Lowry:

> Mike Lowry as well, whose bill differs in slight measure from ours, but nonetheless is on the same subject. I would be happy to have them flank me.

The body language was subtle but clear. Lowry was only a freshman representative. His bill was a nuisance. Wright simply repeated the statement he made before the Senate committee.

Mineta was next. He discussed the importance of past commissions and stressed the important educational value of this particular one. He said:

> Our greatest hope is that the knowledge gained from the proposed commission will guarantee that this tragic abuse of civil rights will never again occur.

This apparent conclusion, however, did not end his remarks. He appended a word of support for the Aleuts and then said:

> I would also like to submit for the record a resolution of the General Conference of the United Methodist Church at their Indianapolis, Indiana meeting in April, 1980. . . .

However innocent the intentions of Reverend Perry Saito may have been, this use of the resolution with Saito's amendment placed the United Methodist Church on record in support of the study commission. Had the Saito amendment not been made, Lowry, not Mineta, would have submitted the resolution, and the effect would have been quite different.

Matsui was next on the panel. He expressed his full support for the Senate amendments, specifically the granting of subpoena power to the commission. Danielson responded with surprise, "Subpoena power?" Matsui laconically replied, "Yes." Matsui spoke of four purposes for the commission: 1) helping effect reversal of the Supreme Court decisions upholding the constitutionality of mass exclusion and detention; 2) objective determination of the appropriate form of redress; 3) the educational value of its work; and 4) the deterrent effect its work would have on potential repetitions of the government's actions.

He acknowledged the need for the commission to have subpoena power. He talked about redress, something neither of his predecessors on the panel had addressed. The commission's educational value will be borne out by history, he said, but Supreme Court decisions can be reversed only by the Supreme Court. And penalties, not education, usually serve as deterrents to illegal behavior, especially on the part of the government.

Having the least seniority, Lowry was the last to speak. His bill, which differed from the commission bill by proposing compensation payments of about three billion dollars, was described by the ever-politic Danielson as addressing "the same problem but in a slightly different manner." Lowry did have a prepared statement, which, significantly, was not incorporated in the published record. His prepared statement began with support for the commission. In his oral presentation, he dropped this and launched directly into his argument for redress:

> It is . . . an honor for me to sponsor, along with approximately 20 other Members of Congress, H.R.5977, which I think cuts right to the quick of what we are talking about in this hearing.
>
> This Government of the United States more than any government in the history of the world has protected and developed the protections for individual rights. The thing that has made this country great is the Constitution of the United States and the Bill of Rights, the protection of individuals against government abuse, against abuse by their own government. That is what started the United States. The Bill of Rights and the Constitution are written to protect individuals against abuse by our own Government.
>
> In 1942, by order of the President of the United States, upheld by the Congress of the United States and upheld by the Supreme Court of the United States, we violated all of those principles. We violated the principles of the protection of property, protection of individual rights, and the guarantee of due process.
>
> When a government that is dedicated to the protection of individual liberties abuses those individual liberties, the answer is compensation.

The committee members did not respond to Lowry's arguments. Danielson attacked the figures of $15,000 and $15 a day. "You have no factual data to support them; is that correct?" Danielson asked. McClory responded by pointing out that his son was married to a Chinese woman and that his grandchildren "look quite a bit like . . . Mr. Matsui." But despite the short shrift given the Lowry Redress Bill, Lowry's presence and arguments attested to the presence of some democratic life in the American body politic.

Stuart E. Schiffer, from the Department of Justice, followed with several technical changes to the wording of the legislative vehicle. Schiffer also addressed the Lowry Redress Bill. There was one ironic statement:

> Our preliminary review indicates, however, that locating these individuals [the victims] could place a costly—and possibly impossible—burden on the Federal Bureau of Investigation.

Mass exclusion and detention took only seven months. Why is restitution so much more difficult—possibly impossible—when the injustice was so readily executed?

Japanese-Americans and the Aleuts comprised the final panel. The Japanese-Americans were John Tateishi of the Japanese American Citizens League, William Hohri (myself) of the National Council for Japanese American Redress, and Mike Masaoka of the Nisei Lobby. The Aleuts were Mike Zaharof and Phil Tutiakoff, both of the Pribilof Islands Association.

Tateishi was first. The JACL once again submitted its 100-page written statement for the record. Only this time, by the time it was published several months after these hearings in the official record, all the statement's earlier plagiarisms had quotation marks, footnotes, and attributions. Stylistically, however, it became even more awkward; it concatenated texts from various sources, as though written by a committee of authors who had never met to discuss their joint effort.

Tateishi was brief in speaking. Each of us was given ten minutes. He brought up several points but argued inconclusively. He addressed the question, "whether or not this Commission can do any more than a committee of the Congress." He indicated a number of things the Commission might do, but did not show why a committee of Congress could not do them. He expressed the JACL's belief that the Commission "can benefit all Americans," but did not explain how this could happen. He expressed the JACL's concern for the future and its hope that "no other group of citizens will experience what we experienced in 1942." But he did not link this concern and hope to the Commission. I had difficulty remembering what he said.

I was next. I began by separating my opposition to a study commission from the Aleuts' support of a commission. I had met the Aleuts' witnesses at the door of the committee room, about thirty minutes before the hearings began. I agreed that they had a legitimate need for a commission to investigate what had happened to them because so little was known. Following this clarification, I expressed my disappointment at the absence of witnesses from other parts of Japanese America. I pointed out that we had taken a poll in Chicago which demonstrated that while almost fifty per cent of the Japanese-American community favored compensatory redress, only twelve per cent favored a study commission.

(This poll was taken by NCJAR board member Tom Jamison. He used the telephone and called a random sample of telephone numbers in a directory of Japanese-Americans in Chicago. He polled 100 persons. About forty per cent of the sample were either uncertain or uninterested. If our poll were performed as a newspaper-like poll—one requiring a positive action by the respondent in order to be counted—we would drop the forty per cent uncertain and uninterested, with the resulting increase in responses favoring compensatory redress from fifty to more than eighty per cent.)

I argued that the amounts sought in the Lowry Redress Bill were nominal. "My own inclination," I said "is to demand one thousand dollars a day. That would come to around one hundred billion." This wasn't extreme, but it was sensational. The press picked it up, though that was not my intent. I criticized the hearings. "What do you hope to accomplish," I said, "by asking Japanese-American victims to parade before a Commission? What are we supposed to say? Are we supposed to prove that we were mistreated and humiliated? Are we supposed to prove that our Constitutional rights were violated?" I labeled the commission a charade. I characterized its function as exploitation. I saw consternation on the faces of the committee and its staff.

I offered a compromise. Of course, it wouldn't be accepted. I suggested that the study commission be combined with the Lowry proposal, so that instead of determining whether any wrong had been committed, the commission would assume that a wrong had been done, and then work to determine how the compensation could be paid within the limitations of the federal budget. I slightly misquoted Supreme Court Justice Jackson's dissent in the Korematsu decision, calling the decision a "loaded gun" rather than a "loaded weapon." But I did not hide my pessimism. I concluded, "Maybe it will be for some future historian to say that America was tested and found wanting."

Mike Masaoka was the final representative of Japanese America. He is an immodest man. "Of all living Japanese Americans," he announced, "I may be the most familiar with the major events of those times." (One event of which he had no experience was that of mass exclusion and detention. Masaoka was never interned.) He waved his credentials of heroism: "I am also an honorary Texan because I was among those who helped rescue the lost Texas battalion in World War II. Together with four brothers," he continued, "we were in the Army of the United States and we all saw some combat together. One died in the rescue of the lost battalion and another is 100 percent disabled. Today, in making my case for them, I hope you understand why I feel personally so concerned about this matter."

Masaoka saved his bombast and ire for the Lowry Redress Bill; he used me, not Mike Lowry, as his target. Masaoka was, after all, a lobbyist; he could not afford to offend a member of Congress. He said:

> Mr. Hohri has made an eloquent plea for H.R.5977 which provides for individual compensation. We, both in the JACL and in the Nisei Lobby, oppose this particular bit of legislation. We do, however, not impugn their motives because both groups, all groups, in fact, are seeking the same general objectives and we may, of course, differ as to procedures and perhaps as to amount, but we find certain flaws in H.R.5977 which I would like to call to your attention.

Referring to the fifteen dollars per diem compensation, he declaimed:

> You have the question, are you going to pay the SAME amount to a child, an infant, as to an adult? Are you going to pay the same amount to a DOCTOR, DENTIST, TEACHER, as you would pay to someone who doesn't have that background or training?[2]

But the Lowry bill, the reader will recall, intended compensation for violations of constitutional rights. Masaoka may have had in mind losses of earnings—he was not clear—which the Lowry bill was not intended to compensate.

Masaoka then attacked the proposed entitlement of heirs of deceased victims to redress. He knew that the purpose of including heirs was to allow redress for the grievances of the Issei, most of whom have died. He found a molehill and made it into a mountain:

> What if they were born outside camp? What if they are the grandchildren? Should they be entitled to the same amount? Should they now?

Danielson, intrigued with this line of reasoning, interrupted:

> Could it be someone who might have been, let us say, living in New York and was never interned or even threatened?

Masaoka, reading the cue, began rising to the occasion:

> Even worse. If you read down further you note that if these individuals and their legal heirs are not in the United States, the Attorney General has to go abroad to find them. So it is quite possible that you will have Japanese nationals who were never in the United States as beneficiaries of this particular legislation.

Then Masaoka said portentously:

> Not only that, but you have certain Japanese who served the Japanese war effort against the United States.

He was not belaboring the obvious. He moved in for the kill:

> You could have situations of brothers, American citizens, who [have] Japanese national brothers, [who have been] fighting each other. In the case one passes away, is the other who has never made an effort to come to America to be given this redress?

Though the words stumbled, the charge was clear: Lowry was proposing that redress be made to the enemy. I could imagine such farfetched extrapolation being made by some rabid, Jap-hating racist. It was shocking coming from a "brother." Was Masaoka being whitey's hatchetman? Was he doing that which no self-respecting legislator would dare to attempt: bury redress with the accusation of treason? Or was it that Masaoka hated his Nisei self?

Masaoka spoke for almost thirty minutes; he consumed about one-fourth of the total hearing time. His long-windedness was preemptive. McClory, not the Committee's chair, interrupted to obtain time for the two Aleuts to testify. They had to shorten their presentations. They had traveled to Washington, D.C. from Alaska—a long way for five minutes before a House Committee. There was no time remaining for the others on the panel to answer questions or to speak in rebuttal. Demagogy perverted dialogue.

The legislation-seeking phase of the redress movement came to an end in these hearings. There were still to be the final acts: the motions, speeches, and votes of the House of Representatives; and the national television news of President Carter's signing of the bill creating the Commission on Wartime Relocation and Internment of Civilians (CWRIC).

NCJAR would not ignore the CWRIC. But we remained skeptical of its purposes and its potential. Its stated objective was to submit a report and recommendations for legislative action. We had learned a lesson about legislative redress; it was, to use the Department of Justice's phrase, "possibly impossible." We had to think about an alternative.

12. TRANSITIONS
SEARCHING FOR ANOTHER WAY

My wife Yuriko and I decided to stretch the 1980 Labor Day weekend into a two-week vacation, driving to Washington, D.C. to visit Jack and Aiko Herzig and then to New York to visit our daughter Sasha and her daughters, Otsu and Tsuya, as well as other relatives and friends. During this vacation, NCJAR took the first, tentative steps towards an effort to seek redress in the United States courts.

On July 21, 1980, the House of Representatives passed the bill creating the Commission on Wartime Relocation and Internment of Civilians. Ten days later, President Carter signed the bill into law. The commissioners were to be appointed within ninety days, by the end of October. But the appointments were delayed. It would be months—going into 1981 and the new Reagan administration—before all the commissioners were appointed and the Commission held its first meeting. The delays gave NCJAR respite. It was a good time to think about something new.

Logic supported seeking redress in the courts. The law might provide the leverage NCJAR needed. The successful enactment of redress legislation would require a constituency and an audience of a size that we could not possibly muster. Japanese America was less than one-half of one per cent of the national population, and a vocal part of Japanese America opposed our efforts. The courts might hear and decide our case on its merits. Historical fact, rather than popular opinion, would affect the scales of informed legal justice. The courts also provided NCJAR with autonomy. We had the field to ourselves. We did not need to negotiate with the JACL, the Commission (CWRIC), with members of Congress, or with those seeking redress in other ways. Finally, the courts were a more appropriate forum in which to express the victims' grievances; the injuries they suffered had been to their legal rights and privileges as American citizens and residents. In the courts, our research would find places for expression. But there was little logic in the way in which NCJAR brought redress into the courts.

We knew little about the law. No one among our board members or within our inner circle of supporters was trained in the law. The American Civil Liberties Union, a leading civil rights organization, had helped to clarify and improve our legislative proposal, but provided no guidance for pursuing redress in the courts. We had a correspondent who thought the courts were a better forum for redress than the legislature; but his support was moral, not substantive. Nor did we draw up a list of law firms from which to make our selection. Choosing a law firm in Washington, D.C. by that method must be as difficult as choosing a Chinese restaurant in San Francisco's Chinatown.

Our way was uncomplicated, if unplanned. Jack Herzig contacted a friend who was an attorney; Jack thought him sensitive and humane—the Yiddish term "mensch" is appropriate. Attorney Benjamin Zelenko and Jack Herzig had served together on a board in Washington. They met and discussed NCJAR's interest in a courtroom approach to seeking redress for Japanese-Americans. Zelenko referred Jack to the Washington law firm of Landis, Cohen, Singman and Rauh. The first and last names are noteworthy. James Landis (1899-1964) had been Dean of the Harvard Law School and had served in Franklin Roosevelt's "brain trust." B. Michael Rauh is the son of the well-known Democratic liberal and attorney, Joseph L. Rauh. Zelenko himself had served as General Counsel to the House Judiciary Committee during the civil rights years from 1962 to 1972.

None of this made much difference to us when Jack, Aiko, Yuriko, and I met with Mike Rauh on September 3, 1980. We simply wanted to learn whether or not there was a judicial route available for seeking redress. Maybe we would be advised that judicial redress was impossible. In the early 1970s I had been a member of Church of the New City; our church had tried to sue to prevent newspapers from publishing advertisements for housing unless the housing was available without racial bias. We had been unable to find a reputable law firm that would agree to represent us. NCJAR's first hurdle was finding good lawyers who thought that a courtroom effort for redress was worthwhile.

Mike Rauh, like many well-informed Americans, knew about the wartime event, but his knowledge was limited. His ignorance of our history was matched by our ignorance of the law. There was a problem of trust on both sides. Could we trust this firm to give us sound legal advice? Could the firm trust us to be responsible and informed about the historical issues? The exchange of views was open and friendly. Mike was candid. He explained that we probably had less than a fifty-fifty chance of success. There were serious legal obstacles. He'd need about a month to decide if we had a case and, if we did, to formulate a proposal for us to consider. He did ask one question: "Why has no one ever before filed such a lawsuit?" This question would occur over and over again in following months. The answer to this riddle would reveal much about ourselves.

It took the law firm two months to respond. During that period, Benjamin Zelenko joined Landis, Cohen, Singman and Rauh as a senior partner. I made a special trip to Washington to discuss their proposal. We were to meet in the afternoon of Monday, November 3, 1980. But before this meeting, Aiko and Jack arranged for me to visit the National Archives. I received my identification card as a researcher. Then I followed them to the Modern Military Archives section in which they had been conducting their research. I remember a three-shelf library truck, which was packed with boxes; each box contained file folders of copies of correspondence, memoranda, and transcripts of telephone conversations. One such truck contained perhaps ten running feet of documents. I was impressed. How many trucks had Aiko and Jack gone through? Aiko gave me a box to examine. She showed me the procedure for identifying papers which we wanted photocopied. We were to enclose such papers within a paper loop. All papers were returned to their folders, and all folders to their boxes.

The National Archives librarian would later do the photocopying for the cost of copies. As beginner's luck would have it, I came across a significant find: documents about the military's response to Mitsuye Endo's petition for release from Tule Lake under the writ of *habeas corpus*, including the military's attempt to obtain legislation suspending the writ. Here was evidence of the strong interest the military maintained in our detention, months after the administration of the camps had been assigned to the War Relocation Authority. Aiko and Jack had retrieved thousands of pages of such documents. I came away from my short visit to the National Archives with great appreciation for their work there.

In the afternoon, Jack and Aiko Herzig and I met with Mike Rauh and Benjamin Zelenko to discuss a lawsuit. The attorneys laid out a simple plan of action. The injuries we suffered were justiciable, i.e., amenable to litigation. The main obstacles were procedural ones which might bar our entrance to the courts. Statutes of limitations require injured persons to sue within a few years of their injuries. We were late by decades. The doctrine of sovereign immunity protects governments from being sued. The government may be sued only if the government consents to be sued. (This sounds like something an ancient English sovereign dreamed up before the rule of law was established. Everyone is subject to the law except the sovereign—an arrangement similar to the right of veto given to a few nations in the United Nations Security Council.) Our lawyers' main task would be to overcome these procedural obstacles.

The obstacles were not insuperable. In the 1960s Mike Rauh's father, Joseph L. Rauh, had successfully represented Japanese-American clients even though deadlines set by statutes of limitations had passed. Funds deposited in yen with Japanese banks prior to the war had been frozen by the United States. After hostilities had ceased, holders of these yen deposits were permitted to reclaim their money within a prescribed period of time, which ended on November 18, 1949. But the disruptions of mass exclusion, detention, and dispersal made impractical notifying the depositors by mail: how could current mailing addresses be found? Instead, the government published notices in the *Federal Register*, which few of the depositors had ever heard of, much less read. (Just think of the impracticality of mass exclusion had the government chosen to limit the publication of its exclusion orders to the *Federal Register*.) When Rauh's clients finally did hear about the availability of their money, the deadline had passed. Although the government agreed that the money rightfully belonged to these depositors, the government could not circumvent the statute of limitations. The elder Rauh successfully argued that the government had failed to exercise reasonable vigor in informing the depositors of their right to reclaim their money, and that therefore the statute of limitations should be tolled, i.e., have its deadline postponed. Eventually, in 1967, the Supreme Court agreed.[1]

Nonetheless, the procedural obstacles in our case were formidable. Overcoming them would require extensive preparation. Mike Rauh proposed that one year be expended in legal preparation. Aiko saw the value of historical research. Rauh agreed but stressed the need for legal research. The firm would hire a young attorney to work full-time on legal research during this year of preparation. NCJAR would have to pay the costs for this initial phase. After filing suit, the firm would seek to recover its costs as part of the settlement. The initial legal fees were set at $75,000.

"I didn't see you blanch," Jack Herzig said to me after we left the office and headed for a Chinese restaurant for a drink and an early dinner. I am inclined to think of money in terms of my capacity to earn and accumulate it. This amount was beyond my comprehension. I had never owned that much. The money would have to be raised from others, from people that we didn't know yet. This was another instance of faith. We still knew very little about the law. I doubt that even our attorneys fully understood the legal implications of what we were about to undertake. Certainly, no one knew what new discoveries we would make among the documents we were researching. Nor did anyone know who our "young attorney" would be. As it turned out, we would be committed to our lawsuit before we would meet one of our principal attorneys. We did not meet her for another year.

Constructing first prison camp at Manzanar, California. *National Archives.*

Processing new arrivals at Manzanar. *National Archives.*

Hiking through the construction to one's assigned barracks at Manzanar. *National Archives.*

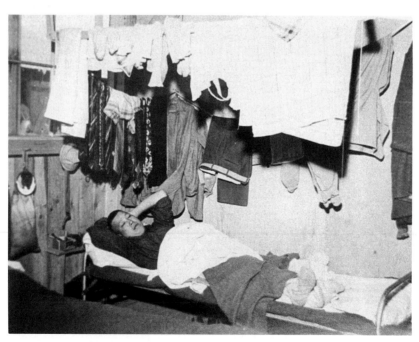

An internee making himself at home on his cot and straw-filled mattress (Manzanar). *National Archives.*

Teaching children in a makeshift elementary school before any equipment was available (Manzanar). *National Archives.*

An internee pruning a tree while a soldier stands guard (Manzanar). *National Archives.*

A Manzanar block was comprised of fourteen barracks for living quarters, one for recreation, a double-sized one for a mess hall, and a row of barracks for latrines and laundry. *National Archives.*

Orphans at Manzanar's Children's Village. *National Archives.*

A committee of Manzanar Block Leaders. Front row, from left: Karl Yoneda, N. Inouye; back row, from left: Bill Kito, Ted Akahoshi, Tom Yamasaki, and Harry Nakamura. *National Archives.*

Nursery school children in Manzanar. *National Archives.*

Serving milk to children under five years old.
National Archives.

A German prisoner-of-war camp at Camp Blanding, Florida. The wooden sidings of these buildings contrast with the tarpapered walls of War Relocation Authority buildings. *National Archives.*

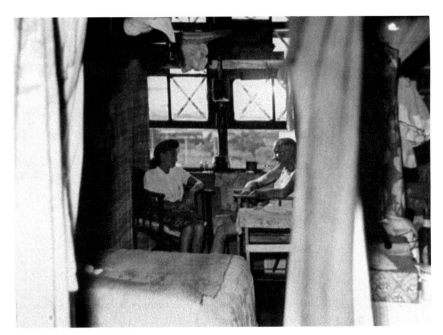

An internal view of a prison camp located in Shanghai, China shows how the Japanese housed its civilian internees there. *National Archives.*

A Japanese-American soldier guarding war prisoners in Hampshire, Illinois. *National Archives.*

A U.S. Army Signal Corps photograph of the Poston camp uses this caption: "Aerial view of a Japanese concentration camp for aliens near Parker, Arizona." *National Archives.*

Harry Ueno, leader of the Manzanar Kitchen Workers Union, who was arrested but never charged or tried for allegedly assaulting a government informant. His arrest sparked the "Manzanar Riot." *William Hohri.*

Joseph Y. Kurihara, a Hawaiian Nisei, World War I veteran, and an outspoken critic of mass exclusion and detention. He was an early advocate of reparations payment. *Hannah Holmes.*

Shosuke Sasaki, William Hohri, Kathy Wong, and Frank Abe at the May 1979 meeting in Seattle which formed the National Council for Japanese American Redress. *William Hohri.*

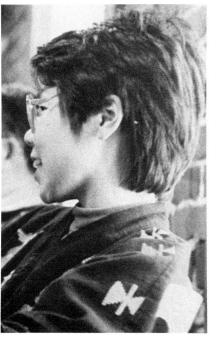

Henry Miyatake, an early leader of the redress movement, at the same May 1979 meeting. *William Hohri.*

Sansei activist Karen Seriguchi. *William Hohri.*

Nisei activist Aiko Herzig and writer-historian Michi Weglyn at the 1980 New York University conference on redress. *William Hohri.*

Gordon Hirabayashi of the Supreme Court Hirabayashi case at the same 1980 conference. *William Hohri.*

Roger Daniels speaking to Mike Masaoka and Jim Wright at the 1980 Senate hearings on S.1647, the fact-finding commission bill. *William Hohri.*

Bert Nakano, leader of the National Coalition for Redress/Reparations, testifying at the CWRIC hearings. *Frank Abe.*

William Hohri testifying at the opening hearings of the Commission on Wartime Relocation and Internment of Civilians. *Frank Abe.*

Nelson Kitsuse, an early leader in the redress movement, at the September 1981 conference on redress at Northeastern Illinois University. *William Hohri.*

Minoru Yasui, a leader of the JACL National Committee for Redress, at the same September redress conference. *William Hohri.*

Karl R. Bendetsen, architect of mass exclusion and detention, testifying at the second Washington hearings of the Commission on Wartime Relocation and Internment of Civilians. *New York Nichibei.*

John J. McCloy, former Assistant Secretary of War and primary decision maker for mass exclusion and detention, testifying at the CWRIC hearings. *New York Nichibei.*

Calvert Dedrick, a Census Bureau statistician who used punched-card census data to help with the massive roundup, testifying at the CWRIC hearings. *New York Nichibei.*

Mike Masaoka, wartime National Secretary of the JACL, testifying at the CWRIC hearings. *New York Nichibei.*

Phil Nash talking to Miyo Hayashi at the same hearings. *New York Nichibei.*

Outside the Supreme Court: Edward Tokeshi; Wesley Yamaka; Joyce Okinaka; and Ellen Carson. *William Hohri.*

April 20, 1987, left to right: unidentified; Kathryn Korematsu; Fred Koretmatsu; Goji Tashiro; and Sally Tashiro. *William Hohri.*

A line of people waiting to enter the Supreme Court, April 20, 1987. *William Hohri.*

Kathryn Korematsu (partly hidden); Fred Korematsu; Grayce Uyehara talking to Chizuko Omori (back) and Colleen Darling. *William Hohri*

Yuriko Hohri (partly hidden); Doris Sato (back); Sam Ozaki; Lydia Omori; and Chizuko Omori. *William Hohri.*

Jack Herzig, researcher, NCJAR advocate and strong supporter, in the Rayburn House Office Building in December 1986. *William Hohri.*

Aiko Herzig, researcher, strong supporter and advocate of NCJAR. *William Hohri.*

Penny Willgerodt, English editor of *New York Nichibei*, interviewing Harry Ueno April 29, 1987 outside the Supreme Court. *William Hohri.*

Karen Kai, Peter Irons, and Fred Korematsu. *William Hohri.*

13. TRANSITIONS
RETAINING A LAW FIRM

The following year was stressful and busy. It went by quickly. Our initial task was to raise $75,000. We set an intermediate goal of $30,000 with a March 1981 deadline. If we could reach that amount by that date, we would proceed. Otherwise, we would discontinue our effort to file a lawsuit. There was some talk among us of seeking grants from foundations and organizations. I thought the initial funds should come from individuals, especially from victims. We had to take ownership of our cause. The lawsuit had to become our lawsuit; we had to assume its costs, its risks, and its promises. The lawsuit would become a test of Japanese-Americans' capacity to act on their own behalf, as well as a test of the moral and legal will of America.

We came up with the idea of using the classic Japanese story of the "Forty-Seven *Ronin*" for fundraising. *Ronin* are masterless samurai. In the story, forty-seven *ronin* avenge the injustice which led to their master's death by killing their master's adversary and then, true to their samurai code, they accepted their punishment for violating their code by taking their own lives. Both vengeance and life-taking are admittedly extreme. We were seeking judicial redress. Still, in a sense, we were masterless. We were not part of the Japanese-American establishment. And we asked *ronin* contributors to give one thousand dollars, serious money. The sum was not equivalent to the passion and blood of the story, but it did mean something to the contributor. We felt that a few *ronin* contributors would make a big difference. Ultimately, they did. Jack and Aiko were the first to contribute money for the lawsuit. Soon afterwards, a hard core of four of us became the first *ronin* contributors: Nelson Kitsuse, Harry Nagaoka, Tom Jamison, and myself. We didn't meet our goal of $30,000 by March 1981. I was ready to discontinue the effort. But the NCJAR board thought we should keep on for a little longer. We extended the deadline to May 1981. We reached our initial fundraising goal by the end of April.

On April 22, 1981, I was once again in Washington. NCJAR had raised $29,000. We had twelve *ronin*. We had almost arrived at our initial goal. We could taste success. We had a few revisions to our formal agreement with the law firm to discuss with the attorneys. Aiko had arranged two other events to make further use of the trip. I spent the morning at the National Archives. We went to the War Relocation Authority section to examine family records. I especially enjoyed finding early mimeographed editions of the *Manzanar Free Press,* the camp newspaper, which had illustrations by my brother Sohei. I also found the account of a softball game in which my team, the Dusty 9, was defeated by Terminal Island by the score of 42 to 2, the two runs being made by us in the ninth inning when our humiliation as high school students was made complete by having to play against grade school children. (During this game we saw a small airplane flying backwards against high winds.)

During lunch hour, we met with a group called the Asian Pacific American Federal Employees Council to discuss the redress movement. We were always looking for a group to help us gain support for NCJAR in Washington. But that did not happen. After the brown-bag luncheon meeting, the Herzigs and I went out for our own lunch and then went to the law office.

At this meeting Benjamin Zelenko said, "Well, friends, this is a historic occasion." We came to agreement on the terms of our relationship. NCJAR would remit an initial $15,000 as soon as we raised $30,000. From then on, we would remit $5,000 a month for one year, which would bring us to $75,000. On May 5, 1981, we signed a letter for NCJAR retaining the firm of Landis, Cohen, Singman and Rauh.

Appointments to the Commission

Before we could get deeply involved in the lawsuit, however, we had to deal with the Commission on Wartime Relocation and Internment of Civilians (CWRIC). We had already begun by lobbying for appointments to the CWRIC.

Although I was national chairperson of NCJAR and NCJAR's most visible public representative through speechmaking and writing, I was not NCJAR's sole, moving spirit. The Seattle supporters had convinced Representative Mike Lowry to introduce our redress bill. Jack Herzig had put us in touch with our law firm. Aiko Herzig had pushed us into many other activities. She had been our lobbyist and had made many contacts for us in the Congress. She had begun the monumental task of research in the National Archives. She also prodded us into proposing candidates for the Commission.

I remained uneasy about the Commission. But her argument that we should try to make the best of a bad deal by working for the appointment of good commissioners made sense. We came up with three names. The Seattle supporters proposed Professor Charles Z. Smith of the University of Washington Law School. We thought Father Robert F. Drinan, former Member of Congress and former Dean of Boston College Law School, would be a good commissioner. And Ralph Lazo, an NCJAR *ronin* supporter, was submitting his own name as a commissioner.

Ralph Lazo, though not nearly as well-known as the first two candidates, has a unique place in Japanese-American history. As a teenager, he was the only American not of Japanese descent to enter a camp voluntarily for no reason other than his desire to remain with his friends. (Other persons not of Japanese descent did voluntarily enter camps, but they were mostly spouses of Japanese-Americans.) Ralph Lazo was living in Los Angeles when the Japanese attacked Pearl Harbor. He was a student at Belmont High School and had many Nisei friends. One of them, Isao Kudow, asked him, "Ralph, what are you going to do without us? Why don't you come along?" So, after consulting with his father, he went down to the Santa Fe Railroad Station and registered for exclusion and detention. As fate would have it, he didn't end up with his friends, most of whom were sent to the camp at Heart Mountain, Wyoming. Ralph was sent to Manzanar. I came to know him at Manzanar High School. He was one of the most popular students in our class.[1] I thought that he was well-qualified to serve on the Commission. But Ralph Lazo was not appointed.

Charles Z. Smith was also an exceptionally well-qualified candidate. In addition to being a professor of law, he had been a judge and was considered an expert in the history of the exclusion and detention program. He was well-liked in Seattle's Japanese-American community. He had served as president of the American Baptist Churches U.S.A. He received endorsements from leaders of the several Protestant denominations. But he, too, was not appointed.

Father Robert F. Drinan was appointed to the Commission. This took some doing. The original bill specified seven commissioners. On December 15, 1980, Senator Warren Magnuson, who had lost his seat in the Senate, appointed former Senators Edward Brooke and Hugh Mitchell. On January 5, 1981, President Carter, who had lost the presidency to Ronald Reagan, appointed Joan Bernstein, Arthur Flemming, and William Marutani. Also in January 1981, the Speaker of the House of Representatives, Thomas P. O'Neill, appointed Representative Daniel Lungren and former Supreme Court Justice Arthur Goldberg. However, even though this completed the original complement of seven commissioners, problems remained. No one had been appointed who could properly represent the interests of the Aleuts, whose plight was also to be investigated by the Commission. And House Speaker O'Neill felt strongly about appointing Robert F. Drinan. So, to solve these problems, a Senate resolution, S.253, was passed by the Senate on January 27 and by the House the next day; it increased the number of commissioners from seven to nine. Once it was signed by President Reagan in February, Father Ismael Gromoff was appointed by the Senate Majority Leader, while Father Robert F. Drinan was appointed by the Speaker of the House.

Following these long delays, the CWRIC convened on March 4, 1981 and selected Joan Bernstein as chairperson and Representative Daniel Lungren as vice-chairperson. After four more months, on July 14, 1981, the Commission held its first hearings, in the Senate Caucus Room.

14. HEARINGS
FIRST WASHINGTON HEARINGS

I was a reluctant participant in the opening hearings of the Commission on Wartime Relocation and Internment of Civilians, which were held in a hot Washington on July 14 and 16, 1981. I knew how the Commission had been conceived in San Francisco, on March 3, 1979. I believed the Commission was a cop-out. It resulted from the JACL's unwillingness to demand redress directly from the United States Congress. The Commission was to do a study, arrive at the obvious conclusion that an injustice had occurred, and then state the victims' demands for them. Similarly, the peasants in *The Seven Samurai* begged samurai to fight for them—only here there was no question of survival, only the JACL's fear of failure. The commissioners did not understand the questionable origin of the Commission, except for Judge William Marutani, who had participated in the San Francisco decision.

In retrospect, no one fully understood the dynamics of the Commission. Everyone involved had a different interpretation. The JACL saw it as their greatest political achievement, a triumph that would overshadow their other successes. I saw it as a charade: tales of woe and demands for restitution signifying much but producing nothing. For some, it was an opportunity to organize the Japanese-American community in accordance with their political theories. For most, it was an opportunity to air their grievances and to argue their opinion before official representatives of the United States—like Dorothy's audience before the Wizard of Oz. For the commissioners themselves, the Commission meant that distinction and prestige would be added to their careers—an additional line, perhaps, in *Who's Who in America*. Their main mission was to conduct hearings in cities where the victims lived. As the hearings took place, an improvised Greek drama developed, with the elements needed to ensure a respectable audience rating.

The news media would serve as an antiphonal chorus, with clips in the evening and morning television news and with newspaper feature stories and editorial comment. As a sort of collective heroic figure, the victims would retell old hurts, fears, indignities, and disgust. They would come together in large public gatherings to speak, listen, and remember. Some victims made memorable presentations, such as Charles Hamasaki at Los Angeles, Kinzo Wakayama at San Francisco, Masao Takahashi at Seattle, Jitsuo Morikawa at Chicago, and Jack Tono at New York. A few well-chosen words would distill the essence of the victims' pain, like Akiyo DeLoyd's: "All our flowers were made of Kleenex." The villains of the piece were the movers and shakers who were still alive who testified, such as John J. McCloy and Karl R. Bendetsen, as well as lesser and less villainous characters, such as Philip M. Glick, Edward Ennis, and Mike M. Masaoka. To provide bitter, comic relief, there were characters to be hooted and hated: Lillian Baker, whiter than white, and Senator S. I. Hayakawa, bleached-out yellow. The drama would be filled with pity and fear, but would have no denouement and resolution. Rather than fulfilling the classic Greek form, the Commission hearings would eventually resemble contemporary soap operas, anticipating resolution in a sequel.

But hidden behind the surfeit of emotions and catharsis of the testimony, the media interviews and commentary, and the repetitive questions of the commissioners, a story-line was developed through the work of a persistent and unheralded researcher, Aiko Yoshinaga Herzig. Aiko, who had worked as NCJAR lobbyist, decided to join the Commission staff as the director of research. She did not get the directorship but did land a job as research associate. Despite this subordinate title, she produced most of the CWRIC research. Ultimately, the documents she retrieved for the Commission from the National Archives and elsewhere formed the basis of the Commission's Report and Recommendations. Other documents that she had retrieved earlier for NCJAR became part of the Commission's files.

This collection of documents had great impact. The documents demolished the doctrine of military necessity, which was the main rationale for exclusion and detention. They revealed the presidential politics involved in extending the exclusion program twenty-one months beyond the cessation of "military necessity," such as it was. They revealed the suppression of evidence and other unethical conduct by the U.S. government which compromised the Supreme Court decisions in the Yasui, Hirabayashi, Korematsu, and Endo cases. Some documents were used in a dramatic, effective attack on these famous, erroneous, Supreme Court decisions. (In 1983, Fred Korematsu, Minoru Yasui, and Gordon Hirabayashi petitioned the court for a writ of *coram nobis* to have their convictions vacated. The evidence was so overwhelming that the government agreed to the vacations.) The Commission's Report and Recommendations, in turn, would find their way into legislative proposals for redress. The documents would support the historic class action lawsuit against the United States filed by the National Council for Japanese American Redress on behalf of the 125,000 victims.

This small mountain of documentary evidence justified the Commission's otherwise shadowy and insignificant existence. The rest was drama, certainly worthy of interest, but with little effect on what was happening in the real world of contemporary American politics.

Of course, most participants thought that they already knew the story line. They would identify the causes of the wartime events as anti-Japanese racism, economic greed, political opportunism, the sensationalism of news media, or the necessities of war. The commissioners' chief task was to organize the hearings and to get the show on the road. The first job was to select an executive director, who had to be Japanese-American. (Who better than the victims understood their injury?) Former victim Paul Bannai, a Republican politician—for Ronald Reagan was President by now—was appointed. The choice was infelicitous, for a controversy arose around Bannai that almost destroyed the Commission. Soon after its first hearings, Cheryl Yamamoto, who served as the Commission's primary liaison with Congress and the general public, resigned. Eventually, Bannai crossed swords with the Commission's chairperson, Joan Bernstein, and was himself forced to resign two days before the Chicago hearings.

The First Day

The first hearings confirmed my suspicions about the Commission. Representatives of the government presented official historical accounts, but these included none of the principals who were still alive. Instead of McCloy, Bendetsen, and Eisenhower, Abe Fortas, James Rowe, and Leland Barrows appeared—all secondary figures in their former governmental roles. Also, Departmental historians testified, relying primarily on published works. This was a rehash of what was already known. During the hearings, staff support was not provided for the commissioners, who, except for Marutani, were not well-informed. Most of the commissioners could have used staff help in formulating their questions. Two of the four test-case challengers, Gordon Hirabayashi and Minoru Yasui, testified, but they were not yet aware of the governmental machinations that led to their convictions being upheld by the Supreme Court. Each of the three redress groups made its pitch: the National Council for Japanese American Redress, the National Coalition for Redress/Reparations, and the Japanese American Citizens League. Several lawyers' organizations and civil rights groups testified, as did a few individuals.

Daniel Lungren

Chairperson Joan Bernstein opened the hearings by summarizing the intent of Congress in creating the Commission. She was followed by the vice-chairperson, Republican Representative Daniel Lungren. Lungren felt compelled from the outset to dampen expectations of monetary compensation:

> I would extend a note of caution, however, to those who would believe that the sole . . . purpose of this Commission is to merely determine the extent to which some form of monetary restitution is to be provided to individuals by the government.[1]

He adroitly blamed the victims for his own reluctance to recommend reparations:

> The issue of transferring taxpayers' dollars in reparation to those interned is one over which there appears to be a split of opinion even within the Japanese American community itself.

He raised the specter of enormous cost:

> Moreover, several of the proposals in this regard which have already been aired publicly have suggested an expenditure well into the billions of dollars.

Lungren attempted to show that the entire Congress shared his qualms over restitution:

> I feel compelled to state that in my judgment Congress would have never chartered this Commission if it felt that restitution were to be accepted by the Commission as a foregone conclusion.

Indeed! Almost two years later, Lungren would be the one stating a foregone conclusion. When the Commission's report was issued, on February 24, 1983, Lungren quoted himself word for word from the preceding quotation, thus demonstrating that nothing in the intervening two years had made him change his mind on Congress and restitution. He was opposed to monetary redress in 1981; he would remain opposed to it in 1983.

Japanese-American Members of Congress

The Japanese-American members of Congress were less nervous about reparations than Lungren. Senator Hayakawa was outspoken in his opposition, but he did not testify in Washington. The remaining four Japanese-Americans did present statements there. But though they were not nervous, they seemed restrained, as though wishing to avoid eye contact with the issue.

Senator Inouye from Hawaii seemed to be appealing to some nobler self-image:

> I know there are many expectations about what this Commission will recommend. I have never and will not now express my own thoughts about what should be your recommendation to Congress. This I can tell you. If nothing else results from this inquiry other than a reasoned, thorough, and accurate record of what took place and why it took place, you will have done your job well.

He seemed willing, too, to yield to probable defeat:

> It may come to pass that a budget-conscious Congress will find itself unable to provide any significant form of monetary redress or reparations. But no Congress, President, or Supreme Court can ever underwrite the words of your report. So make them good words, even great words. Make your report one that will awaken this experience enough to haunt the conscience of this nation, haunt it so that we will never forget that we are capable of such an act, so that we will never again be able to do this to ourselves, and so that we will be able to pay tribute to the suffering, the fortitude, the patriotism, and ultimately the triumph of the people who lived through this experience.

The other Japanese-American Senator from Hawaii, Matsunaga, did little better than Inouye:

> Such damages and injuries [suffered by Japanese-American victims] can never be fully compensated at this late date, for many of the internees are dead and gone, while others continue to bear irreparable psychological scars. However, a formal recognition of the wrong committed against the internees and an offer of token compensation to every former internee or, if deceased, to his or her legal heir or heirs would once again prove that this great nation of ours is so strong and so steeped in righteousness that it is unafraid to admit its mistakes of the past and to make whole those whom it may have wronged.

The two Japanese-American members of the House of Representatives were even less forthright. Neither Representative Matsui nor Representative Mineta appeared personally. Instead, they issued a joint statement, which Commissioner Bernstein read aloud. The statement said nothing about redress; it apologized for their inability to be present, stressed the importance of a commission and the necessity of studying primary documents, and ended, "As you begin your work, we wish you success, and we look forward to a thorough review of the entire internment and relocation experience."

These statements by the Japanese-American members of Congress were not a clarion call to redress. As Dwight Chuman's poll would later show, these cautious statements were inconsistent with the sentiments of most Japanese-Americans, who overwhelmingly supported monetary redress. Apparently, the Japanese-American members of Congress, except Hayakawa, wished to remain on their Olympian heights, far above the battle, keeping their hands clean and their reputations unsullied. They left the task of raising the banner and mobilizing a movement to others. These leaders kept polished their best "Quiet American" and "Model Minority" images.

Perhaps these Japanese-American community leaders had their own, covert agenda for redress. Eventually, the Japanese-American members of Congress would introduce redress bills in Congress. Still, the Commission had become a functioning reality. The commissioners were ready to accept recommendations from members of Congress as well as ordinary citizens. The democratic process is by definition open and public. Whether they wished to be or not, the Japanese-American members of Congress were the leading spokespersons for Japanese America. Senator Hayakawa seemed to understand this, and he exploited the role to maximum advantage. He spoke against redress. His Japanese-American colleagues failed to counter him by speaking for redress.

Once the parade of congressional witnesses had testified, living representatives from the World War II government bureaucracy testified.

James Rowe

James Rowe spoke for the Department of Justice. During World War II, he was second to Attorney General Francis Biddle. He said he hadn't prepared a written statement for want of time. With some self-deprecation, he described himself as cynical. Perhaps he was exercising the prerogatives of old age. As he said, "Well, at my age, I don't really care." He characterized military necessity:

> If you had a military uniform on, you'd say "military necessity." At least in this very early stage, people bowed down [to it.] I remember Ennis, at one time, said [that] there was no evidence whatsoever [of] either sabotage or espionage. And, I gather, they never did turn up. But the rumors were floating around. One congressman came to me one day when Ennis was making this argument and said, "Just what if you're wrong? What if the Japanese do this?" Ennis replied, "Well, just take us out and shoot us."

Commissioner Marutani asked Rowe:

> What should this Commission recommend to see that we do not have a recurrence of this type of infringement upon fellow citizens?

Rowe replied:

> Well, I would remind people about the Bill of Rights. I'm not sure we get it when we need it.

Rowe continued with casual contrition:

I'm probably too cynical this morning. I don't know what you could do except emphasize— get attention—get public attention. It is a precedent in a way. You know, when the problem comes up, we will remember the Japanese, and what a mess we made of that—and to an innocent people.

Then, as if given sudden enlightenment, he asked:

I'm not quite sure what your charter is, what you're supposed to be doing—anyway.

Leland Barrows

Leland Barrows was next. He had been Assistant Director of Administrative Management for the War Relocation Authority. As Barrows said, "I was invited to speak here because my old friend and former chief, Dillon Myer, who directed the War Relocation Authority during all but the first three months of its existence, is unable to be here." In the Los Angeles hearings, Lillian Baker later presented a statement which she claimed was on behalf of Dillon Myer, thus giving the impression Myer was not otherwise represented before the Commission. But Barrows clearly contradicted this impression. He spoke authoritatively about the WRA. Dillon Myer, he related, picked his initial WRA staff from among his former co-workers in the Department of Agriculture. Barrows discussed the budget-making process; he recommended the final reports of the WRA published in 1945 and 1946; he mentioned voluntary exclusion, the private employment of around 10,000 internees from the camps in 1942, the famous Salt Lake City meeting of April 7, 1942; he described the camps' infrastructure of blocks of barracks, hospitals, schools, agriculture, employment, clothing allowance, food and rationing, and the Geneva Convention on Prisoners of War. He discussed self-government, temporary and indefinite leave, military service, registration and the loyalty oath, segregation, political pressures from the press and from politicians, the closing of the camps, and the scattering of Japanese-Americans throughout America. In all this long survey of WRA activities, he did not once discuss terminology, not once did he mention "concentration camp" or the propriety of "relocation center." Baker, by contrast, gave the impression that Dillon Myer spent much of his energy on the narrow question of proper terminology for the camps.

Abe Fortas

Abe Fortas's testimony received the most press attention. He had been Under Secretary of the Interior during World War II. He was wise and eloquent, but he seemed to be too forgiving. He referred to war hysteria as an influence on Supreme Court decisions. But the most important decisions, Korematsu and Endo, were rendered in December 1944, when the war was all but over. Fortas was simply unaware of the machinations and deceptions that had lain behind the judicial process.

C. William Lengacher

There were also three contemporary representatives from the Department of Justice, Department of the Army, and the Department of State. Parts of their statements were

FIRST WASHINGTON HEARINGS

noteworthy. C. William Lengacher, Chief Judgment Enforcement, Civil Division, Department of Justice, made this uninformed statement:

> Although precise figures are unavailable, we estimate that the period of detention of internment of evacuees averaged about two years.

In 1946, the Department of Interior published a detailed compilation of statistics with the title, "The Evacuated People: A Quantitative Description." A quick perusal of this publication shows that well over half of the persons in the camps were still interned in January 1945. The median stay, accordingly, was close to three years.

David Trask

Dr. David Trask was the Historian of the Department of State. He confirmed the linkage that existed between the American treatment of Japanese-Americans and the Japanese treatment of Americans. After describing two exchanges of nonofficial persons other than prisoners of war between the United States and Japan, Trask discussed the status of "evacuees" in detention centers:

> One point of contention about the evacuees centered on the issue of forced labor. Should the Japanese inmates of the relocation camps be compelled to contribute to the war effort by working? No, said the Department of State. Although the United States consistently denied that the camp inmates were internees and thus subject to the Geneva Convention, State believed that any practice or regulation that fell short of the Geneva standards could provoke Japanese reprisals against its American civilian internees.

Trask illuminates the U.S. government's ambivalent application of the Geneva Convention. In March 1983, at a University of Utah Conference, "Relocation and Redress: the Japanese American Experience," John J. Culley of West Texas State University presented an informative paper entitled "The Santa Fe Internment Camp and the Justice Department Program for Enemy Aliens." In his paper, Culley informs us that once a Japanese translation of the Geneva Convention on the treatment of prisoners of war was obtained by the "enemy alien" inmates of the Santa Fe Internment Camp, they negotiated with their camp's administrators and established a *modus vivendi*. The application of the Geneva Convention standards to the ten WRA detention camps would certainly have benefitted their inmates. For example, the Geneva Convention standards would have required both the quantity and quality of food to be that of the U.S. armed forces. But the American citizen inmates of WRA camps did confront a legal anomaly: whereas citizens of Japan could appeal to the Japanese government, through the Spanish embassy, citizens of the United States had no comparable recourse. They could not, as U.S. citizens appeal to the government of Japan, and they were denied the writ of *habeas corpus*, which meant they could not obtain any judicial relief and protection from their own government.

Mutual reprisals almost became real according to Trask's description of the trouble at Tule Lake:

Discontent erupted into violence at the Tule Lake camp in November 1943. Assistant Secretary of State Breckinridge Long expressed concern to Senate investigators that the situation threatened Americans held by Japan. Indeed, Radio Tokyo had already broadcast ominous veiled threats regarding the 10,000 American civilians in its custody. Long had reservations regarding the transfer of disloyal Japanese Americans to U.S. Army control; he feared the impact on Japan's American prisoners. He also revealed that Japan had demanded clarification of U.S. relocation policy prior to the continuation of exchange negotiations.

The inmates of the ten WRA detention camps were fortunate that Japan exercised restraint.

The Second Day

Senator Jackson

The second day's hearings also began with congressional speeches. Of these, Senator Jackson's, though at first muddled, was unusually realistic:

Finally, it seems to me two fundamental issues . . . need to be addressed. One, should there be compensation? I question seriously whether you can provide for a monetary settlement of a problem that goes beyond that kind of solution.

Jackson's doubt over "a monetary settlement of a problem that goes beyond that kind of a solution" is unclear. It became clearer during the questions. Commissioner Goldberg pressed the question of compensation. Jackson responded:

Well, I appreciate very much, Justice Goldberg, your thoughtful comments. I think in that connection, if the Commission should make a recommendation in terms of some dollar compensation—it would be a tragedy if you came up with a figure that Congress would not appropriate. And then we're back to square one.

At least *someone* discussed the possibility of Congress's failing to appropriate an adequate sum to redress the Japanese-American victims.

Mike Masaoka

When Tuesday's hearings had run out of time, Mike Masaoka, who was scheduled to testify then, consented to be moved to Thursday. He spoke extemporaneously and at great length, and had to be asked to close his remarks. He spoke like an old man when he said:

Some of my experiences go back further than most Japanese Americans living today. And as Congressman Yates and Senator Jackson pointed out, I have been here a long, long time.

He described the Commission as "democracy trying to correct one of its abuses" for the benefit of the commissioners, plying his lobbyist wiles to place the commissioners into a state of mind favorable to his words. He used his considerable firsthand knowledge and his histrionic skills to make himself appear "bigger than life." He addressed the question of whether President Roosevelt ever visited a camp and said, "To the best of my information and knowledge, he did not." But he erred when he said that German and Italian aliens were "not included in the Executive Order 9066." The order referred only to "any and all persons" and made no distinctions by race or nationality. Individual exclusion orders by the authority of EO9066 were issued to Americans not of Japanese ancestry, mainly to Americans of Italian and German ancestry. He displayed his high regard for the powerful by dropping names of members of Congress and Mrs. Roosevelt in many anecdotes. He rambled. Bernstein finally asked diplomatically, "Mike, are you going to leave some time for the Commission to ask you some questions?" After several more minutes, he concluded by describing effigies made by his enemies who then smeared them with human feces. I had never heard of this kind of hostility towards him.

JACL

Masaoka was followed by spokespersons for three redress organizations: NCJAR, National Coalition for Redress/Reparations, and JACL. The JACL had devised several strategies for having many JACL leaders speak before the Commission. In its official testimony as one of three redress groups, Dr. James Tsujimura, the JACL's national president, made the first presentation. He used his time to introduce Mrs. Lily Okura, vice president of General Operations of the JACL board, Dr. Clifford Uyeda, immediate past national president, and Mr. Pat Okura, past national president. (Tsujimura would make his own statement later at the Seattle hearings.) He then deferred to Minoru Yasui, who had already testified on Tuesday as one of two who took test cases to the Supreme Court. Yasui was the chairperson of the JACL's National Committee for Redress (NCR). After some words, Yasui, in turn, deferred to John Tateishi, who had preceded Yasui as NCR's chairperson and had become its executive director. Later in the day, two other JACL people would testify as part of a lawyers' group. And so it would go throughout the hearings. The JACL had a great interest in the hearings; the Commission was their creation.

The JACL would seek and screen persons who wished to testify. It offered coaching sessions on how best to present one's testimony, urging people to "spill their guts" and to speak eye-to-eye to the commissioners, instead of reading their statements. In cities where hearings were held, the JACL held parties for the visiting commissioners and arranged public relations events such as talk-show participation and press interviews. JACL members were heavily represented in the hearings. The Commission hearings were their notion of the democratic process at work.

Lillian Baker

The dramatic highlight of the first hearings was the appearance of Lillian Baker, speaking on behalf of Americans for Historical Accuracy. She was about the same age as the victims and described herself as a historian. According to *Who's Who in American Women*, Baker's two books were *Collector's Encyclopedia on Hatpins and Hatpin*

Holders and *100 Years of Collectible Jewelry, 1850 to 1950*. It's hard to understand why *Collectible Jewelry* made her a historian or why *Hatpins and Hatpin Holders* made her knowledgeable about mass exclusion and detention. Her interest in the issue was of long standing. She had battled tenaciously against the emergence of the term "concentration camp" as a replacement for the official euphemism "relocation center." She had failed in her struggle to keep the replacement phrase from being cast in bronze on commemorative plaques for the two California camps, Manzanar and Tule Lake. She was one of those persons who believes in her country right or wrong, which means, of course, that her country was always right, never wrong. The name of her organization, "Americans for Historical Accuracy," was hardly suitable. In her view, history was a partisan matter, requiring neither a historian's objectivity nor fidelity to documentary evidence. Her technique, which she seemed to believe was authentic historiography, was to select from documents whatever supported her view. She cited Supreme Court Justice Hugo Black's statement that the camps were not concentration camps, from an opinion that failed to recognize that the placement of victims in "assembly centers" was as much detention as their placement in "relocation centers." She argued that detention had not occurred because anyone could leave the camps; but she was ignorant of the zones of exclusion that were declared for the six camps outside the exclusion zone which made it unlawful for persons of Japanese ancestry to leave camp. To listen to her was to relive the times of World War II. She was a 1981 manifestation of the normal thinking of white America on this issue during the 1940s. This kind of talk is rarely heard nowadays, either through the realization of error, or because of a wish to hide racism. She was stalwart in her beliefs that history would prove that the camps were benign and that America would "come out smelling like a rose."

There she was, sitting at her appointed place, all ready to testify even before the hearings reconvened following lunch. Her blond hair and white suit glowed in the bright television lights. She was prepared for battle against all those "Japs" who would sully her beloved white America.

But she hadn't reckoned with the likes of Arthur Goldberg, who knew the decisions of the Supreme Court and what they meant. She was smart enough to recognize when she was outmatched, "Now you didn't expect me to argue with a Supreme Court justice?" Goldberg, smiling, confirmed the disparity, "No, don't do it." The sedate Japanese-American audience tittered. But the Justice was interrupting. When Chairperson Bernstein informed her that her time was up, she protested that she'd been interrupted and hadn't been permitted to complete her statement. She was given a few more minutes and then once again told that her time had expired. She fought for more time and had to yield. She stood up with her cane and left angry.

Dwight Chuman

The JACL did not control all the Japanese-American testimony. Dwight Chuman testified near the end of the first Washington hearings. Chuman is English editor of the largest Japanese-American newspaper, the *Rafu Shimpo*. (I asked my mother-in-law, who speaks Japanese fluently, what "Rafu Shimpo" means. The Japanese are prone to abbreviate then concatenate the abbreviations. The "Ra" of "Rafu" is the Japanese pronunciation of the "LA" for "Los Angeles." The "fu" is Japanese for big city. "Shimpo" is news. Hence, "Rafu Shimpo" is Los Angeles News.) Chuman described a survey his newspaper had taken earlier in the year:

> Our newspaper printed the survey in both Japanese and English to enable all those victimized, especially our rapidly dying off Issei first generation to speak for themselves on this issue. Perhaps the most important misconception we feel this survey sets aside is rhetoric implying that our community is deeply split on redress.

He first attacked, then demolished, Representative Lungren's earlier charge that, "There appears to be a split even within the Japanese American community itself," with these figures:

> [There were 3749 surveys returned.] 3575 respondents, or more than 96 per cent, answered that they felt Japanese Americans should seek redress; and 3,350, or 89 per cent, said an appropriate form of reparation is direct monetary payments to individuals affected by Executive Order 9066, or their immediate heirs.

Chuman also introduced some uncomfortable questions for the commissioners to consider:

> I ask specifically that you command your staff to examine documentation available in [the] National Archives which show[s] the Japanese Americans in the camp[s] may have been subjected to scientific programs of behavior modification, rumor experiments, and that the relocation centers may have been laboratories for government studies on the control of population of defeated enemy nations; that conditions for[ced] euthanasia to become a regular practice in some camp hospitals, that members of the Japanese American Citizens League may have served as government informants prior to and within the camps, and by doing so exacerbated dissension and suspicion among internees.

> Please tell us why members of the JACL, our only nationwide organization, became the targets of violence in the camps. And help us to understand why the JACL, which discouraged court challenges to the legality of evacuation in the camps, [in its] documents indicate[s] that JACL national secretary, Mike Masaoka, in 1942 publicly characterized Minoru Yasui as a "self-styled martyr out to do nothing but capture headlines."

> Perhaps [your] staff can determine whether [such] circumstances had a chilling effect on other Japanese Americans exercising their rights as citizens.

> We ask the staff to help us understand why the JACL national secretary in March of 1942 recommended that Japanese "be put into labor concentration camps to be farmed out to large sugar beet combines as cheap laborers, that Japanese internees should be brought in for roadmaking, and that Japanese be branded and stamped and put into supervision of the federal government."

Commissioner Marutani responded to Chuman as though Chuman's questions lacked substance because they failed to mention other key individuals such as DeWitt, Gullion, Bendetsen, Knox, and Stimson. Marutani, who was usually precise and perceptive, revealed here his own predisposition to defend and protect the JACL and Mike Masaoka. In the course of the hearings, others addressed the questions raised by Chuman. In response to a specific request from the JACL president in the Seattle hearings, the

Commission gave Masaoka the opportunity in the second Washington hearings to respond to the quotations cited. But in their report to Congress, the commissioners ducked these issues.

These first hearings were a historic event. Though the Commission was off to a shaky start, few realized this and the expectations of the public were high. The news media were there in force. Both the NBC and CBS television networks did interviews of key individuals for the news programs. ABC's "Nightline" program after Thursday's hearings included some of the participants. Stories appeared in many major, daily newspapers. The Japanese press was very interested. Of course, the Japanese-American press was also present. In addition to Dwight Chuman, there were Takako Kusunoki, English editor of the *New York Nichibei*, Peter Imamura, editor of the *Pacific Citizen*, playwright Frank Chin, Seattle radio reporter Frank Abe, and others. Japanese-Americans from the East Coast were there in large numbers, as well as many from the Midwest and the West Coast. These were, after all, the first official hearings on redress.

The hearings then moved from the nation's capital to the communities where we lived. Chiye Tomihiro of the Chicago Chapter of the JACL characterized the process as catharsis. But that may have been premature. After all, the drama had just begun.

15. HEARINGS

LOS ANGELES HEARINGS

The first field hearings were held in Los Angeles on August 4-6, 1981. A room in the Los Angeles State Building was selected because it was in a government building, but it was far too small for a large hearing. (This was one of several lessons that the Commission's executive director learned the hard way.) Hundreds of people came to testify and to listen. An overflow room had to be arranged. These were not only the most poorly planned hearings, but also the rowdiest. Frank Chin characterized them in the *Rafu Shimpo* as "A Circus of Freaks." He wrote:

> They cheered, applauded, commented, and [Representative Daniel E.] Lungren sitting, as chair in place of Joan Bernstein, left them to clap and boo. They booed and jeered S. I. Hayakawa. They made Hayakawa look good. Hayakawa made the news.
>
> . . . . No matter how they felt as individuals, the members of the audience, joining in one big boo, with hate on their faces, are wrong to mob Hayakawa. . . . They are there to listen, not to influence the commission or the witnesses . . .

Chin extended his criticism to the testimony of the victims:

> Listen to the stories, friends. You've heard them all before, at so-called writer's conferences, in group therapy. The endless procession of newspaper-interview-famous-Nisei bleeding the same stories before Asian American Studies classes that didn't use books. You've seen these tears before, staining the mimeograph program of yet another narrated slide show and panel of former internees remembering camp at Pine Methodist Church in San Francisco, or the Oakland Museum—thirty years of interviews, articles, seminars, pilgrimages, where the Nisei have shown up to weep in public.
>
> . . . . Pity! Pity! Pity! Open weeping. Wild applause.[1]

This article drew predictable anger from readers of the *Rafu Shimpo*, some of it, unfortunately, bordering on anti-Chinese racism. I was not in Los Angeles to see and hear what happened. But as I read the transcripts of the Los Angeles hearings, it became clear to me that much of what Chin wrote was uncomfortably true. One is overwhelmed by the stories of individual hardships and suffering. They seemed adversarial. It was as though the former victims were pleading their case in court. Given the relative powerlessness of the Commission, their exhibition of suffering and pain seemed degrading. Why were these victims sharing the intimacy of their pain with these commissioners? What were the commissioners able to do for them? There was little time for dialogue between the witnesses and the commissioners. Not only should the hearing room have been larger, the number of days allotted should have been increased. The victims were once again victimized. All the commissioners could say with any certainty was that their testimony was going into the record. (And even that remained uncertain until the very end of the Commission's life, and then it proved illusory. The transcripts were not published and never formed a record accessible to the general public, despite the best efforts by the Commission's small staff, combined with the efforts of dedicated Nisei volunteers.) And I must agree with Chin that the booing, however heartfelt, degraded those who booed more than Hayakawa, the object of the booing. As Chin argued, the testimonies obscured the overriding issues of official culpability and governmental wrongdoing—which Hayakawa strived to have forgiven and forgotten.

S. I. Hayakawa

Senator Samuel Ichiye Hayakawa was the first to testify, because of his rank as a United States Senator. Also, as a Senator, he was not subjected to time limits. He spoke at length. He attempted to set forth a definitive statement about the mass exclusion and detention. He began with the history of anti-Oriental prejudice in America. He touched on "Social Darwinism," which orders human evolution along racial lines of white, yellow, brown, and black. This is where the booing began, though he wasn't actually advocating "Social Darwinism."[2]

Hayakawa argued that the exclusion order came about as a result of popular racism. He also gave wartime hysteria as a cause of exclusion. But he failed to distinguish military intelligence from popular opinion when he said, "How frightening were those nightly blackouts during that black winter of defeat! Would Japanese carriers come to bomb the cities? Would their submarines sneak through the Golden Gate to shell San Francisco? Would they actually mount an invasion? Nobody could tell." This was clearly the response of an hysterical populace, but it was not the thinking of military intelligence. It was frightening to the public to behold how the Japanese outblitzed the Germans in their speedy advance through Southeast Asia. The Japanese wanted the resources of Malaya, Java, Borneo and Sumatra. A few months earlier, the combined embargo of American, British, and Dutch shipping had denied them these resources. This was clearly Japan's sphere of interest. Japan had begun the war with forces in place in Indochina, and a major military outpost in Taiwan. The U.S. military expected a war with Japan. General Douglas MacArthur told Washington that he expected war to start about April 1, 1942.[3] Hayakawa ignored the distinction between military and popular opinion and observed, "The relocation was unjust. But under the stress of wartime anxieties and hysteria, and in the light of the long anti-Oriental agitation in California and the West, I find it difficult to imagine what else could have occurred that would not have been many times worse."

Hayakawa pontificated. He exploited his academic credentials. He tried to convince the commissioners by drawing conclusions from ad hominem arguments and unsupported characterizations. He characterized Dillon Myer, the director of the War Relocation Authority, as a "wise and humane man" and a "firm believer in democracy and justice," in order to infer that "Mr. Myer did everything possible to make life tolerable for the internees." This inference was about to be overwhelmingly contradicted by three days of testimony.

The booing of Hayakawa was lamentable. Public hearings should be orderly. A citizen's right to freedom of speech should be honored. By some accounts, the booing was orchestrated; that too is inconsistent with democracy. (But I am not sure whether I would have been able to contain my hostility.) Hayakawa, however, was not without guile. He knew where to prod and how to provoke. He said, "I emphasize this last point because relocation centers were not concentration camps . . ." A disruption from the audience followed. Vice-chairperson Lungren implored, "Please, let's have no public display here. Again, let's try and run an orderly hearing so that we can hear the people whom we have come here to listen to." Hayakawa insisted that only the Nazis had concentration camps. Hayakawa, calling upon his reputation as a semanticist, said, "to call the relocation camps 'concentration camps' as is all too commonly done is semantic inflation of the most dishonest kind." But, as a matter of historic fact, "concentration camp" was used to refer to the camps by President Roosevelt in his press conferences of October 20, 1942 and November 21, 1944. In addition, in an October 7, 1943 letter to General Delos Emmons, newly appointed Commander of the Western Defense Command, Chief of Staff George C. Marshall writes, ". . . bad actors had been largely eliminated from Arizona concentration camps and transferred to northern California."[4] Hayakawa was conducting his semantics lesson for the wrong audience.

Floyd Schmoe made an effective, if not conclusive, rebuttal a month later in the Seattle hearings. Schmoe had visited all sorts of camps worldwide and confirmed that the "relocation centers" were indeed concentration camps. However, as overwhelming as the arguments were against Hayakawa's position, "relocation camps" would prevail over "concentration camps" in the Commission's report to Congress.

Hayakawa prodded again. He said that the internees had had a good time in the camps, for ". . . how else, Mr. Chairman, can one account for the fact that for many past . . . years, graduates of camp high schools . . . have been holding . . . anniversary reunions?" Again there were disruptions. Lungren felt compelled to threaten the audience. "Please, I would like to tell the audience that the Chairman is not disposed to make threats," he said and then proceeded to make one, ". . . if we are going to have outbursts with respect to whatever one agrees with or disagrees with, we may just have to close the hearing to the public."

Hayakawa continued with his upbeat description of a camp life he had never experienced by discussing camp artists and musicians and characterizing internment as "a three-year vacation from long years of unremitting work on farms, in fishing boats, and in little shops [in which] they used their leisure, Mr. Chairman, to recover and to relive the glories of their traditional culture." Hayakawa thus overthrew, with his semantic bulldozer, the theory and practice of imprisonment.

He then launched into a discourse on his version of the Japanese trait of *giri* as the sense of "duty to one's community, to one's employer, to one's nation," explaining that the "Nisei, although much Americanized, are in some respects profoundly Japanese." In order to arrive at such a sweeping generalization—in 1942 it would have been an indictment—a social scientist would first have to define *giri* authoritatively and then by some technique, determine whether Nisei exhibited the defined trait.

Hayakawa was no fool. He was an academician, and knew the rules of scholarship. I am not the semantics expert that Hayakawa is acknowledged to be, but his definition is incorrect, and I think he misreads the culture of Japanese-Americans. *Giri* is more properly equivalent to English terms such as "social obligation," "propriety," and "duty." Because of the term's dependence upon the expectations of social obligations, Japanese-Americans could develop *giri* only in a culture where such expectations occurred. But, according to Edwin O. Reischauer, even in Japan, where *giri* is superseded by *gimu*, the cultural burden of this trait has caused "restiveness among the young."[5] His characterization of the Nisei was a little better than General DeWitt's infamous "A Jap is a Jap." Fortunately, Hayakawa lacked the power the General had. He may not have been talking so much about all Nisei as about himself. He felt so strongly Japanese that demands for redress made his "flesh crawl with shame and embarrassment." One would think that a member of the United States Senate would invoke American values, especially those found in the Constitution, rather than Japanese values. The testimony of other Japanese-Americans overwhelmed his facile and fraudulent characterization of the internment experience.

One effect of Hayakawa's long statement was to reduce the time available for the testimony of others. By mid-morning, Lungren had to warn, "I'm afraid I'm going to have to reiterate that we're running about an hour behind schedule now. If you do have written statements, they will be made a part of the written record *in toto*, which means we will have the benefit of reading them." Who would yield? For many, this was the moment of a lifetime. Hours had been poured into writing each statement. To distill years of frustration and hopelessness into five minutes—two pages, double-spaced—was a difficult test of mind and spirit. How could one cooperate with such a request?

Hannah Tomiko Holmes

Hannah Tomiko Holmes testified that morning. She is about my age and was interned in Manzanar with me. We'd become good friends through the redress movement and through correspondence. She did not graduate from Manzanar High School with me in 1944, however. She graduated four years later, from the Illinois School for the Deaf. Exclusion and detention were bad enough for "normal" people; they were a disaster for the disabled. Education for "normal" children in the camps was minimal. The Manzanar school system would never have withstood measurement by the educational standards of the state of California. But for Hannah, education did not exist. Educational facilities did exist for the deaf in the "outside" world; but deafness did not excuse one from exclusion by reason of "military necessity." Hannah testified through a reader:

> When the war started, I was a thirteen-year old student at the California School for the Deaf . . . sponsored by the State of California in Berkeley. I was one of eleven Japanese students at that school who were forced to leave because of the war. A twelfth student, Ronald Hirano, was allowed to stay . . . but I'm really not sure how that was arranged.

Akiyo DeLoyd

Other, more common, disabilities also took their toll. Akiyo DeLoyd's mother was a diabetic. Diabetes, of course, requires nutritional care; improper nutrition may be life-threatening. Akiyo DeLoyd related her story:

> My mother died in Poston, Arizona. She was a diabetic. I can remember the time I went to the kitchen for milk. I was told the milk was for babies and small children. The diet of rice, macaroni, and potato was hardly a suitable diet for a diabetic.

And then, remembering, she added:

> As far as that goes, it was not an adequate diet for anyone.

Here one is faced with the problem Frank Chin brought up:

> Where is the expert testimony? Where are the penologists, the cultural anthropologists? . . . There certainly were enough of them working in the camps. Where are the psychologists, the historians? The experts and specialists? It's clear the victims of the experience did not understand much beyond the immediate orbit of their family. They don't know what happened to anyone but themselves. . . . They are neither technically nor temperamentally equipped to speak knowledgeably, factually and candidly about the depth, degree and kinds of damage they absorbed because of camp.[6]

Akiyo DeLoyd's individual story suggests a more general conclusion: camp diets had a deleterious effect on all diabetics. Studies on this subject had been done. In 1980, Rita Takahashi Cates wrote a 641-page doctoral dissertation entitled "Comparative Administration and Management of Five War Relocation Authority Camps" for the University of Pittsburgh. If allowed, she could easily have testified for three days before the Commission and added substantially to our understanding of the camps. Her dissertation's five camps are Poston, Gila River, Heart Mountain, Manzanar, and Tule Lake. On page 208 of the dissertation, she cites a report of the Block Managers Evacuee Food Committee of March 20, 1943. The report is based upon a survey of all the Heart Mountain camp's thirty-three mess halls. It stated:

> It will be noted that out of 1,545 meals served, 914 or 59% were not suited for stomach patients, 923 or 60% were not suited for hypertension patients, 854 or 55% were not suited for diabetics . . .

What remains unknown is the number of such patients and the effects such diets had on them. Individual stories, not general conclusions supported by hard facts, were the principal products of these hearings. Still, Akiyo DeLoyd's story has its own special power:

> In a way, the stress of going into camp, [the] poor diet, and [the] worry hastened the death of my mother. She was fifty-two years old. She had to be cremated. There was no choice. My sorrow to this day is that I could not put a fresh flower on her grave. All our flowers were made of Kleenex.

Mary and Albert Kurihara

Mary Kurihara testified twice, first for herself, then for her husband, Albert Kurihara, who was hospitalized with a stroke. Albert Kurihara is a cousin of Joe Kurihara. "The stroke was a result of thinking . . . [about] his camp experience and his cousin Joe Kurihara," she said. The Kuriharas conformed to the five-minute rule. Albert Kurihara described camp and its aftermath:

> I remember I had to stay at the dirty horse stable at Santa Anita. I remember thinking, "Am I a human being? Why are we being treated like this?" Santa Anita stunk like hell. I had to do hard seasonal labor during that time, harvest and sugar beets work, which no one else wanted to do.

> After the camp I was treated like an enemy by the other Americans. They were hostile and I had a very hard time finding any job. I had to take so many different jobs that it made things very insecure. This was the treatment they give to American citizens.

Mary Kurihara gave a graphic description of the problems of resettlement after camp:

> In 1945, we managed to go back to Los Angeles where we stayed with three other families at a home belonging to a distant relative. The times during the camp and after camp was very hard.

The Kuriharas' description of incarceration and its aftermath hardly fits Senator Hayakawa's depiction of camp life as a three-year vacation, a happy time.

Sally Kirita Tsuneishi

Mrs. Tsuneishi described her resettlement:

> After the war, we were allowed to return to Hawaii. But there was no home for us. Our store and our home were confiscated by the plantation. And we were to start a new life in Honolulu. Without funds, the only place we could afford was under a house—not a basement, but underneath a home. The landlord's washtub was our bathtub, our kitchen sink, and even our laundry tub.

Charles Hamasaki

Witnesses struggled with their writing. Most of the testimonies were grammatically correct. One singular recollection, however, though grammatically flawed, was authentic in idiom and content. Charles Hamasaki, eighteen at the time of expulsion, lived on Terminal Island and had just graduated from San Pedro High School. (Only the name "Charles" does not sound quite right. Most Terminal Islanders I knew went by their Japanese names.) Charles spoke extempore:

> As far as I remember, in 1942, February second I think it was—you know—two guys walk in my house. And they came to my bedroom. And they said, "Hey! Hey! Buddy, wake up!"

> I wake up. And I asked them, "Who the hell you guys are?"

> You can laugh right now. But I wasn't laughing. You know. "So, let me see your I.D."

Then they flashed FBI. He say, "FBI."

So I say, "What the hell did I do?"

Then they look at each other, and they say, "Hey! Hey! We got a young one here." You know. They were running into a lot of old guys, you see. So, one of the guys says, "Hey! Get your coat on, man. I'm taking you in."

I said, "What for?"

"You are an enemy alien."

I told them, "Enemy alien?" Man, I told them, "The enemy aliens live across the Pacific Ocean." I told them, "Don't take me in."

He says, "Get your coat."

So I got my coat. And they took me to Terminal Island—the immigration station, over there. It was like a jail, over there, you know. At that time, they didn't have that Terminal Island Federal Penitentiary. It was next to that thing.

So, they took me in over there. Four days I stayed over there. Meanwhile, I know how to talk both languages. That's why I interpreted for this other fisherman friend, and translated everything. So, I thought that maybe they might let me go, since I was doing them a favor.

Hell no! Man!

(Wait a minute! Give me time, man!)

Then, they took us all from the Terminal Island Immigration Station to the Union Depot over there. I remember that. And there was about ten or twelve cars over there. And they herded us into that car. When we walked in, they told us to pull the blinds down, you know. So, I said, "What the hell for?" You know.

He said, "Never mind. That's an order. Put the blind down!"

We can move. For four days we traveled.

During the time we was traveling, these guys, you know, they asked me—you know, old man—he say—old man, you know, "Hey! Where we going?" When I peeked, it was Fresno. You know. And they stopped.

They stopped. And they put more guys on. And then, they keep on going. It took about a day to go over there.

The next thing I know, it was Stockton; Sacramento; Redding; Portland; Seattle; Tacoma; and Spokane. And we couldn't move from where we sat down—except to go to the head, you know. And, you know, what happened?

You know, my feet start swelling. You do nothing but sit down. You know. You guys try that. You guys never did, because you don't know.

Then, when I looked—the next thing I know—we was in Montana. The train stopped. They cut the train in half. And half went further east. So the next place we stopped at was Bismark, North Dakota. Fort Lincoln. Fort Lincoln.

And, they told us to get off. Well, before that, you know. One thing I got to say. On that train, they fed us real good. Yeah. You know, we are a poor family—poor fishermen at Terminal Island. And all we eat is fish, you know. On the train, you know. The first time I ate a steak. Yeah. I'm serious, man.

You know what some of them old men said? The old men say, "Hey! They are feeding us, because we are going to die. They are going to kill us." You know, just like the execution chamber—before you die. That's what he said.

105

I said, "No! No! No! This country—they ain't going to do that kind of stuff, man. You know, this is a democratic country—Bill of Rights, the Constitution, and all that stuff. And the Japs go with it. You see, they not going to do this. This is democracy."

You know what my old man say? "No! This is not democracy. This is democratic shit!" he said.

"So, by God, maybe this guy got a point," I said. He might be right.

Then, we get off that train. When we got off the train—hey! Twenty-four degrees below zero! Man! I'm from Southern California. I had my moccasins—not a shoe—moccasins with me—and a T-shirt and an overcoat. In that time, bell bottom trousers was in style. You know, forty-one.

So, when we got off the train—it snowed there: ten feet high. Cold like hell! Twenty-five degrees below zero! And they line us up in the freezing weather to count the head, so nobody escaped.

They got to have an exact count. And we did that every morning—every morning, man, for one month. During that time, we stayed—that's what I call a concentration camp. That one. They had barbed wire. They had towers, machine guns, and searchlights—and everything. That's a concentration camp, you know—not like a relocation camp. I call that a concentration camp. This Lillian Baker or Barker or whoever she is—she said, "Not concentration." But, I call it "concentration camp."

At first, you know, when these guards—there was about five guards every night—they got to come inside the barracks, you know, to inspect. You know, when you have the brain so cold, you put your blanket over your head. Then, when they come, they say, "Hey! Buddy, stick your head out." They got the rifle, and they go like that.

They was scared of fishermen, because there was a rumor that fishermen is a mean, wild bunch of guys. Hell, no! We was gentlemen.

After a while, they got used to us. Hey! These guys not bad. So, they throw their rifles and guns and everything away. "Hey! Buddy, what's doing? How you doing this morning? Cold weather, eh? No. Hot. Cold." You know. Daily, routine talk—conversation, you see.

After that—Oh, let's see—my mother and sister—they didn't know where we went. After one month, they let us write letter. But, letter was censored, you know. So, they found out where we were. And then, after that—(I don't need this no more. Whoever wrote this thing—there is a little error here.)

So—oh!—then, they had a hearing, you know. So, I told you this was a democratic country. We got a trial now—coming up, anyway. So, we had a trial, you know, to answer: are you—oh! yeah! yeah! "Are you loyal to this country? Or, are you loyal to Japan?" he ask me.

I told him, "No, I am loyal to this country." You know, then, okay. They ask me a whole bunch of questions.

They even asked me, "What if Japanese Army invade this land over here, and we give you a rifle—what would you do?"

So, I told them what I do, "Japanese Army come this far in, you don't have to worry about that kind of thing." That's what I told them. So, I say, "I'm going to be loyal to this country."

So, after a couple of weeks, . . . they say either you get released, paroled—(oh! Well, one more thing, anyway. oh!)—interned. So I got released. So, they send me to where my mother and sister were. I came to Santa Anita.

When I came to Santa Anita race track over here—that was in August, 1942. It must have been. You know where I slept? In a barn. I'm a fisherman. I'm not a farmer. The first time I smell that smell, that you know—you know what I mean—you know what I mean—what I am referring to—the smell. But, like me, I was a fisherman. I know how stinky fish smell. So, this wasn't too bad. That's the way it was. Life in Santa Anita, you know—it's not too good.

Well, after that. Let me see. Yes. After that, we went to Rohwer, Arkansas. It's the same thing again. Swamp. Hot. Chiggers. All that kind of stuff, you know.

Then, this question came up—loyalty question. "Yes, yes" or "no, no." So, I signed "yes, yes." So, they said, "Okay, you sign yes, yes. You are loyal. You can go out of the camp."

Okay. So, I went out of the camp. I went to Kalamazoo, Michigan. There, the WRA gave me that job. And what a lousy job they gave me. Nobody wanted that kind of job. It paid $11.32 every week. So, I get $31 or $29—something like that I get. So, I quit that job. And then, I started fooling around all over the place, you know. I went to five or six different other camps.

Then—(I'm getting to the end. Wait a minute. I'm short.)— and now that I look back, after all these years, I'm still maybe bitter or angry. You know, arresting me as a Japanese fisherman—just because I was a fisherman, and I knew how deep the water was, and this and that. All that thing—you think I knew all that stuff? I didn't know nothing.

So, Lillian Baker said some Japanese is going to go to the Palos Verdes and wave flags over there for the battleship. I heard that on the radio—that KABC, one night. Flag. Wave flag. Come this way, maybe 100 yards. Turn left, and go 200 yards. Some people, they say fishing boats getting torpedoes. Where in the hell I'm going to get torpedo? Ridiculous, man!

That's why I say I was bitter. I wasn't there with my mother and them to evacuate—48-hour evacuation. They lost all the property and every damn thing! You know, in 1948, when I came out of the Army, . . . they pay me thirty-three dollars—thirty-three bucks! I still remember. I was at San Pedro, some place, up there, and they talk, talk, talk. And they gave me thirty something dollars! That's right! You know, this monetary reparation kind of deal.

Hey! You know. Like Senator Hayakawa—he don't know nothing. That guy, in my opinion—(I don't know what you are clapping for)—my opinion of that guy; he got a lot of money. He's a rich man. If he was in my shoes, and poor like me. He says Japanese are proud. Sure, we are proud people. If you put the word "proud—p-r-o-u-d" and put twenty-five grand on the side or fifty thousand or whatever it is—which side you going to take? I bet if you was in my shoes, you would take the twenty-five G's. That's what everybody is going to do. Yeah. That's what I'm going to do. I don't care. Proud or no proud.

Hamasaki's grit pulverized Hayakawa's facile sophistries. He knew that he had been screwed, and that accounts had to be settled.

Lillian Baker as Dillon Myer

There were dozens of stories related at the hearings. As I read them, many seemed repetitive. They were only a sample of more than 125,000 stories. Various themes ebbed and flowed. Story-telling sometimes turned confrontational, as when some witnesses challenged the commissioners for the lack of time, as if there existed some official device for creating time. Sometimes the unrelenting tales of woe were relieved by a welcome sense of humor, as in Charles Hamasaki's testimony. According to Frank Chin, there was even a moment of improvised melodrama:

> The 100th/442nd Association president was winding up to pitch his organization's stand on redress. He was about to climax another JACL-inspired show. A good public show of Nisei veterans and vet organizations, laying their resolutions and great American slogans on the record. Kawaminami was dissociating the 100th/442nd from a letter to the editor by Lillian Baker, the blonde avenging angel. A Japanese flag, taken as a war trophy, was on display in Gardena. The Manzanar Committee objected. They took the flag as a racial slur. Lillian Baker's letter claimed the 442nd vets organization joined her in supporting the display of the war trophy.
>
> Then Lillian Baker stood up from the sixth row of the audience. "Be careful, because Lillian Baker is here," she said, rising to her [feet with her] aluminum, four-legged cane. The crowd [jeered], "Sit down!" Then, "Out! Out! Out!" and "Nazi!"
>
> Lungren was slow, slower than slow, about bringing his gavel into play and calling for order. Rachel Grace Kawasaki, a white woman, stood on a chair by the witness table and faced the crowd and shook her fist and shouted back at the crowd, calling them racists. Lillian Baker leaped and hopped to the [witness] table and grabbed at the notes in Nisei vet Kawaminami's hands. The security police moved in. A white woman cop and a black male cop. A strange wrestling match between uniformed police, a Nisei vet in his seventies, Lillian Baker, in her white pantsuit and hanging on to her four-legged cane, towering over him, and Rachel Grace Kawasaki standing on a chair. And the jeering crowd. It's as if Hayakawa was right about the "small but vocal minority."
>
> The blonde woman cop and black male cop hustled Lillian Baker and Rachel Grace Kawasaki out of the hearing room, without drawing their batons or using much force. No scratches. No punches. A little shoving. A lot of grabbing of wrists, perhaps an elbow. And the crowd applauded.[7]

Lillian Baker formally appeared at the end of the first day's hearings, in order to read a statement written by the former director of the War Relocation Authority, Dillon S. Myer. This was "fishy." Leland Barrows had already testified on behalf of an ill Dillon Myer in Washington. His testimony had been comprehensive and authoritative. He had served at a high level within the WRA. Of course, most in the Los Angeles audience were unaware of Barrows's earlier testimony. But the commissioners must have known.

Before Baker began, most of the audience rose and left. She asked to begin after the commotion of their leaving had ended. Her statement, attributed to Myer, was filled with serious inaccuracies:

> My name is Dillon S. Myer, and I was appointed by President Franklin Delano Roosevelt, June 1942, to head the War Relocation Authority, which had been established under Executive Order 9102 March 21st, 1942.

Executive Order No. 9102 was signed on March 18, 1942.

> Executive Order 9102 was a completely separate and distinct order under the Presidential wartime powers, and was a civilian agency. Unlike Executive Order 9066, February 19th, 1942, which gave the Western Command extraordinary powers to wage war successfully by specifying that "any and all persons" may be removed from military designated areas, Executive Order 9102 established an agency of the government responsible for

establishing centers into which persons of Japanese ancestry could reside or relocate away from the red zones of the military designated areas on the west coast.

Why would Dillon Myer distinguish Executive Order 9102 from 9066? After all, numerous executive orders were issued. Moreover, 9066 did not specify the Western Command—which is, of course, the Western *Defense* Command; it was a broad delegation of authority to the Secretary of War and to "the Military Commanders who he may from time to time designate." Nor was any order issued to authorize detention centers. EO9102 simply created the WRA as a civilian agency to administer the program of exclusion, detention, and relocation.

The rest of Baker's lengthy statement, allegedly made on Myer's behalf, is filled with similar inaccuracies, which reveal Baker's ignorance of the details of the WRA's program, and sounds much like Baker's own statements made wherever and whenever she could obtain a platform. No witness gave testimony under oath, so there was no possibility of a perjury indictment to discourage fabrication. Unfortunately, Baker was not questioned. Hers was the last testimony of the first day. The commissioners must have been happy to see the day's proceedings come to a close.

Amy Iwasaki Mass

Earlier, Amy Iwasaki Mass, a clinical social worker who specialized in working with Japanese-Americans, made a more fitting benediction to the Los Angeles hearings. She herself had gone through a period of self-examination to renew her memories of her childhood experiences at the Heart Mountain concentration camp. She said:

> As a clinician in the field of mental health, I tried to understand why so many Americans, Japanese and otherwise, were able to justify, rationalize, and deny the injustice and the destructiveness of the whole event.

She continued:

> I have come to the realization that we lulled ourselves into believing the propaganda of the 1940's so that we could maintain our idealized image of a benevolent, protective Uncle Sam. We were told that this was a patriotic sacrifice necessary for national security. The pain, trauma, and stress of the incarceration experience [were] so overwhelming [that] we used the psychological defense mechanism of repression, denial, and rationalization to keep us from facing the truth.

She went on to the heart of the matter:

> The truth was that the government we trusted, the country we loved, the nation to which we had pledged loyalty had betrayed us, had turned against us. Our natural human feelings of rage, fear, and helplessness were turned inward and buried. Experiencing and recognizing betrayal by a trusted source leads to a deep depression, a sense of shame, a sense of there must be something wrong with me. We were ashamed and humiliated; it was too painful for us to see that the government was not helping us, but was, in fact, against us.

Then, in response to Commissioner Marutani's question of how one is to adjust one's belief in America to the objective reality of racial prejudice, she said, finally:

I find that the greatest psychological damage is for those people who still cannot admit that they have been hurt, that they don't belong, that it was all fine. . . . [But] when people come to terms with the reality that we are, indeed, not accepted—that kind of truth frees us to be more creative in our adaptation to reality.

16. HEARINGS
SAN FRANCISCO HEARINGS

Next, the Commission traveled to San Francisco, where it held hearings at Golden Gate University, on August 11-13, 1981, before another overflow crowd. The hearings in San Francisco were subdued in contrast to those in Los Angeles. Again, I was not present, but read the transcripts.

There was no recurrent theme to the testimony of different witnesses. Roy Sano tried to enunciate a theme, but no one else picked it up. There were no controversial characters like Senator Hayakawa and Lillian Baker. Colonel Boris Pash spoke against redress and displayed remarkable ignorance of official intelligence reports of that period. Ernest Kinzo Wakayama emerged as another dissenter to the government's program of exclusion and detention. Several persons replied to Senator Hayakawa's Los Angeles testimony. Once again, time pressures nagged at the witnesses. Once again, spoken and written statements were consigned to an evanescent "record."

Roy Sano

Roy Sano, a theologian from the Pacific School of Religion, was one of the first witnesses. Witnesses were grouped by topics which didn't accurately describe the testimony. Sano was one of a group with "Resolutions." This group followed "Elected Officials." But rather than read the resolution on redress from the 1981 California-Nevada Conference of the United Methodist Church, he submitted it for the record and presented a thesis instead. The resolution's preamble of "Whereas" statements was similar to the preamble of the 1980 General Conference resolution on redress. A copy of the resolution was given to each commissioner.

Sano's thesis used the imagery from Ruth Benedict's essay *The Chrysanthemum and the Sword*:

> Both a sword and a chrysanthemum are a part of the picture. The Japanese are, to the highest degree, both aggressive and unaggressive, both militaristic and adaptable, submissive and resentful of being pushed around . . . brave and timid.[1]

Benedict's work was based on studies of Japan and of Japanese-Americans. Sano's thesis was that Japanese-Americans had both the chrysanthemum and the sword but had buried the sword. He used a moving recollection of Pearl Harbor day by Frank Chuman:

> My father went to a dresser in his bedroom where he kept two samurai swords, one long for two hands, the other short. These were family treasures handed down from the Satsuma clan. I looked forward to owning these swords some day, and many times had secretly taken them out to admire the magnificent blades. My father removed the swords from the beautiful, inlaid cases, and he took them out into the back yard. There, he thrust both blades, bare and glistening, deep into the ground, and we buried them. I was disconsolate and sad. Disposal of these beautiful pieces of Japanese workmanship seemed to be a symbolic rite. It was as though a tangible cultural tie with Japan was being severed.

Sano contended:

> We became all chrysanthemum without a sword. We were the "flower people" before the "flower children." The ethnic movements from the late 1960's and the early 1970's have tried to restore a wholeness to a distorted people. The struggle for reparations represents one of a continuing series of efforts, and you may be assured that more will follow.

As appealing as Sano's thesis was, Commissioner Drinan was struck, instead, by a clause in the California-Nevada Conference resolution, "Whereas, the American Convention on Human Rights, to which this country is a signatory, states that "every person has the right to be compensated in accordance with the law in the event he has been sentenced by a final judgment through a miscarriage of justice."" Drinan asked if "that would be the Inter-American Convention on Human Rights, and which President, if you recall, signed it?" Sano was not sure. As he said, he was "only delivering the message and had not checked out all the documentation."[2] I found it heartening that two years after the redress movement had cited this document's clear definition of compensatory redress as a human right, it finally attracted the attention of a legal mind as astute as Father Drinan's. Drinan said, "Well, we are a signatory. Some President signed it. But I know the U.S. Senate has not ratified it. But even so, it is binding in a certain sense, and it is very, very relevant."

The Unabashed Colonel Pash

The next group was "Statements by Retired U.S. Army Officers." Colonel Boris T. Pash, U.S. Army retired, former "Chief of Counter Intelligence Corps," led off. Pash was an unabashed apologist for mass exclusion and detention. For an intelligence officer, he was remarkably uninformed. His testimony was clouded by his brief job title. Even though he gave his full title when introducing himself, "Chief of Counter Intelligence, Western Defense Command, Fourth Army," he had apparently identified himself to the Commission as Chief of the entire Corps—which would be like Lt. General DeWitt identifying himself as Chief of Staff. Furthermore, in answer to a direct question by Commissioner Brooke, "Colonel Pash, . . . your job at the time in 1940, as I understand it, was Chief of Counter Intelligence Corps?" Pash replied, "Yes." This and other questions and answers between Brooke and Pash consumed valuable time.

Commissioner Mitchell asked, "I am just wondering what consideration was given by your Intelligence Corps to the General Mark Clark recommendation, the FBI recommendation, the Munson Report, and the Commander Ringle Report—that the mass evacuation was not necessary. Were any of those given consideration at the time, trying to reach some other solution in your office, your Intelligence office of that day?" Pash admitted his ignorance of those reports. He recounted anecdotes from the period and remembered "facts" which were incorrect. Pash said that he was told "that all Japanese in the United States, including Nisei, were considered to be Japanese citizens and at the age of 18 must fulfill their military obligations in Japan." Commissioner Marutani pressed, "Colonel Pash, did the United States government recognize dual citizenship?" Pash did not respond. Marutani asked further, "Are you aware of whether or not we did or didn't?'' Pash, "No, I am not aware of it.'' The United States government did not recognize dual citizenship, but in practice dual citizenship was widespread among the world's nations. After 1924, moreover, Japan no longer automatically conferred dual citizenship on foreign-born children of citizens of Japan; these children acquired dual citizenship only if their parents registered them at the Japanese consulate within fourteen days of birth.[3]

For all his ignorance, Colonel Pash did make one significant observation:

> One of the disturbing factors was that at no time prior to Pearl Harbor or thereafter, particularly during the critical early months of the war, was any information received from local Japanese sources on suspected clandestine or anti-American activities or attitudes within the community. No reports on persons from the local areas who had gone to Japan.

Although Pash was once again incorrect—such "sources" did materialize—he did make clear what he expected as a demonstration of loyalty: informing on one's neighbors. This was the dirty underside of loyalty. Informing took a painful toll in the Japanese-American community during World War II. Former informants still keep their lips sealed, probably still believing in their righteousness, and still not recognizing their own victimization; and their victims continue to wonder if the informants will ever understand the human costs of their derogatory allegations. Colonel Boris T. Pash made it clear that officials such as he remain comfortably unperturbed by their wartime demand for Nisei to bear unsubstantiated, if not false, witness against their neighbors.

Ernest Kinzo Wakayama

The "Impact on Japanese American Veterans" panel was next. Its first witness was Ernest Kinzo Wakayama, age 86. In 1981, he was a resident of Fukuoka, Japan. He made a special trip from Japan to testify at the San Francisco hearings. He was a veteran of the U.S. Army in World War I. In 1943, he also initiated a legal challenge to exclusion and detention, using the writ of *habeas corpus*. (He was another of the group of dissidents who had remained hidden behind the question: "Why was there no resistance to the camps?" The question was more a misstatement of fact than a query.) His statement was prepared in outline form; it was a densely worded presentation.

Wakayama was first evicted from Terminal Island. He correctly recalled that the first notice was eviction within twenty-four hours, but this was changed, through intercession of local churches, to forty-eight hours. He went to Santa Anita, then to jail for seventy-two days, then to Pomona, then to Manzanar. He recalls the uprising: "Tear gas and shooting. Two or three persons died and several wounded, I learned later. Segregation commenced. Was ridiculous [for] veterans to answer questions therein printed, so I objected and refused.'' He is, of course, referring to the loyalty oath. His refusal brought him much trouble.

"Picked up at midnight by three armed guards," he continued. "Came by ambulance and was taken to Lone Pine Prison once again. Reason not given. Prison: was detained about ten days, no questioning," he said. The WRA disregarded the Constitution and international law. "Neutral country Consul representing Japanese government came and released all aliens. I was left alone in jail because of my citizenship status," he continued. What he means by "citizenship status" is that he was an American citizen. The Government then employed what can only be called "political cruelty." Ernest Kinzo Wakayama said, "Sent a message to my wife. She went to see a man from the Justice Department and requested protection. The reply was, 'If protection wanted, tell your husband to become an enemy alien.' " Citizens of Japan were able to appeal for justice to their government through the Spanish consulate. Citizens of the United States had no appeal. Wakayama summed up, "Hard feelings, extremely disappointed, lost hope, and anger intensified when such irresponsible reply came out from high Justice Department personnel."

Wakayama was still intensely aware of the many legal violations he suffered:

> Summary: [My appeal for release under] [t]he writ of *habeas corpus* created vengeance by the administration, and my arraignment [was] top news in Los Angeles newspaper, made the front page with my picture in it, [and] read by 50,000 or more people. Was very efficient to stir up the public sentiment, to make me the target of all events occurred thereafter at various camps I was taken to. Destroyed my pride, honor and dignity.

> My Opinion:

> 1. In regards to the arraignment, I would like to know who planned the charges: "Attempt to overthrow the United States Government." This is a serious and a great challenge, as it is subject to supreme punishment by death. It was also a great insult to an innocent citizen and to a veteran. Where was the legal procedure? Why and its reasons?

> 2. Imprisonment twice again without due course was another inexcusable insult also. On what ground, evidence and proof that such action was taken?

> 3. Pertaining to problem of disloyalty, do I have to die twice to show and establish my loyalty? Why? My honorable discharge certificate from the [U.S.] Army was not given the slightest thought at all, had no recognition and verification to my loyalty. This may be just a scrap of paper, but to me it is valuable because I obtained it in exchange for my most precious life!

This may be too densely worded; an explanation may help. When a Japanese soldier goes to war, he assumes he will not return; he gives his life. This thinking was perceived as fanaticism and became part of the racist stereotype of Japanese. Racial hatred and fear of the Japanese impelled the government to demand all Japanese-Americans to take two loyalty oaths:

> Are you willing to serve in the armed forces of the United States on combat duty wherever ordered?[4]

> Will you swear unqualified allegiance to the United States of America and faithfully defend the United States from any or all attack by foreign or domestic forces, and forswear any form of allegiance or obedience to the Japanese emperor, to any other foreign government, power or organization?[5]

There were many problems with these oaths. In the 1940s women didn't think of themselves as proper candidates for combat duty. For many men, the government's denial of their citizenship rights abrogated the government's claim for their military service. For Japanese-Americans who were citizens of Japan, forswearing allegiance to the emperor was tantamount to statelessness. For Japanese-Americans who were U.S. citizens, the expression, "forswear any form of allegiance or obedience to the Japanese emperor" implied prior allegiance or obedience. Any deviation from or qualification of a "yes-yes" response was deemed disloyal. For Wakayama and other World War I Japanese-American veterans, the requirement of taking the oath raised unacceptable doubts about their *demonstrated* loyalty to the United States.

Marshall Sumida

Marshall Sumida, a former officer of the Military Intelligence Service, was on the same panel as Wakayama. Sumida has studied and written about the issue of redress. He made an interesting observation about military security under combat conditions:

> In the Korean War, I was a combat counter intelligence officer with the Eighth Army in Korea. I went in there one week after it started. We were in there during the heaviest fighting period. Assignment: counter espionage and espionage. . . .

> In the actual combat area, it was unfeasible and impossible to intern civilians for a few suspects among the hundreds of thousands of refugees crossing our lines. Facilities were limited to even hold enemy prisoners of war. Men were needed to fight the war.

> Counter measures other than imprisonment were used to deter espionage and sabotage. On the West Coast, where the military imprisoned 120,000 civilians as suspects against espionage and sabotage to safeguard the Western Defense Command in case of possible enemy landing [— that] is stretching legal justification to the point of being ludicrous.

Many of us Japanese-Americans assume that detention was appropriate; our quarrel is with the racial criterion used for selecting detainees. Sumida, on the other hand, questioned mass exclusion and detention as a solution to the problems of espionage and sabotage. In a hot war, resources of troops and materiel are the critical issue. Troops are needed for combat, not guard duty. Nor does a sensible commander imprison tens of thousands of potential troops and war workers to pander to the paranoia of those who think loyalty is genetically determined or, in the case of John L. DeWitt, genetically undermined.

Ruth Colburn

Ruth Colburn had worked as a paid volunteer as the librarian in Manzanar. Her simple observations illuminated the realities of camp life. On compensation for labor: "I worked with a staff who [each] received sixteen dollars a month, and I received one hundred and sixty-seven dollars a month." On armed guards: ". . . you could take an oiled road along the barbed wire fence. . . . Over the barbed wire fence, there were these watch towers with MP's who had guns. This situation kind of shook me up a bit. I was short, and with a bandana over my head to protect myself against the dust and wind, I could have been mistaken for an evacuee. I thought there could be a trigger-happy MP up there." On providing the recreation of reading: "Remember, these people had been there since 1942. And a third of the camp was Issei. Not until 1944 did our camp library have these 400 [books in Japanese, which were donated by Mr. Kondo upon his release from Manzanar] for all the Issei people!"

In the course of the hearings, I found the observations of white American volunteers among the most perceptive. The harsh realities of camp life are portrayed more clearly by those who encountered them from a "normal," unvictimized perspective. Ruth Colburn's statement shows vividly the exploitation of internee labor, the threat of violence, and how neglected the Issei were.

Ben Tong

One panel had the ambiguous title, "Multiple Impact." It was followed by two with similar titles, "Socio-Psychological Impact" and "Psychological Impacts of Incarceration." Dr. Ben Tong presented his statement on the "Psychological Impacts" panel. He had rehearsed and assured the commissioners that he would take 8.6 minutes. Tong, a second-generation Chinese-American, made several important points:

> I wish to emphasize this afternoon that the case can and must also be made for certain similar kinds of positive behavior during the Nikkei internment, whether it took the form of organized protests, which camp officials and obliging social scientists recorded later on as "mindless riots," or work slow-downs or strikes, or the gallant sacrifices of the 442nd. Courageous and heroic behavior must be recorded, validated and legitimized.

> The record would otherwise not be complete. Extraordinary situations in life do indeed bring forth the best as well as the pathological in human beings, and Nikkei concentration camps were no exception to this ironic historical truism. Not documenting courageous and heroic behavior would prompt the present generation of Americans, Asian American and otherwise, to continue to uphold, unwittingly perhaps, the racist stereotype of Japanese Americans as essentially passive and accommodating victims and nothing more.

He then began to speak about the absence of a much needed "*language* for talking about the experience" of the camps. He felt that metaphors like rape and incest are inadequate. He explained the phenomenon of the victims' repression of their memories. He also raised the issue of "the wholesale imposition of Euro-American theories and concepts by certain White social researchers in the 1940's who were obsessed with making a name for themselves." But then he was warned that he had only one minute. He was to be denied 3.6 of his 8.6 minutes. (Somewhere earlier in the hearings, a clock was brought into play to announce with a bell when one minute of a witness's five minutes remained.) So, unable to go into details, he skipped ahead to his conclusion:

> I wish to emphasize that redress must not be limited to eloquent and moving governmental apologies, no matter how sincere or heartfelt. There has been much talk about there being no adequate material recompense for confiscated property and damaged lives.

> This is not a negligible matter. As a professional psychologist, I can say, perhaps with some confidence, that the potent symbolism inherent in money is critical to the mental health of the former internees and their families. It does represent, as little else will,

a valuable measure of the sincerity of the American government's attempts to make right a most hideous wrong.

As a matter of fact, I would strongly suggest, in the name of therapeutically sound collective activity, that Japanese America proceed to sue for damages if compensation in eight figures is not forthcoming.

I found it remarkable that a psychologist should demand a lawsuit. Probably Dr. Tong believes that a lawsuit would help solve the other problem of language and definition of the injury. The wrong is obvious. But throughout the hearings, most victims were unaware of the extent and nature of the wrongs, nor did they understand the legal remedies available to them. A detailed and comprehensive compilation of documented causes of action—the actual violations of constitutional and civil rights—is necessary, as is the corresponding demand for appropriate and substantial remedies.

Attorneys

But Tong's uncompleted point was left unmentioned by the attorneys who testified next. Lorraine Bannai had worked on this issue with a group of attorneys called "Bay Area Attorneys for Redress." She addressed broad constitutional issues. She said, ". . . if any suit is brought . . . and the U.S. is sued or has a claim to pay, it's got to be [paid] by Congress, anyway." This was changed in 1976; it is no longer true that Congress must appropriate funds to pay for damages assessed against the U.S. on a case-by-case basis. But this continued to be presented as a reason why only legislative redress is practical. On the other hand, our lawsuit received unexpected support when Patricia Takayama of the Northern California State Bar Subcommittee on Japanese American Redress and Reparation stated that group's support for "enabling legislation allowing the waiver of procedural barriers to thereby permit the adjudication of claims for damages."

Wayne Collins is also an attorney. He is the son of Wayne Collins, Sr., an attorney who became the namesake for the sons of many grateful Japanese-American parents, whom he had helped to retrieve from renunciation and expatriation. (He had also saved many Japanese-Peruvians from deportation to *Japan*, not Peru, their homeland.) The junior Collins pointed out that it is the renunciants and Peruvians who suffered most and who accordingly most deserve reparations. Commissioner Drinan made an interesting distinction between "damages" for property loss and personal injuries and "reparations." Drinan suggested that there is resistance to "reparations" because the word implies an intentional wrong; he proposed "damages" as being more palatable to Congress. Collins added, "Reparations implies a political wrong was suffered."

Drinan revealed a fundamental weakness in legislative redress: the unwillingness of Congress to admit to intentional wrongdoing by the United States. Thus, when Shosuke Sasaki's proposal for redress legislation was transformed into the Lowry Redress Bill, all of Sasaki's "Whereas" statements were removed. Congress would never admit the reasons for the three billion dollars in reparations that the bill sought.

The Ephemeral Record and Absent Dialogue

Without a published record, the hearings would be ephemeral. Commissioner Mitchell sensed this when he said, "I've been asked whether that record will ever be printed and available. . . . I can say that the proofs of the Washington hearings have been received, which should prove to you that they are being printed and will be printed." Ernest H. Weiner of the American Jewish Committee stated emphatically, "*At the very least*, these hearings can serve as a mechanism to *indelibly* impress on the minds and hearts of America that the evacuation and incarceration of Japanese Americans was not and cannot be flicked aside as a simple error of bureaucratic judgment" (emphasis added). Mitchell had been misled by his staff. The transcripts of the hearings will not be printed, even though the Commission's life extended until June 1983. The hearings will not be a mechanism to impress anything indelibly on the minds of Americans. A simple error of bureaucratic judgment would flick aside this responsibility.

The hearings suffered from severe time limits on testimony, the sheer weight of many stories and analyses, and the attempts by organized groups to influence rather than enlighten. The hearings were an exercise in the bureaucratic productivity of words and paper. Soon the Commission's public relations firm would tell the world about the more than 700 persons who testified and the hours consumed in listening and the number of cities in which hearings were held. But there was no dialogue. There was little interplay of different ideas and interests and interpretations. There was little learning or understanding or reconciliation or acceptance. If there had been a fullblown debate on the issues over a period of days, without time restrictions, if audio tapes and video tapes had been made and distributed, if transcripts and formal papers had been published, then some of these results might have been achieved. Tong, the psychologist, argued for the legitimation of heroes, ranging from dissenters who fought against detention to volunteers for the all-volunteer combat team. Collins, the attorney, placed the highest priority on redress for the renunciants and the Peruvian Japanese. Mike Masaoka of the JACL argued passionately against redress for renunciants and draft resisters. Military experts could have been brought in and addressed the issues of security in a hot war, brought up by Sumida. Members of Congress might discuss the "political realities" alluded to by Drinan. The issues that divided people during the war continued to divide people. Without dialogue—and without a fair amount of confession, I suspect—the persistent disputes among Americans on this issue will not be resolved.

17. HEARINGS
SEATTLE HEARINGS

The Seattle hearings were held at Seattle Central Community College on Wednesday, Thursday, and Friday, September 9-11, 1981. Again the hearing room overflowed, and a room downstairs was used for those people who couldn't crowd in without exceeding the limitations imposed by a local safety ordinance. Again, I did not attend these hearings; this account is based on my reading of the transcripts. Several themes ran through the Seattle hearings. A group from Hawaii spoke of their experiences. The role of the Japanese American Citizens League (JACL), both past and present, was discussed and made clear. Of course, there were more individual stories.

Senator Jackson and the JACL

These hearings were chaired by Commissioner Hugh Mitchell, former senator from the state of Washington. The other commissioners present were Brooke, Marutani, and Gromoff; Flemming would show up later. Commissioner Brooke read Senator Henry Jackson's latest postion on redress. Jackson had chaired the Senate hearings on the Commission bill, S.1647. At that time, he had asked the JACL spokesperson, Jerry Enomoto, what the JACL would like to see result from the Commission's work. After Enomoto fumbled, Jackson had answered his own question by saying, "In other words, the Commission should be free, obviously, to make whatever recommendations they deem appropriate?" To which Enomoto had replied, "Yes." At the first CWRIC hearings in Washington, Jackson had warned the Commission against recommending restitution in an amount that Congress might fail to appropriate. This failure would return the entire redress effort, as he said, to "square one." By the time the Commission reached Seattle, Jackson had a more modest and less failure-prone recommendation:

> I recommend that the Commission study and develop further a proposal of redress that would establish a foundation in memory of the Japanese Americans who were interned. This foundation would be established with an initial endowment from the Federal Government and would serve as a visible and living memorial to the sacrifice the Japanese Americans were forced to make during World War II. The "foundation" will provide a mechanism to begin to make a positive social atonement for the terrible wrong that was committed. Furthermore, the foundation should serve as a symbol of democratic values and ideals to help show that never again would an episode like the relocation and internment occur.[1]

This is the foundation-for-good-works idea. It is the same idea enunciated by the JACL's old guard, including Mike Masaoka, Minoru Yasui, and William Hosokawa. The Hosokawa version of the idea, read at the hearings by Tak Kubota, is particularly revealing. Kubota later expressed his concurrence with the foundation idea, and said that he had discussed it with Senator Jackson. Hosokawa wrote:

> Let's take another look at the objectives of the redress campaign. I have been assured by earnest advocates that the main aim is to impress on the American people the

injustice of the evacuation and to establish funds for carrying on an education program. This being the case, is there any real justification for seeking individual cash payments? As an alternative, why should we not seek a lump sum appropriation, let's say 200 million dollars—a tenth of the amount presently targeted and therefore possibly closer to attainment—to establish an American foundation for human rights in memory of the wartime sacrifices of Japanese Americans?

There certainly ought to be a better name for such a foundation but no better goal. It seems to me something like this would be a clean, simple way to get our point across, would not be handicapped by the appearance of being self-serving, would be of benefit to all segments of the nation, and still be a memorial to the experience of Japanese Americans during World War II.

Operating in a manner somewhat like the Rockefeller Foundation, for example, its primary purpose would be to support research, education and promotion of human rights. It could provide scholarships, support publications, finance experimental projects. If a $200 million endowment could be set aside, from $15 to $20 million would be available annually from income for operations. One of the foundation's temporary functions, to be phased out in time, could be to give direct assistance to needy Issei and Nisei or even other victims of disasters like the Indochina boat people who have exhausted other sources of aid.

Japanese Americans should have substantial input into this proposed foundation's organization and operation. But its strength, its beauty and its acceptability would be based on the determination of Japanese Americans to see that the injustices they experienced would never be repeated against any minority. Such an idea would eliminate the feeling that we are trying to "punish" the U.S. Government and the American people for what was inflicted on us, a vindictive theme that unfortunately crops up in arguments for redress. The foundation I have in mind would be a living memorial to our sacrifice. And it would avert the criticism that the Japanese Americans, the "most successful minority," are trying to rip off the Government for billions. This is an inevitable criticism that will stir old hates, hinder our program and destroy much of what we seek to accomplish by seeking reparations.

To summarize, a foundation for human rights would seem to be a constructive project and something that could be made into a viable, useful organization with substantially less than billions of dollars. It would avoid the need for trying to determine who gets paid off and the bureaucracy for making the payments. It would be a contribution to understanding, not a proposal to get a handout.

Note the striking consonance of this statement with positions taken by the JACL during the war years. Hosokawa characterized the massive violations of the Constitution as "wartime sacrifices of Japanese Americans." The exclusion and detention were merged with the voluntary sacrifices of the all-volunteer combat team of Japanese-Americans. This merger implies that all sacrifices were voluntary. The implication is untrue; few victims voluntarily excluded themselves or willingly entered into detention centers. The military commander of the Western Defense Command gave the exclusion order, and violators were subjected to criminal penalties, including imprisonment.

Moreover, the injuries suffered by Japanese-Americans were injuries to their individual civil and constitutional rights; the redress of such injuries through individual compensation is inseparable from the rights themselves. The recognition of these injuries, and their redress, are as inseparable as the constitutional test cases and the actions of the Heart Mountain draft resisters. During World War II, the JACL fiercely opposed these challenges to the destruction of Japanese-American citizens' rights, and urged Japanese-Americans to cooperate with the government's program of mass exclusion and detention.

The proposal of a foundation for human rights, instead of redress, is clear evidence of the disregard key persons in the JACL still had in 1981 for the constitutional and civil rights of Japanese-Americans. The Hosokawa statement subordinates the struggle for civil rights to the image-making of public relations. The statement is sprinkled liberally with cues such as "most successful minority," "self-serving," "rip off," and "handout." Hosokawa's reduction of a demand for two and one-half billion dollars to two hundred million dollars is a gratuitous accommodation to the government's budgetary problems.

In the Senate hearings, Senator Jackson recognized an ally: the JACL would be "reasonable," certainly not vindictive, and would defer to political power and prestige, much as the JACL had done in the difficult war years.

The Hawaiian Stories

Other public officials followed Senator Jackson, but the panel of Hawaiians who followed them made the Seattle hearings unique. The removal and internment of 1,500 Hawaiians had been overshadowed by the mass exclusion and detention of 120,000 mainland Japanese-Americans.

Franklin Odo

Franklin Odo of the University of Hawaii at Manoa set the background:

> Pearl Harbor ended, for an entire generation, any real possibility that Japanese Americans could draw from the culture reservoir so carefully constructed in the previous half century. The pattern of arrests and detention on and after December 7th strongly suggested that the common denominator was not evidence of potential danger but close association with things Japanese. Prior to that day, the FBI had listed 400 suspects and designated only 50 or 60 as "sinister." As early as December 19, 1941, however, President Roosevelt and his cabinet had agreed to [the] removal [of] all Japanese aliens to some island other than Oahu—probably Molokai. But pressure to include the Nisei continued to mount and in March, 1942, the Joint Chiefs of Staff recommended that 100,000 of the total of 157,000 Japanese be forcibly removed to mainland concentration camps. The President approved it and an initial target number of 15,000 to 20,000 was to be selected.
>
> Legal and logistical problems intervened, however, and the President subsequently agreed to a maximum of 15,000. Eventually, the figure dwindled to 1,500, close to the number actually detained in Hawaii and the mainland.

Patsy Saiki

Patsy Saiki, author of *Ganbare!*, described an event that occurred at the Sand Island Internment Camp, where Hawaiian-Japanese were held:

At Sand Island Internment Camp, a whistle blew frantically one day. And the two hundred Japanese internees—including priests and bishops—were ordered to line up in the afternoon sun and strip. They and their piles of clothing were examined; their sleeping tents were overturned in a thorough search. What were the MPs looking for? Two spoons! Two spoons which could be converted, they were told, into contraband weapons!

They stood naked in the hot sun until finally allowed by the captain to wear their clothes again. How much humiliation was needed to let the men know they were prisoners? This stripping was more than a physical one—it was a psychological stripping that implied "all that belongs to you is your skin. We control what you have."

Iwao Kosaka

Iwao Kosaka read a Japanese poem:

If you live long enough

You will recall the olden days

Then, even the bad times

Will become fond memories.

He then described the illogic of his detention with simplicity:

I was born in 1914 in Honolulu but was taken to Kure City in Hiroshima by my parents. In 1937 I returned alone to Honolulu. I spent the next four years studying English in the mornings and teaching Japanese in the afternoons to support myself.

Suddenly in July of 1942 the FBI ordered me to report to the Honolulu office. Once there, they took me directly to the Immigration Station without even giving me a chance to change my clothes. About a week later, I was taken to Sand Island Detention Camp. While at the Immigration Station, we were treated like prisoners, including compulsory cleaning and dishwashing.

I had not burned my draft card and had broken no laws here in America. I did receive my education in Japan, but that was due to circumstances beyond my control. I had gone to Japan just before the war, but who would not have been concerned about his family after the series of deaths?

I had indeed taught in a Japanese language school, but that was to earn a living. I told the FBI that I had received military training while in school in Japan, but that was compulsory for all but the handicapped.

The Sand Island camp was surrounded by two concentric circles of barbed wire and armed guards kept watch 24 hours a day. One night the air raid siren sounded and lights flooded the camp. Guards surrounded the camp to see that we could not escape. Any attack from the skies would have left us as a most inviting target. The internment centers were supposed to provide American citizens protection, according to some, but how could this be true? Life in the camps was exactly like being in a prison.

Henry Tanaka

Henry Tanaka's experience confirmed the "crime" of ethnicity. He said, "As a loyal American citizen, I felt that it was my duty to assist my country in any way that I could. So, when a call for special policemen was made, I volunteered and was assigned to work in the office." But he was soon arrested by the FBI and went to jail. The interrogation he received was revealing:

> One day, several of us were taken to the County Building which was presided over by a Military Intelligence officer and three plantation managers. "Where were you born? Have you been to Japan? Who will win the war? Are you expatriated? Did you visit the Japanese training ship, *Taisei Maru*, when it visited Kauai?" These were some of the questions put to me. It is important to note that during these proceedings and during the entire length of my imprisonment, no specific charges were made against me.

The questions referred not to criminal activities but to activities that a person of Japanese ancestry might have undertaken. Was it criminal to have visited Japan? Should a visit to a Japanese training ship have resulted in over two years of detention? Should a man, because of his Japanese ancestry, have been discreet in his expression of political opinion?

Seiyei Wakukawa

The other half of the "crime" of ethnicity was its stupidity, amply demonstrated in the experience of Seiyei Wakukawa, editor in chief of a daily bilingual newspaper in Honolulu. Wakukawa was obviously an educated, intelligent person. He said:

> I was visited at my residence a few times by FBI agents, Army or Navy Intelligence officer, but each visit ended in a congenial exchange of views on the war with one exception of enigmatic note, and that was an indirect suggestion from the officers that I was expected to cooperate with authorities in ferreting out possible subversive elements. But I knew no subversive elements, nor did I think the situation warranted my being an unofficial informer.

His unwillingness to become an informer may have been his undoing. Law enforcement officials, including FBI agents, considered failure to inform as disloyalty to the United States. Wakukawa continued:

> As for myself, at no time since the outbreak of the war did I have any fear of being even remotely suspected of being an enemy alien inimical to the best interest of the United States, far less to be apprehended and incarcerated as such. To my great disappointment, however, what to me was unthinkable did happen. One day in April, as the fall of the Philippines became imminent, I was hauled in along with a large number of young Kibei Nisei. After being confined in the Honolulu Immigration Station for over a month and another month on Sand Island, with only one cursory hearing, I was shipped to stateside to be interned at Lordsburg, New Mexico.

> From Lordsburg, I dashed off a letter of protest and appeal to the White House, resulting in my being paroled in February, 1943, the first internee from Hawaii to be so treated. After parole, I was invited to teach the Japanese language at the University of Chicago Civil Affairs Training School. In the spring of 1944, I was asked to join the staff of the Navy's Taiwan Research Unit at Columbia University. A few months later, an invitation from Harvard University took me there, where I spent the remaining months of the war teaching and doing research work on matters related to military government and civil administration. Part of this work was published by Harvard [University] Press in the book, *Japan's Prospects*, and used by MacArthur's headquarters in bringing about far-reaching changes in Japan's land ownership and farm tenancy system.

My wartime internment reflects the irony of the entire internment system. If I was such an enemy, deserving of internment, then why was I so easily released to serve in the wartime effort and ultimately to assist in the occupation of Japan? My experiences after the parole incident only serve to emphasize the misjudgement and error of those responsible for internment.

The Hawaiians seemed to have been less victimized by their experience, even though their detention was every bit as harsh as that experienced by mainland Japanese-Americans.

Opinions from White Americans

The Seattle hearings were unusual for their witnesses who opposed redress. Only one was from the Lillian Baker brigade; she was more a pathetic nuisance than a challenge. Most were ordinary citizens who made the usual arguments against redress: confusing Japanese with Japanese-Americans; confusing the risks and hardships faced by soldiers with the violations of civil rights suffered by those detained; defining the program of mass exclusion and detention as patriotic duty.

Henry Kane

Henry Kane, a former assistant attorney general for the state of Oregon, said, "Japanese American internees served their country during the crisis period of World War II by their relocation and internment." This, of course, is exactly the line the government wanted us to swallow—except that the government would not permit the use of the term "internment." Then Kane said, "Internment of resident aliens of Japanese citizenship during the war with Japan was constitutional . . ." This is only partly true. Section 21 of Title 50 of the United States Code states: ". . . all natives, citizens, denizens, or subjects of the hostile nation or government, *being of the age of fourteen years and upward*, who shall be within the United States and not actually naturalized, shall be liable to be apprehended, restrained, secured, and removed as enemy aliens" (emphasis added). The law clearly stipulates age fourteen as the lower limit. Yet children were rounded up, even deaf and orphaned children. More to the point, Kane ignored the fact that the government did act to remove "enemy aliens" under such statutes and also under Presidential Order 2525, and limited this roundup of such persons to around two thousand. He misses the indiscriminate nature of mass, racially based detention. His errors might be excused were they made by an ordinary citizen. Kane said, "I state as a matter of fact and law that the United States committed no 'crime' that compels, merits or suggests 'redress' or 'reparation.'" It would be interesting to know if he would have supported a test of this assertion in a courtroom.

Arthur Barnett

The white Americans who spoke against redress were outnumbered by white Americans who supported redress. Some were persons involved in Japanese-American history, such as attorney Arthur Barnett:

It's interesting to sit here. Gordon Hirabayashi has appeared before you, and his case before the United States Supreme Court is a matter of record. He consulted me before he decided not to obey [the exclusion order.] Then, we raised a defense fund, and I was a witness. I accompanied Gordon when he surrendered to the local FBI [on] the day after he was supposed to have reported.

Louise Crowley

Others, like Louise Crowley, illuminated the event by explaining the damage that occurred to white America as well:

I'm a native Seattleite. I graduated from Broadway High School in 1937. Broadway had a high percentage of Nisei students, so a lot of my friends were of Japanese descent.

Now I want to talk about the effect of the evacuation and internment and the effect it had on a white person that wasn't interned. The high school and college years are the ones when a young person begins to make deep . . . and lasting friendships. Many of my own were prematurely and very painfully disrupted and shattered by that evacuation. I felt then and I still feel a passionate sense of outrage, helplessness, and betrayal. There was nothing anybody could do about it, absolutely nothing. It happened so fast. Suddenly, with ten days' notice, half of my friends and their whole families were imprisoned behind barbed wire, cyclone-topped fences around the fairgrounds at Puyallup, bound for who knew where—without having done anything at all to deserve it.

I must have been a pretty naive kid. I hadn't known such despotism was legally possible in the United States. Well, I learned, and I haven't forgotten.

[On] weekends, other white friends and I would drive down to Puyallup to visit them. We could smell the assembly center long before we got to it. [The camp was] overcrowded, muddy, with open latrines. The camp [was] so hastily thrown together, there was no provision for proper sanitation. We had to talk to our friends through the fence, with armed national guardsmen standing by. We couldn't bring them presents. I remember that Shig, who was an artist, wanted paper, paints, even just pencils, but there was no way we could give them to him.

A Critique of the JACL by Frank Chin

Dr. James Tsujimura, President of the Japanese American Citizens League, raised an issue for the Commission to consider:

Mr. Chairman, there is another serious matter which I wish to address at this time. At the Commission hearings in Washington, D.C. in July and at these hearings in Seattle, serious accusations have been made against the Japanese Americans from the west coast and the incriminating role of the JACL in the formulation of the infamous loyalty oath.

As national president of the Japanese American Citizens League, I wish to request officially for the record that Mr. Mike Masaoka, on behalf of the JACL and its membership, be allowed to respond to these very serious accusations at the Washington, D.C. hearing scheduled in October, in order that these matters may be put to rest.

It is my belief that the issues of evacuation and redress placed before this Commission are of great importance to this nation and that they transcend indictments of individuals and of organizations.

Two months later, the Commission did invite Masaoka to return for a second appearance; the request and its fulfillment demonstrated the JACL's influence with the Commission.

The accusations to which Tsujimura referred in the Seattle hearings were earlier made by playwright Frank Chin:

> I am a writer with Chinese ancestry, one of those people Sax Rohmer would call inscrutable; . . . I'll try to be as "scrutable" as possible here.
>
> My testimony is on the loyalty oath, and I summarize.
>
> The loyalty oath, questions 27 and 28, was invented and created by the Japanese American Citizens [League] in late 1942 as a publicity stunt to convince the government the Japanese American Citizens League was the only leadership organization over the Japanese Americans.

This was a statement which required supporting evidence. Chin provided documents later, but they only suggested that there might have been a link.

Chin continued:

> The loyalty oath was, in JACL's opinion, a kind of graduation competence test from the WRA-JACL confirmation program. By Mike Masaoka's reckoning, the JACL and WRA were partners in creating "Better Americans in a Greater America." The general policies they submitted to Eisenhower on April 6, 1942 leaves no doubt as to his organization's intention to use the camps to modify Japanese American society, culture, history, and individual behavior.

Perhaps Chin erred by confusing intentions with actions. The JACL recommended policies far beyond its power to implement. In February 1942, the JACL made ten such recommendations before the Tolan Committee, which were ignored. These included the advice that "evacuation . . . be conducted . . . in a manner . . . consistent with the requirements of national defense, human welfare, and constructive community relations in the future"; and that "the resettlement of evacuees from prohibited areas should be within the State in which they now reside"; and that "competent tribunals be created to deal with the so-called hardship cases and that flexible policies be applicable to such cases." Thus, though the JACL did support the WRA's use of the camps to modify Japanese-American society, the following statement, made by Mike Masaoka on April 6, 1942, cited by Chin, seems to be little more than an aspiration to power:

> We believe that all projects should be (1) directed to create "Better Americans in a Greater America"; (2) to maintain a high and healthy morale among the evacuees; (3) to train them to cope with the difficult problems of adjustment and rehabilitation after the war; (4) to permit them to actually and actively participate in the war effort of our nation; and (5) to develop a community spirit of cooperative action and service to others before self.

Masaoka's five points were as ineffective as the earlier ten recommendations had been in affecting government policy.

But the points did support Chin's following analysis:

> Mr. Masaoka led the JACL in taking the stand that Japanese Americans were sacrificing their citizen rights and voluntarily entering the relocation camps in order to prove their loyalty and their contribution to the war effort. Therefore, he reasoned, "Paradoxical as this may seem, we are opposed to hearing or determining boards of commissions which might attempt to determine the loyalty of those in these resettlement projects . . ." The loyalty oath accomplished that later.

Masaoka spelled his indoctrination program to Eisenhower:

> We do not relish the thought of "Little Tokyos" springing up in these resettlement projects, for by so doing we are only perpetuating the very things which we hope to eliminate, those mannerisms and thoughts which mark us apart, aside from our physical characteristics. We hope for a one hundred percent American community.
>
> One thing is certain: there should be no Japanese language schools.
>
> Special stress should be laid on the enunciation and pronounciation of words so that awkward and "Oriental" sounds will be eliminated.

Later, many Japanese-Americans would incorporate Masaoka's program as "proper" behavior in their relationships to the white majority of America.

Here was the core of Chin's argument for the JACL's responsibility for the government's loyalty oath:

> The loyalty oath, key phrases, and the forswearing of all forms of known and unknown allegiances to the Emperor of Japan are virtually identical in the JACL loyalty oath of 1942 and questions 27 and 28 of the WRA leave clearance application.
>
> You are familiar with questions 27 and 28. I will read the JACL part here in 1942:
>
> > I do solemnly swear that I will support and defend the Constitution of the United States against all enemies, foreign and domestic; that I will bear true faith and allegiance to the same; that I hereby renounce any other allegiances which I may have knowingly or unknowingly held in the past; and that I take this obligation freely without any mental reservation or purpose of evasion. So help me God.
>
> Now this process also included oral interview that contained certain questions that had to be answered yes, like:
>
> > Would you assist in the resettlement program by staying away from large groups of Japanese?
> >
> > Would you avoid the use of the Japanese language, except when absolutely necessary?
> >
> > Would you try to develop such American habits which will cause you to be accepted readily into American social groups?
> >
> > Are you willing to give information to proper authorities regarding any subversive activities that you might know of or which you might be informed about directly or indirectly, both in the relocation centers and in the communities in which you are resettling?
> >
> > Would you consider an informer of this nature an *inu*?
> >
> > Would you conform to custom and dress?

In short, the loyalty oath in printed form and in the interview required any who would be cleared to leave to seek life outside the camp to endorse the JACL program, to agree to discriminate [against] the Issei, and display respect for the *inu* and turn informer to the Government against their own.

The greatest damage, in my opinion, that the Government inflicted on Japanese Americans was the imposition of the Japanese American Citizens League as the leaders of the Japanese Americans inside the camps. A leadership that would be repudiated by the Japanese Americans themselves, according to Solon T. Kimball, community analyst and anthropologist, recorded in the success and failure of the Government program of the internment camps.

I find Chin's conclusion off the mark. I do not agree that the "greatest damage . . . the government inflicted on Japanese Americans was the imposition of the Japanese American Citizens League as the leaders of the Japanese Americans inside the camps." The greatest damage inflicted by the government was the massive abrogation of civil and constitutional rights of over 125,000 Americans solely on the basis of race. But Chin does hit the mark in stating that the WRA's leave clearance program, requiring those who would leave camp "to agree to discriminate against the Issei, and display respect for the *inu* and turn informer for the Government against their own," was consonant with the position of the JACL.

The JACL's position required Japanese-Americans to accommodate themselves to the government's program; this placed the burden on Japanese-Americans to demonstrate their loyalty and their acceptability. But this was fundamentally illogical. Disloyalty had never been proved, so why was a demonstration of loyalty necessary? Should all blue-eyed husbands be required to prove they are not wife-beaters? The criteria for acceptability were white racist criteria of conformance and assimilation. Why was Masaoka so certain that "there should be no Japanese language schools?" How else were children to learn how to converse with their Japanese-speaking parents? Was not freedom of speech guaranteed by the Constitution? Why were Japanese-Americans to eliminate "mannerisms and thoughts" which were part of their identity? Could they not make these characteristics their unique enrichment of American culture? The JACL's version of the loyalty oath reached even deeper into the Japanese-American psyche, with its renunciation of allegiances Japanese-Americans might have "unknowingly held in the past." Was it true that buried deep in the Japanese-American there lay the sneaky, cruel, copycat, yellow-bellied "Jap?"

Throughout the hearings, I sensed the absence of a proper focus on the government's wrongdoing. What Chin analyzed is an injury deep within the Japanese-American psyche: the accommodationist role of the JACL is both symbolic and real. The symbol is expressed by terms such as "Quiet American" and "Model Minority." That's what Japanese-Americans have become as a result of their harsh mistreatment by the government. That's the direction the JACL has urged upon them with its motto, "Better Americans in a Greater America." The motto's corollary, also adopted by the JACL, was "The Greatest Good for the Greatest Number." The motto and corollary implied that "Better Americans" are more "American," and more "American" was what the majority of Americans were: white Americans. Japanese-Americans were to become as much like white Americans as possible; failing that, they were to be quiet and accommodating.

Underlying the symbol is the harsh reality of the JACL's bowing to governmental pressures to inform on Japanese-Americans: the resultant arrests, incarcerations, stigma, separations, and suffering. Real fathers of real families were removed, without the benefit of the rules of evidence and proper legal representation. The wound to the psyche may not be repairable by human intervention; its repair may come only through the cycle of death and birth—like Old Testament sins that inflict their pain until generations have passed.

Though the hurt was and continues to be real, and though the human failure was a legitimate issue for the hearings, there were more important issues than the JACL. Governmental officials are sworn to uphold the Constitution, and had failed to do so. Responsible officials had inflicted the most serious injuries on Japanese-Americans. If the hearings did not rise above human interest stories and Japanese-American weaknesses to focus on these more pervasive injuries, the hearings will have failed. But the stories themselves were not to be denied their telling.

Stories Heard in Seattle

Tomio Moriguchi

Tomio Moriguchi is president of Uwajimaya, a Pacific Northwest food distributing company. He arrived at a simple measure of economic injury:

> Since then the business has grown at over 20 per cent, compounded the last 36 years. What would the growth rate have been without those years in camp? Four years at 20 per cent compounded growth rate would double any business. Perhaps it could be argued that if it had not been for the internment, our family business would be twice the size it is today.

One of the benefits of the Commission's research was the discovery that an estimate of assets of Japanese-Americans at the time of their mass exclusion and detention as 400 million dollars was unfounded. Somehow this figure had been placed into an early historical account as emanating from the Federal Reserve Bank of San Francisco, and through repetition became factual. But no documentary evidence was found to substantiate this figure. Still, the 400 million dollar figure has been used to arrive at total reparations, adding interest over the years, of about two and one-half billion dollars.

Other studies have arrived at different figures. Moriguchi was proposing, at least for his family, a much simpler method: use the present assets of Japanese-Americans.

Elaine Ishikawa Hayes

Elaine Ishikawa Hayes described the difficulty encountered when a family member was stricken by tuberculosis, a common affliction among Japanese-Americans in that period:

I was evacuated from Sacramento, California with my mother and four sisters on March 23, 1942 to Walerga Assembly Center, and from there, in August, to Tule Lake. I was 18 at the time, and my youngest sister was 6. My father was confined to Weimar Tuberculosis Sanitarium, approximately 50 miles from Sacramento. My father's confinement was particularly tragic, as he was separated from the rest of us for the duration of the war. [He was, perhaps,] the only Japanese left alone in that hostile period in northern California.

June Oyama Takahashi

There was also testimony from Japanese-Americans who lived in the territory of Alaska. June Oyama Takahashi's story was painfully honest:

At the time of Pearl Harbor I was a student in my second year of high school in Petersburg, Alaska. My brother was a student at the University of Washington in Seattle. Our family was in the hand laundry business, and my father was the local photographer. Exact dates have escaped me, but I do remember that it was soon after Pearl Harbor that my father was the first man to be picked up by the local authorities and taken to the Petersburg jail for reasons unknown to us.

When I used to go home from school, I walked by the jail house, and there was a little barred window from which my dad used to call and wave to me. I am ashamed now to say that I would take another route home because it was embarrassing for me. I am left with terrible guilt about avoiding him and regrets about not being able to talk to him about this.

Masao Takahashi

The Issei seemed to speak with particular passion. Of course, the Issei, as "enemy aliens," were the most feared. Masao Takahashi made those fears look foolish:

I am 87 years old, and I first came to the United States in 1913. My eyes are very dim in my old age now. I am asking my daughter to read my testimony for me in English.

On the very day of my eldest daughter's eleventh birthday, February 21, 1942, I was roused from my sleep very early in the morning. The FBI searched my house. I was allowed to dress, but under observation, even in my morning toiletry. Apparently, I was part of a second group of men to be taken by the FBI. I am a perennial optimist. I had done nothing wrong. So, the anxiety of my fellow inmates had little impact on me. I recall feeling confident that I would be released in time to have birthday cake with my family that evening. However, when we were stripped naked and thoroughly inspected, my optimism was shaken by the very humiliation of the process. I assumed that cooperation would lead to an early release, and resolved to accept the inevitable. But that was not to be. Days added into days. Terrible food, tense boredom, and wild rumors were our daily preoccupation. From the window of the detention center, I could see my house. Many thoughts would enter my mind as I looked out that window. My family came to visit with regularity. I remember a friendly guard teasing my visiting 5-year-old daughter by slamming the bar gates closed and telling her she was now a captive. She flew into my arms, saying "Oh boy! Now I can stay with Papa!" Mama had tears in her eyes. I wished I could cry, too.

Masato Uyeda

Another Issei, Masato Uyeda, age eighty-six, was born in Hiroshima, Japan. One wonders how many Americans would be as persistent and persevering as he in achieving their citizenship:

I arrived in Seattle on November 10, 1911, when I was 16 years old. I moved immediately to a mining camp in Frontier, Wyoming where my father was working.

An unknown arsonist burned my store and warehouse to ashes on December 14, 1941. Our family savings of 12 years and all the hard work were lost. I was arrested by the FBI as an enemy alien and sent to the Seattle Immigration Office. I felt so sad; I almost went crazy at that time. This is a thing I have never been able to forget in my whole life. My three-year-old child asked me to take her with me to the immigration office. But it was not possible. And she asked me to buy ice cream on the way back from the immigration office.

The FBI was not able to find any evidence against me after searching my home. I have never committed any hostile acts or participated in any espionage against the U.S.A. Yet, they arrested me and forced me into an immigration office, leaving my wife and children in our home. My group was transferred in a train with blinds closed to Fort Lincoln, Bismarck, North Dakota.

Our life in Fort Lincoln was like that of birds in a cage. We were surrounded by barbed wire fences, and we had no freedom. The food in the camp was no good, but sufficient amounts were provided even under wartime conditions.

The hearings for internees in Bismarck were very one-sided. Our opinions and wishes were totally ignored. After six months in Bismarck, we were transferred by blind-window trains again to Lordsburg, New Mexico. Speaking Japanese or in loud [voices] was prohibited. Internees were ordered to raise their hands for permission to go to the lavatory, and we had to line up and wait our turn. No one was able to see outside the train.

The camp in Lordsburg, New Mexico was an internment camp. Internees had to wear uniforms similar to prison garb and had numbers [on] their backs. The camp was surrounded by barbed wire fences, and the U.S. Army patrolled the fences with machine guns mounted on Jeeps.

We, the internees, felt that it was very strange, since none of us was trying to escape. The government official said that the soldiers were there to protect us internees. In six months, we were again moved to an internment camp in Santa Fe, New Mexico.

After I was in Santa Fe for four months, I was paroled in November, 1943, and I was able to join my family in Camp Minidoka in Idaho. I returned to Seattle in April of 1945. I was prohibited from working outside the Seattle area, so I had to work as a gardener from my home. I was also obliged to report once a week to the immigration office, telling them where I went, how many times, and what I did.

Even though I was parolled in 1943, I had trouble when I applied for citizenship in 1954. When I appeared in court, the judge questioned my loyalty due to my internment, and I had to bring in my attorney to prove my loyalty to the U.S. government. I don't know why only the Nikkei were given such hardship in the United States.

Jim H. Akutsu

If the victims draw sustenance from stories of injury and perseverance, they draw strength from Jim H. Akutsu's story of resistance and imprisonment. The myth of the "Quiet American" who silently endured may be as comfortable as it is untrue. Without resistance and the price of resistance, we can view life as simple and uncomplicated, without difficult choices of social importance. But Akutsu's story, like Kinzo Wakayama's in the San Francisco hearings, shows what Japanese-Americans can be:

My name is Jim H. Akutsu. I am 61 years old. [I was] born and raised in Seattle, Washington. I would like to share some of the traumatic experiences I had during the Second World War.

The price of liberty and freedom is a constant vigil, and that vigil is democracy. Before getting too far into our discussion, I want to show the will I made on December 26, 1941. [I fulfilled] my obligation as an American citizen [and responded] to the call for duty. I took my physical and waited for induction, but the call never came. This is my will. And there is a gentleman sitting in the front row who witnessed it for me.

Classified 4-C, an enemy alien, I entered [the] Puyallup Center with others. Several months later, we were transported to our final destination: Minidoka, Idaho. It was my understanding that we were to get the same kind of food as served in the Army base mess hall, [the] same type of living quarters as in an Army base, and clothing to suit the climate. After months of enduring poor food and primitive living conditions, I felt someone had to speak out. My complaints were [first] addressed at the block level. But without any response, I elevated it to the administration level. For this, I was placed on a stop list and also [placed under] surveillance as a possible agitator. Therefore, I was not able to leave camp for school or to seek employment outside. This affected the outcome of my whole future. As expected, the winter in 1942 was a very rough one.

To make things worse, segregation got started with the infamous questionnaires by the Army and WRA: join the Army or face possible deportation. The questionnaires went off like a bomb, creating much frustration and anxiety and disruptions in families; [they] caused tremendous mental, physical, and psychological strain throughout the camp. My biggest question was: can the government deport me? Only if I were an alien and enemy agent. I would have to wait for my day in court.

News came that my father was sent to the maximum security prisoner of war camp in Louisiana, and that he was very sick. This was a most trying time for my mother. I could see it was tearing her apart mentally, physically, and yet, there was nothing I could do.

In the winter of 1943, we got a wire instructing someone to meet my father at the gate by noon. On the way, an old man asked me where the Akutsu's lived. I pointed the direction for him. After waiting three hours at the gate, I returned to my barrack. I couldn't believe my eyes. The old man whom I had directed earlier in the day was my father. We hadn't recognized each other. Although my mother felt relieved that my father was back, it was a shock to see him in such emaciated condition. Shortly thereafter, she started to get weaker and finally succumbed to a total physical breakdown. She was under emergency care for many days, hovering between life and death. My mother's death, a few years later, was directly attributed to the evacuation.

All my pent up feeling exploded. I was mad, furious. I went to the administration to tell them that I was writing to Washington, D.C. and to the newspaper to expose all the irregular things going on in camp at our cost. Shortly after, when I got back to my barracks, I found an envelope slipped under the door. It was a copy of a letter sent to my draft board by a WRA official asking the Board to seek my induction.

I was being trapped and railroaded. I wrote to General Hershey, Washington, D.C. immediately to express my dismay. I did not get any response. But I found out later that I would be accused of stealing a government document: [the] copy of the letter.

I was not surprised when I received my induction notice. I received the notice nearly three weeks after I was to have reported at the camp hospital. I was then prosecuted for draft evasion and [for] stealing government documents. I spent over two years in maximum security in the federal penitentiary in Washington at McNeil Island.

New Insights, and Old Facts Confirmed

Rita Takahashi Cates

Some of the testimony brought noteworthy facts to light. Dr. Rita Takahashi Cates was from the Eastern Washington School of Social Work and Human Services and Graduate School of Public Administration. She said:

> Government exploitation [of evacuees] occurred before and during the evacuation, relocation and internment processes, when government officials assessed advantages to be derived from the evacuees' resources. In many instances, government officials took advantage of the captive population and deliberately used their services to achieve government objectives. One example is the following:
>
> > On February 18, 1942—which was one day before Franklin D. Roosevelt signed Executive Order 9066 and also one whole month before WRA was established by another executive order—George P. Clements wrote to the Commissioner of Indian Affairs, John Collier, saying, "It seems to me that the temporary internment of the Japanese on the reservation would enable the Indian Department to put the ground in shape for agricultural occupation by the Indian on removal of the Japanese, possibly without any expense for that preparation. Give that a thought. It seems to be the most [rational] program so far presented."
>
> The evacuees were relocated on Indian reservation land, since the evacuees could be used for clearing the land and preparing it for agricultural use. A teletype message from the chief engineer and general manager (H. A. Van Norman) in early March, 1942 identified the advantages of relocating the Japanese to the Colorado River Relocation Center, otherwise known as Poston: "The Japanese could be employed to clear, level and put into production the additional acreage needed which would result in a permanent improvement that could be settled by [returning] soldiers at the expiration of the war." Gila River, the second relocation camp that was located on an Indian reservation, was selected because of its potential for continual vegetable production throughout the year. This is fully documented in the records. It was anticipated that evacuee farmers with years of experience and skill in vegetable production could be tapped for production at Gila, especially since approximately half of Gila's 16,000 acres were "undeveloped" land. The evacuees were expected to clear that land.

In addition to this, she revealed that there was significant negligence by the government in public health matters:

> In all camps there were many cases of government negligence, in that officials had knowledge of unsanitary and unhealthy conditions. For example, bacteria counts in milk remained excessive at Gila River for months, and reached as high as 2,500,000 per cubic centimeter. The U.S. Public Health Service condemned milk when counts exceeded 50,000.

Donna L. Leonetti

Dr. Donna L. Leonetti disclosed:

> The impact of the wartime incarceration can be seen in a number of social and economic variables in the postwar resettlement period, as communities on the west coast were reestablished. The postwar housing shortage was acute. . . . Although Japanese Americans no longer favored extended family household arrangements if they could be avoided,

during this postwar period, many three-generation households were set up as a means of dealing with economic problems and the housing shortage. In 1945, 70% of the Nisei couples in our sample resided with parents. By 1955, this figure decreased to 20%.

In addition to the squeeze of postwar housing, she disclosed data on birth rates and infant mortality rates:

The accompanying effect of the war and postwar economic difficulties was the disturbance and . . . delay of family formation. Birth rates had increased above expected levels for the age groups involved during the internment years, as marriages were arranged in the face of the threat of separation at the time of evacuation or armed services induction. In addition, with the stresses of internment, infant mortality from all causes during the war years rose to 58.3 per 1000 from 21.7 per 1000 in 1939-41. After the war, the birth rates dropped significantly below expected levels for the age groups involved with the poor economic conditions and the necessity for many women to take employment. For those married, births were delayed. For those not married, marriages were delayed. For those women born in the late 1920's and early 1930's, average age at marriage was over 25 years, and for men, even later. Only about 40% of the women were married at ages 20-24 years compared with over 65% in the majority population at that time.

By 1950, birth rates began to rise and infant mortality rates dropped to 24.6 per 1000.

James Tsujimura

The facts supplied by Dr. James Tsujimura were not new but were impressive in their conciseness:

On May 12, 1942, a Mr. Kanesaburo Oshima was shot and killed by a sentry at the Fort Sill internment camp in Oklahoma.

On July 27, 1942, Messrs. Toshio Kobata and Hirota Isomura disappeared under mysterious circumstances while being transferred to the Lordsburg Internment Camp in New Mexico. The internees at Lordsburg were informed that these two men were shot and killed by sentries while attempting to escape.

On December 6, 1942, Messrs. Ito and Kanagawa were shot and killed by armed guards during a riot at Manzanar Concentration Camp in California.

On April 11, 1943, James Hatsuaki Wakasa was shot and killed at Topaz by an armed sentry named Gerald B. Philpott.

In the summer of 1943, an unnamed victim was shot and killed by an armed sentry at Gila Concentration Camp.

In May, 1944, James Soichi Okamoto, an internee at Tule Lake, was shot and killed by an armed sentry.

Floyd Schmoe

Floyd Schmoe represented the North Pacific Yearly Meeting of the Religious Society of Friends. He convincingly confirmed the applicability of the the terms "concentration camp," "prison camp," or "prisoner of war camp" to the detention centers:

I wish only to emphasize one point . . . that although these camps were called assembly centers and relocation centers, they were in fact prisons. They were concentration camps. They were prisoner of war camps.

In my years of work with the American Friends Service Committee and the United Nations, I have become involved in five different wars in a dozen countries. I was, myself, for a brief period a prisoner of the German Army on the Polish front. I visited German prison camps in France and Palestinian camps in Jordan and Gaza and Mau Mau internment camps in Kenya, in Korean camps in South Korea, and more recently I have been in Southeast Asia and [have] seen the conditions of the people there. I have seen thousands, tens of thousands of prisoners, hundreds of thousands of refugees.

In the internment of the Japanese Americans, I visited . . . five of the ten so-called relocation centers. I spent many weeks in two of them, namely Minidoka . . . and Heart Mountain . . . I wish to state here that none of these camps differed in any material way from those which I have just mentioned. They were prisoner of war camps. They looked like prison camps; they felt like prison camps; and they had the same emotional and psychological impact upon internees that prisons have on any person so interned.

Emi Somekawa

Emi Somekawa's revelations may have been the saddest. She described euthanasia:

I was a registered nurse. Unfortunately, there were not that many registered nurses of Japanese ancestry during those years. I worked at both Tule Lake and Minidoka camps. I know that our facilities were not adequate to take care of the population of thousands in the camp.

. . . . After doing and seeing these things happen, week after week, month after month, and trying to take care of the sick human beings, eventually it got to me. It is painful to talk about these happenings. I do not wish to use any names. But I am speaking of a professional person who actually observed euthanasia performed.

A doctor was begged by a family to please administer this patient some kind of medication to put her out of any further misery and pain. These situations arose due to many traumatic and psychological effects that affected the internees due to the evacuation process. This was and still is a very sensitive area, because it involves Japanese American doctors and nurses, as well as families who were subjected to euthanasia.

In given circumstances, knowing that euthanasia was and still is considered a crime, taking people out of misery was the only humane course to take. Had the patient been a member of my family, I would have felt the same way.

The psychological and personal damage caused by the performance of euthanasia is incalculable. The government, by its policy of imprisonment and traumatizing us, by not providing adequate medical accommodations to care for all the needs of the patients, brought death to many patients.

I would also like you to know that no thought or care was provided for the handicapped and the mentally retarded patient. With small enclosed living quarters [that] many families were living in, they had a very difficult time coping with these situations. No allowances were made in the latrines, laundry room, mess hall, or any place where a handicapped person could go. The mental and physical anguish that these patients and their families suffered was more than I could put into words.

Theories and Criticisms

Frank A. Tsuboi and Marie Horiuchi Ooka

Other witnesses propounded theories. Frank A. Tsuboi, a flight engineer for Western Airlines, said, "Well, this is my day in court," a metaphor perhaps, but not fact. But Marie Horiuchi Ooka came uncomfortably close to the truth when she said:

> I discussed life before World War II, the war years, and post-war experiences with my children many times, in order to instill in my children that this should never happen to another group.

> One haunting question asked by them was, "If the United States was losing the war against Japan, do you think the United States government would have annihilated the Japanese Americans as Germany did to the Jews?" This question remains unanswered.

The historical circumstances are not the same. Anti-semitism is at least as old as the Christian Church. The Nazis were explicit in their racism, and they wholeheartedly believed in their theories of Aryan superiority. Americans, by contrast, were struggling with racial prejudice. We had rid ourselves of slavery; we felt discomfort with lynchings; and a few persons protested racial inequality. America was not searching for a Final Solution. But we were in the middle of a hot war, and a balance of threats was established. Had the Japanese victories continued, and had the Japanese developed a more systematic program of harsh treatment of American civilian and military prisoners of war—especially of white Americans—America would have attempted to save these prisoners. Japanese-Americans were available, imprisoned in remote locations. The threat of reprisals against imprisoned Japanese-Americans is documented by the February 5, 1942 memorandum of Secretary of War Stimson to Secretary of State Hull. Would the concentration camps have become death camps? Would there have been any protest? Ooka's children's question is unanswerable.

Lawson Inada

Lawson Inada, Professor of English at Southern Oregon College, propounded another uncomfortably compelling theory:

> Now, apart from the actual evacuation itself and apart from all the individual tragedies that occurred as a result, my findings indicate that the single most source of widespread damage was incurred by the instituting, in 1943, of the "Application for Leave Clearance," otherwise known as the "Loyalty Oath." Thus, for your purposes, the "Loyalty Oath" can be a point of focus and a means of access to the entire experience. The camps irrevocably altered the course of Japanese America; the "Loyalty Oath" practically destroyed it. On the surface, this innocuous looking questionnaire resulted in the transfer of 18,711 evacuees between centers for the purpose of segregation and in 4,224 cases, eventual repatriation. Impressive statistics, certainly, but there is more to the story. In actuality, the "Loyalty Oath" served to segregate generation against generation, religion against religion, family against family, and wreaked havoc on households and individuals—a veritable civil war with no winners. The common term for this, of course, is "blaming the victim." And when they emerged from the experience, they were not to be whole again. The damage would extend through the lives of future generations, and for this there can be no redress.

> Thus it was, then, that 52,798 deliberately chose not to return to their former homes, taking their separate ways, instead, of exile in this country. Compulsion was to disperse as much as possible, to "disappear." For above and beyond the despair associated with "home," above and beyond the stigma to bear, "When did you stop being a Jap" had to be answered.

> There was now an additional element perpetrated by the "Loyalty Oath," and this was nothing more than even a loathing of one's very own kind. Those that did return, the

effects of the "Loyalty Oath" were there to confront them on a day to day basis, with Japanese Americans themselves, in effect, accusing one another of being "Japs" or even "Americans." And if there could have been a magic pill to eradicate one's "Jap-ness," I shudder to think how many would have taken it.

Had Inada been aware of President Roosevelt's theories of racial mixing of Asians and Europeans, revealed by Christopher Thorne in his history, *Allies of a Kind*, and of the striking fact that it was President Roosevelt himself who proposed that Japanese-Americans be widely dispersed throughout America, his statement would probably have been a bombshell. Even without these objective facts, his arguments are compelling. There are a great many Japanese-Americans who tried to take the magic pill to dissolve their "Jap-ness."

Frank Abe

Criticism of the Commission sometimes brought a response from the commissioners. In the case of Frank Abe, it was not his own thoughts but his characterization of those of Shosuke Sasaki:

> Sasaki was among the first to criticize the Japanese American Citizens League for its failure to carry the reparations program to Congress. He regards the passage of the Commission bill as primarily an effort by the five Nikkei Congressmen to avoid taking a clearcut position on redress. Sasaki's principles are so clearly defined that he refuses to testify here today.

Commissioner Marutani responded:

> Doesn't the Commission serve the function to inform many, many citizens who otherwise would not be aware of what happened to Japanese Americans?

To which Abe replied:

> Your Honor, I don't want you to misunderstand me. I certainly do not begrudge the fact the Commission exists. That's why I am here today, to bring you this information on the popular support for redress. My mentioning Mr. Sasaki's feelings is only meant to bring you another point of view [which is] popular in the Nikkei community. To them, time is a-wasting.

Commissioner Marutani, responding to Abe's "Your Honor," used a judicial example:

> It reminds me of a criminal trial where the victim comes in and said, "Look I know what happened. Let's dispense with trial and hang him." I am a victim, and you are a victim. We're all victims, and I can appreciate that understanding. The question is to Mr. Sasaki— for example, and [to] many of us who feel that way—yes, we were victims, but shouldn't the facts be laid down before we take action?

Abe tried to speak on behalf of Shosuke Sasaki:

> I think Mr. Sasaki's feelings are testimony to the fact that there is a strong feeling in the Nikkei community that redress be legislated by the Congress, and anything short of that is a severe disappointment to them.

But Sasaki is difficult for another person to represent; he is very much his own man, with his own ideas and ways of expressing them. It was unfortunate that Sasaki was not present to respond. He might have pointed out that the facts were already available; that many published volumes containing accounts of the events had been published; that none of the testimony in these hearings would be admissible in court because none was sworn; that most of the testimony avoided the crucial issues of governmental culpability; that the Commission had done little to build a solid case against the government; that all of the Commission's proceedings thus far have amounted to little more than catharsis for the victims and a sounding board for white folks who feel apologetic or vindictive. But Sasaki's rebuttal will remain unheard.

Commissioner Brooke was not satisfied that Sasaki's silent demurrer had been adequately answered, so he pursued his own ideas:

> Mr. Abe, . . . let me just say . . . that if this were left to the Congress, the Congress would probably have maybe one or two days of hearings in Washington, D.C. . . . And then this matter could be taken up by the Congress. But I think you certainly understand that this is an issue which, as Judge Marutani has said, needs to be known by the American people. Politicians generally follow the public, as I am sure you are aware.
>
> Not only is there a need for education and information involved, but there is also a need for an advocacy. Commissions, after having hearings and working on recommendations, go into what we call an "advocacy phase." In other words, they go to the country and try to generate support for their recommendations which will be made to the Congress. This is the accepted procedure.

Commissioner Brooke used the same truism Congressman Danielson had used in the 1980 House Hearings: the government is the people. That must be one of the most frequent aphorisms used by members of Congress to deflect criticism. If one examines the relationships, one sees that people vote to elect members of Congress, while members of Congress formulate, amend, and vote on legislation. The voting public does not legislate, any more than the housewife who calls the plumber fixes the plumbing. But Brooke went beyond a rhetorical feint; he really stretched the role of the Commission when he assured Abe that there would be an "advocacy phase." Such a phase never occurred; the Commission never attempted to build public support for its recommendations.

Chizuko Omori

Not all criticism of the Commission evoked a response. Chizuko Omori attacked on a broad front, including the Commission:

> I'm a little disappointed that there are not more of the Commission members here.
>
> The five minutes allotted to me are such a short time that I feel at a loss for words to tell you all that I would like to say.
>
> My family was deeply divided during the three and a half years in camp. My parents were very embittered by what was done to us and wished to leave the country. At 13, I was a captive of their choice, and it was with dawning horror that I began to realize

what that meant. I could not accept that fate. I fought with my parents over and over again, and what I would say was that I was an American and didn't want to become a Japanese. The answer from my mother was, "Well, if you are truly an American, what are you doing in this camp?" I couldn't answer that, and I still have no answer. It has left me a somewhat divided person. This conflict was to poison my relationship with my parents forever, and I felt that I hated them sometimes.

I would like to put in a word to the five Nikkei Congressmen who are so conspicuously missing in the debate about redress. They should feel ashamed for their betrayal of the basic American principles of their Nikkei constituents and . . . their parents. And where are all the constitutional lawyers and the great civil libertarians and thinkers of our land?

She is on target. Most notably absent from these West Coast hearings is Chairperson Joan Bernstein. If she was too busy for the few days the hearings required, she probably will be too busy to read much of the transcripts. And five minutes are too few to grapple with Omori's mother's question: "Well, if you are truly an American, what are you doing in this camp?" And why, she might well have asked in 1981, must you plead your case before an ineffectual Commission whose chairperson has more urgent business to conduct? Nor is Omori's criticism of the five Nikkei members of Congress far from the mark. She is wrong about Senator Hayakawa, who has been engaged in the debate. But the four Democratic members have not taken leadership positions. Do they support reparations to individuals? Or do they support the foundation approach? Where do they stand and why? Nor have the civil rights and civil liberties organizations been forthcoming. The American Civil Liberties Union has been uncharacteristically quiet on this issue. Subsequent history will demonstrate that the ACLU was on the trailing rather than leading edge of court challenges. And the commissioners all but ignored her words, as they did most of the testimony.

18. HEARINGS
CHICAGO HEARINGS

The Chicago hearings of the Commission were held on September 22-23, 1981, at Northeastern Illinois University. This was probably the biggest event ever held on this campus. Professor Shirley Castelnuovo of the University's Political Science Department had developed a strong interest in the movement for redress and was largely responsible for directing the Chicago hearings to the spacious facilities of the University's Alumni Hall. The event was most certainly the biggest Japanese-American event ever to take place in the Midwest.

Maryann Mahaffey

These were the only field hearings in which the Commission's chairperson, Joan Bernstein, participated and over which she presided. Mercifully, we were spared the usual opening parade of political witnesses fulfilling their obligatory roles before a captive audience. Instead, Maryann Mahaffey, president pro tem of the Detroit City Council and a professor at Wayne State, opened the hearings with a ringing personal and political statement describing her experiences as a volunteer worker at the camp called Poston II—one of three camps at Poston, Arizona:

> I volunteered as a recreation worker in the closing days of World War II to help with the relocation of those of Japanese ancestry who had been interned for four years.
>
> My assignment was to help reassure the evacuees that "outsiders" cared and to serve as a bridge back to the world from which they had been separated.
>
> With the innocence and enthusiasm of a dedicated and serious 20-year-old Iowa college senior, armed with textbook knowledge of family life, social problems, and psychological stress, I felt confident about my mission.
>
> I think I did some good. I think that I helped, but I will be forever haunted by what could not be done [for] the irreparable damage inflicted on an innocent, helpless, and defenseless population.
>
> On July 1, 1945, I was driven in a camp van through the Mojave Indian reservation, past the barbed wire enclosure and saw for the first time the primitive, loosely constructed wood barracks that housed the evacuees. I heard the Army MP who accompanied us brag about his connivance in obtaining this assignment so that he could control the camp and display his macho superiority over the detainees.
>
> I learned that only ten evacuees were allowed at any one time into the neighboring town of Parker because of the intense resentment by the permanent residents.[1]

On March 4, 1943, two years earlier, the exclusion zone had been reduced in Arizona, leaving the camps at Poston and Gila River in "free" America. In January 1945, the mass exclusion order was rescinded. All America was now "free." But it is clear from Mahaffey's testimony that the inmates of the camps still had their movements severely restricted. She continued with a description of a visit:

At one point I obtained permission to escort a group of young girls into Parker, their first visit to town in three years. Some had been only four years old when they came to the camp. They saw merchandise in store counters for the first time. They bought their first ice cream cones. They had their first glimpse of cement sidewalks, and they were the objects of cold and suspicious stares by the townspeople.

The girls were subdued and quiet. We were nervous for fear our children would be hurt. I started a teen canteen where regularly the teenagers talked about their fears of the racism they would meet on the outside—but they wanted out. They wanted desperately to be normal, American teenagers.

Mahaffey then summarized her feelings retrospectively:

In the more than 35 years since that agonizing summer, I have thought often and poignantly about my role, about my country, and about justice.

As a mother, as a social worker, and as an elected public official, I feel so inadequate, so humble, so full of shame about what our government has done. Internment camps, concentration camps in reality—I realized then and I am more convinced now—are alien to our democratic philosophy and repugnant in any civilized society.

Mahaffey was followed by Studs Terkel, a radio interviewer, writer, and Chicago celebrity, who described his own culpability and that of the media, especially Walter Lippmann's, and said that he favored redress. (Hardly anyone opposed it. Something was wrong.) Next was the bearded Jay Miller of the American Civil Liberties Union, Illinois Division, who repeated the myth of National ACLU opposition to the exclusion and imprisonment, even though he did describe it as "the ACLU, under the leadership of our Northern California affiliate." He announced that the ACLU "strongly and unambiguously supports redress, including financial reparations, which we consider to be in the nature of compensation and punitive damages for the severe violation of constitutional rights." (But a year earlier the ACLU unambiguously failed to support the Lowry Redress Bill.) He was followed by Yvonne Delk of the Office for Church in Society of the United Church of Christ. She announced her church's support for redress/reparations for "all those who suffered evacuation/incarceration as a result of E.O. #9066."

C. Harvey Gardiner

The panel of participants entitled "On Japanese from Peru" was the bombshell of these hearings. Professor C. Harvey Gardiner of Murphysboro, Illinois, read his prepared text in a slow, methodical fashion. It was only five double-spaced pages. For the past forty years he had studied contemporary Latin America and Japan and had lived in both areas. He had published twenty-five works on the topic. His latest was *Pawns in a Triangle of Hate*. He read:

In twelve Latin American countries, in Central America, in the Carribean and South America, U.S. officials were primarily responsible for kidnapping and impoverishing thousands of men, women, and children. During World War II, the State Department and the FBI kidnapped thousands of people. The American Army and Navy transported them to America, and the U.S. Immigration and Naturalization Service housed them in Texas-based concentration camps. The U.S. encouraged violations of Peruvian laws and then manipulated the illegal entry of thousands of Latin American Japanese. All of this was totally unrelated to what we did to the 120,000 Japanese Americans.

He continued at a deliberate, methodical pace:

> For one of the 12 countries, Peru, I have studied 46 large boxes of the Immigration and Naturalization Services records and many thousands of pages of the diplomatic and FBI records concerning 1,800 Japanese Peruvians who were seized and shipped to this country. No charge of wrongdoing and no evidence of wrongdoing was ever adduced against any one of the 1,800 Peruvian Japanese. Repeatedly, the wartime history of the FBI has been written, but the World War II operation in 12 countries has been ignored. The FBI never had a case against any of the 1,800 Peruvian Japanese, nothing that hinted of espionage, sabotage or any wartime operation. Oh, yes, while the FBI was helping to kidnap and imprison thousands without meaningful evidence, J. Edgar Hoover never had an agent in Peru who could speak a word of Japanese.

(What was the Federal Bureau of Investigation doing in Latin America anyway?)

> During the war, 12 shiploads and three planeloads of Japanese Peruvians were transported and, in turn, interned in Texas. On one voyage, more than $10,000 worth of internee property, jewelry, and cash was seized. On one occasion, hundreds of men were compelled to labor for months without compensation in violation of the Geneva Convention.

He was obviously going to take longer than the mandatory five minutes. The horrors continued:

> A man with an inoperable case of cancer of the tongue died within a month of being shipped to the United States without any medical examinations. Three tuberculosis victims were denied access to a known streptomycin treatment. During four suicide attempts by one internee, the Immigration and Naturalization Service insisted that the Department of State was responsible for his presence in this country. The State Department, lacking medical facilities, turned to the War Department, insisting that it had experience in handling insane soldiers. Finally, after a bungling exhibition of insensitive bureaucracy, the ailing Japanese was admitted to a Texas state hospital.

> When a young widow traveled more than 4,000 miles to claim her husband's body, she had to wait more than a year to receive his corpse.

Gardiner describes our high-level culpability:

> Consider another sketch of official responsibility. In April 1942, when Washington was violating the rights of the Japanese Americans, Ambassador Norweb, our man in Lima, was advancing suggestions based on our handling of the Japanese residents in the U.S. Ambassador Norweb concluded that his embassy could propagandize the Japanese threat in Peru. Next, aided and abetted by those linguistically inept FBI agents, our Ambassador persuaded Peruvian officials to approve a deportation scheme. Norweb wanted the ouster of between 200 and 300 Japanese Peruvians, men he labeled "undesirable." Norweb arranged for the transporation to the United States of those men. In mid-summer—

Interrupting Gardiner in mid-sentence, Commissioner Bernstein began to press for a conclusion. Gardiner tried. But he was already summarizing a 225-page book. Now he was being asked to summarize a summary. Even his pace could not be hurried, try as he might:

In mid-summer, only three months after his first move, our Ambassador concluded that "the most satisfactory solution would be the removal to the United States of all the persons in Peru of the Japanese race."

By then, Norweb was thinking of more than 25,000 men, women, and children of Japanese ancestry. That was the way one wartime American internment program in Latin America originated and mushroomed.

One American wartime diplomat who was in Peru, John Emmerson, has said, "We found no reliable evidence of planned or contemplated acts of sabotage, subversion or espionage." Of the U.S. program of deportation and internment, Emmerson has also said, "It was clearly a violation of human rights and was not justified by any plausible threat to the security of the Western Hemisphere."

Commissioner Flemming interrupted on behalf of Bernstein to urge Gardiner to summarize rather than to continue his reading. Gardiner replied that he had been summarizing, that he had only one page left. Bernstein asked that he summarize the remaining page. Later, I learned that he was suffering from a brain tumor which forced his deliberate pace.

When he had finished, he was followed by a group of former Peruvians who doubtlessly presented the most difficult stories of the hearings.

A woman who was a young, nursing mother when deported from Peru told how her breasts had dried under the stress of the kidnapping. She had packed cans of milk to feed her infant. When she boarded the transport ship, the cans were taken away from her by her brutal captors. When she tried nursing her infant, her breasts produced only blood. As she and other Peruvians entered the U.S., they were stripped naked and sprayed with DDT. They were completely stripped of all their identification papers, including passports, visas, birth certificates, driver's licenses, vaccination cards, and such. At war's end, the U.S. deemed they were illegal aliens because they lacked papers. They were threatened with deportation to *Japan*, not Peru. Attorney Wayne Collins of the Northern California branch of the ACLU came to their defense. Collins had already represented thousands of Japanese-American renunciants, singlehandedly. He would later represent Iva Toguri in her trial for treason. He was able to save hundreds from deportation to Japan. Those who were shipped to Japan had received no assurances that the Japanese government would accept them. For those who remained in the U.S., life was marginal. They remained in the status of illegal aliens for ten years. Some went to Seabrook Farms and worked in sweatshop conditions. Their movements within the United States were restricted. They could not travel outside the United States.

Fred MacDonald

The afternoon's testimony began with Professor Fred MacDonald, professor of history, Northeastern Illinois University. He propounded an interesting thesis: the government's deliberate use of the popular media to agitate against Japanese-Americans, thereby creating the atmosphere enabling their eventual exclusion and detention:

If you would know how 110,000 innocent people could be robbed of their liberty and property, robbed by a nation proffering notions like "liberty," "freedom," "justice," and "innocent until proven guilty," you would understand the role of the mass media.

He explained:

The 110,000 Japanese-Americans . . . were the innocent victims of an orchestrated press and political campaign commencing in the last week of January 1942. Not until seven weeks after Pearl Harbor did this campaign begin. Then political and publishing leaders on the west coast deliberately stoked the fires of popular distrust and racism toward Japanese-Americans. They irresponsibly circulated false charges of fifth-column activities, sabotage, and disloyalty on the part of Japanese-Americans.

The goal of this deceptive campaign was to panic public opinion and, thereby, compel state and national military planners to bolster military defenses along the west coast. At the heart of the press and political campaign was the failure of the Federal and then the California state governments to respond adequately, in their mind, to the need for defense.

According to MacDonald, the problem was in the difference between the military's reluctance to bolster West Coast defenses and the perceived need by West Coast politicians for more defenses:

The Army, which has been given a lot of discredit for its role in the concentration camps, at least at this point was uncommitted to taking a military posture on the coast.

As late as February 4th, in a meeting in Washington, D.C. of the Senate Defense Committee, chaired by one of the Senators from Oregon, General Mark Clark and an admiral explained that their defensive position is to put the military on the Pacific Islands and train them and then from there launch an offense. [They also explained that to make] a military commitment along the west coast would . . . invite the Japanese Navy and Army to use the west coast as the battle zone. So, they would not put a strong number of people along the west coast.

It is by the fourth week, the final week in January, that the press and political campaign is launched [to counter the military's view.] It is launched on January 25th, when Senator Hiram Johnson, dean of the west coast delegation in Congress, the senior Senator from California, let it be known to the press that he intends to organize the delegation, already recognize[d as] a formidable political force, to organize that delegation to press for more defense commitments and Naval craft along the west coast.

As appealing as this theory is, it lacks documentary support that directly links popular opinion to military policy.

Masaru K. Yamasaki

Masaru Yamasaki spoke briefly about his own experiences and then discussed those of his father, Manhichi Yamasaki. His father's experience directly contradicts the written statement of Karl R. Bendetsen (discussed in the second Washington hearings) that the government harvested all crops, sold them, and deposited the earnings into the detainee accounts:

Instead, negotiations were made through the Farm Security Administration to then sell the crop and all farm equipment to a Caucasian. A loan was secured by this Caucasian to pay Manhichi for the agreed upon price. Before the loan arrived, Manhichi was sent to the Walerga Assembly Center. The Caucasian George Faris—I will never forget his name—returned the loan to the Farm Security Administration, clearing himself of his debt. The sum involved was $2,000, approximately $2,000, but to my dad that represented his entire life savings during his struggles to raise his family as model American citizens.

During our confinement at Tule Lake, we had the Legal Aid Department. I contacted the Legal Aid Society and an attorney, Henry Taketa of Sacramento, California. Mr. Taketa wrote letters to the Farm Security Administration from Tule Lake but to no avail. To this day, my dad never received a penny from that particular sale.

The commissioners could have confronted Bendetsen with Yamasaki's testimony at the second Washington hearings where Bendetsen testified. But they did not.

Jitsuo Morikawa

The Reverend Jitsuo Morikawa introduced a theme that reflected my own feelings about the hearings. He is an eloquent preacher:

The Commission on Wartime Relocation and Internment of Civilians appears to be an act of moral concern on the part of the United States Government, to discern if injustice was inflicted on 120,000 civilians in their relocation and detention in internment camps. After forty years, when memory is faded and a majority of the population have either forgotten or never heard of the event, the U.S. Government has appointed a commission to determine if a wrong was done, and if a wrong was done, what measures could be taken to redress the wrongs, long after those who suffered most have gone to their grave and long after the rest have suppressed their painful memories into their subconscious, and long after the key figures involved in the Executive Order 9066 are not available for questioning.

A nation which through its executive powers acted with lightning speed in the wholesale suppression and internment of 120,000 persons of Japanese ancestry, without due process of trial, without protection of the courts, without reference to the law, has given itself forty years in which to bring itself under question through a process they have determined, to judge whether even any wrong was committed. The timing of the Commission compounds the wrong. The protracted silence adds to the injury. Evasion of guilt and denial of mistreatment reinforce the injustice.

To further deepen the affront, witnesses to testify before the Commission are allowed a few minutes to tell their story of months and years of internment, of confinement, of deprived civil rights. Even in the course of a Commission hearing, we appear to be under executive orders to neutralize, minimize and restrict our testimony. Is it a way of disarming us under the pretense of listening to our protest, impressing the public of a fair procedure? How can we voice our pain and agony in a testimony limited to a few minutes? It's an insult to our integrity, an affront to our being as humans. The pathos of the hearings is that both [the] public and our people have the impression of their magnaminity, eager to hear the deep melancholy notes of tragedy and suffering, but the hearings are structured so there is no possibility of such to happen.

To even further accentuate the injustice, we the victims, are expected to bear the moral burden to determine the nature of the redress, removing that burden from those identified with the [perpetration] of the injustice. We have suffered enough without adding the burden of begging or even demanding reparations for our suffering, and offering the privileged luxury to those ultimately responsible of simply saying yes or no to our painful demands. Let the U.S. Government struggle with the moral issues involved, go through the painful agony of dredging up forty years of hidden guilt and let them be exposed to the light of day. And if we are a nation committed to human rights and look with scorn on their violation in other nations, we can scarcely escape the indictment, "physician heal thyself," without seriously righting a wrong which remains permanently as a blot in our history and leaves a permanent scar of shame on 120,000 Americans and their offsprings.

No easy redress is possible. The acts of redress must be as costly as the pain and agony of the injustice. There is no easy way to redemption. The cost is always high. Will that price be paid by the Japanese Americans to further add to their suffering, or will it be the American nation through its elected state?

Morikawa's statement stung. The spontaneous applause that followed—the first to occur—suggested that he had struck a responsive chord in the crowd. The commissioners responded defensively.

Alice K. Esaki

Alice K. Esaki is a Nisei who happened to be in Japan during World War II:

By the time the war started, I was fully bilingual, bicultural and felt very good about my dual cultural background. I have always considered myself American. . . . We had no communication with our parents and felt totally deserted. I was confident that my parents would be safe, although my Japanese friends and neighbors felt differently.

You can imagine my surprise and disappointment and fear when we heard that all of the Japanese Americans were evacuated from the West Coast. Speculation, rumor, and fear that we would never see our family again became a daily concern.

One day, someone threw a rock in our yard. The rock was wrapped in a large flyer with a photograph of children [and] adults looking longingly through barbed wire fences. The camp was situated in the desert with a guard on the watchtower looking down at the internees. I kept on saying, "It is only a picture. I don't believe it." My Japanese friends and relatives would say, "Where is this democracy that you always talked about? Did you know that they could only take the things that they could carry?"

My grandmother and I would spend hours arguing whether this was true or just propaganda. I did not want to believe that such a thing could really happen. I kept denying that this was . . . true. But seeing the newspaper and hearing the news over the radio, I slowly [became] convinced that this was a reality. A year or so later, we received a letter from my father stating that he was in Minidoka, Idaho.

Esaki's testimony breaks through the barrier of our all-American parochialism and forces us to see ourselves as the world sees us. The mass exclusion and detention program does raise serious questions about American democracy. Former Nazis have confronted American critics of their horrible deeds with the historical facts of this American act.[2]

Rev. Seiichi Michael Yasutake

Rev. Mike Yasutake spoke about those in the government who should be held accountable for their actions:

I was subjected to answering a loyalty oath twice, . . . once in the camp and another as a student at the University of Cincinnati. It would seem that Japanese Americans were required to be more patriotic and more loyal than the rest of the population. Because of the loyalty oath, the records show that many people suffered, and many were sent to Japan.

The governmental bodies and agencies responsible for such oppressive activities as I have just described were not and are not now held accountable for what they did. The FBI hired and possibly intimidated Japanese American individuals into informing and spying on their fellow Japanese Americans in the concentration camps. All of this tended to create division and suspicion among groups, among friends, and even among family members. Informers and those spied upon were all victims of oppression. . . .

In view of this, my recommendation is that those who had been decision makers and implementers of policies on evacuation [and] detention be subpoened. I am referring to such people as the then Assistant Secretary of War, John J. McCloy, and the then Army Officer, Karl R. Bendetsen. Such people should be questioned in depth by examiners who are well-informed of the events under consideration.

Very few of the victims were aware of the responsibility of McCloy and Bendetsen. Very few held them accountable as Yasutake did. Most concentrated on their own private injuries, as though expecting the Commission to find the culprits for them. But what this showed was the depth of their injury: the silence that still could not break, despite all their storytelling. Injuries require both victims and victimizers. Yasutake was one of the few who were willing to point to the victimizers.

The rest of the first day of hearings was anticlimactic. The JACL presence was obvious. JACL members handed out copies of the hearing schedule together with a JACL leaflet. JACL members were seen sitting in the press section. Senator Brooke wondered aloud why no one voiced opposition to redress. Not one racist testified. Most of the witnesses had been screened by the JACL. The closest thing to opposition was the characterization of monetary redress as "thirty pieces of silver" by Ben Yoshioka. Many witnesses supported the JACL's proposal for a foundation to perform good works. None attacked it. Most spoke in favor of individual compensation. Perhaps the most innovative proposal came from Shiro F. Shiraga. He, too, was not interested in compensation. Instead, he wanted the government to erect monuments on the scale of the pyramids of Egypt at each of the ten camp sites. They were to last a thousand years, a long-term memorial of the injustice.

Chicago Hearings: The Second Day

The largely Nisei audience in Alumni Hall broke into sardonic laughter when, on the second day of the hearings, John Corey, an emissary from Chicago's Mayor Jane Byrne, addressed Joan Bernstein as "Mr. Chairman" and then introduced himself as the representative of Mayor Daley. He was rude to be a day late. He was ruder still not to include Tule Lake and Rohwer in his recitation of camps in his prepared text. He was squeezed into a panel of white persons who actively supported the victims during World War II. It might have been more interesting if he had discussed his own activities during this period.

Maynard C. Krueger

Professor emeritus Maynard C. Krueger led off this panel. He identified himself as the running mate of Norman Thomas on the Socialist ticket in 1940. Krueger spoke extempore, making good use of his years of experience as a professor and a stumper for the Socialist Party. He told how he and Norman Thomas visited every camp:

> These visits of mine were by invitation of the residents of the camps. It was the first time I had ever seen people behind barbed wire. . . . It never seemed to me, however, that the physical conditions of the camps came anywhere near being as serious as the ultimate insult and the violation of human dignity which was involved in . . . people being forcibly put there.

> My problem was what to say when I stood up before an audience of residents of a concentration camp. . . .

> What does one say to an audience of internees in a concentration camp in the United States? I can tell you what I decided to say and that I did say in every one of the camps.

> I do not repudiate the doctrine of military necessity. Every political order which has any self-respect has some kind of a safety to provide for instances that are not provided for in a constitution. Thomas Jefferson had that problem when he had the opportunity to buy the Louisiana Territory. The military counterpart of civilian prerogative in the government is called "military necessity."

> When I was asked in the camp, "How could those generals believe that we are a danger to the military security of the United States?" I had something to say. I said the best I could say, that the minds of the generals must have been warped so that they made a decision which did not correspond to the fact. And I asked my friends in the camp to try to understand that there was a race prejudice in the United States, and that there was nothing about military education which reduced it in generals; that there was economic interest in the United States, and that there was nothing about military education which would make generals impervious to the pressure of organized agriculture and organized commerce and organized labor—all of which ran in the anti-Oriental direction.

Krueger saw racial prejudice and economic interest as underlying reasons for the government's decision to exclude and detain. Krueger thought that the military necessity rationale was logical, though based on false premises. The military invoked military necessity for the sake of defending the West Coast. He did not consider the military necessity of hostages available for reprisals. He continued:

> When I was asked, "How long is this likely to go on?" I would have to tell them that I thought it would go on until the end of the war. It would go on for the duration. Don't depend on the United States Supreme Court's reversing a decision of the United States Government which is based, they said, on military necessity.

He also discussed restitution with the internees:

> I would tell them there will come a time . . . when the consciences of the people of the United States, operating through their elected executive and their elected legislature— when the people of the United States will say that this was a wrong decision, and that there will be an act of apology, and there will be some attempt at restitution.

> By whom? By the political and by the executive and the legislative political agencies of our social order, [but] not by the courts.
>
> "How long would it be?" I would be asked . . . and I would have to tell them that the children of Israel wandered in the wilderness for 40 years before they found their way to the promised land, and it is quite likely that the people of the United States may take that long.
>
> "Forty years? Why forty years?" Because forty years is long enough for one generation to die off and another one to take its place. . . .

He did the audience and the commissioners the service of showing the majority population's need for redress. Speaking in reference to reparations, Krueger said:

> And if you now propose to the people of California that the Government of the United States wants to take the lead and asks California to join, I think you might get some special support from the people of California on a kind of action. . . . If there were some feature of the penitential program—whatever it is to be called—. . . which made it possible for people in general—school children, union locals, churches, local groups of all kind and individuals—to make some contributions to the thing. . . . Whatever is to be done, in my opinion, should not be done entirely by government but should be open to popular participation in the financing of it.

Jan Linfield

Jan Linfield was a teacher at Poston. She spoke of her experiences:

> In 1944, I had just graduated from Northwestern University, and I accepted a position as high school teacher at the Poston Relocation Center Camp III, located in the desert of Southwest Arizona.
>
> I am quite sure that I learned much more in the fifteen months that I spent in Poston than I taught. Behind the polite exterior presented to the caucasian teachers, I soon saw the deep anger and despair of young people my own age, having spent the last three years of their lives in incarceration, having left behind in California college classes and beginning careers. Some of them taught in the school, teaching the same classes as I but paid pennies by the government for the dollars paid to me.
>
> I never deluded myself that I shared in the suffering of the Japanese Americans at Poston, even though I chose to live in one of the tarpapered barracks in the camp rather than the white clapboard houses provided for caucasian administrators and teachers. The essential difference, of course, was that I could at any time cross that barbed wire perimeter and with a wave from the armed soldier in the guardhouse leave the camp for a weekend in Los Angeles or Phoenix or Tucson, which my Japanese American friends could not ever do.

I remember a teacher at Manzanar High School, Helen Ely, who also lived in the barracks. Helen Ely, like Jan Linfield, was exceptional in her awareness of the injustice of the camps.

Linfield then connected this past experience with her current experience in Chicago's black ghetto:

> Racism, in its simplest definition, is the use of a double standard. Blacks in this country have been acutely aware of this double standard. It still exists for most Blacks in most areas of their lives. They even anticipate when and how it will happen.

How else can one explain the widely-held belief in Black communities like Woodlawn that the government has already prepared detention centers for inner city Blacks to be sent to in the event of civil disorders? Variations of this story spread and proliferate because they find credence in the Black community's long experience with the double standard.

It would be a serious mistake for us to dismiss these rumors and say that could never happen here, when, as a matter of historical fact, it did happen here in 1942 on the West Coast.

United Methodist Clergy

The theme of Krueger and Linfield was reinforced by a panel of United Methodist clergy, including Rev. Martin Deppe, Bishop Jesse DeWitt, Rev. Martha Coursey, and Rev. Gregory Dell. Deppe, speaking for the General Board of Church and Society, said, "It is altogether shocking and shameful that we should be gathered here today, almost 40 years . . . after the so-called 'resettlement' of Japanese-Americans. Shocking because . . . a minority people . . . have still not received just recompense. . . . Shameful because the majority people . . . have not demanded an accounting by our government." Bishop DeWitt said, "To confess error is to open the way for national healing and forgiveness." Coursey, pastor of the Parish of the Holy Covenant, said, ". . . the time is past for symbols and apologies. . . . It is ridiculous to question 'whether' any wrong was committed. . . . Let us be about redress and reparations." All the United Methodists supported redress legislation and legislation to enable the victims to file lawsuits.

Greg Dell, speaking as copresident of the national Methodist Federation for Social Action and as a pastor, made a strong statement. After citing Amos and Jesus as authority for seeking justice, he quoted Abraham Lincoln:

"If by the mere force of numbers a majority should deprive a minority of any clearly written constitutional rights, it might, in a moral point of view, justify revolution, certainly would if such a right were a vital one."

What a brushing aside of all the specious rhetoric about the Commission's fulfillment of democratic principle! Dell struck home:

It is that witness, that heritage, both theological and ideological, which makes this hearing and this process a virtual insult. We respect and are grateful for the concern and commitment of the members of this Commission. We are deeply dismayed over its existence. That a commission should be created for the primary purpose of inquiry, when the facts of racist injustice are so evident, is in itself an extension of injustice.

Winifred McGill

Winifred McGill was one of NCJAR's first board members, when NCJAR was trying to organize a coalition. She and Sam Outlaw joined the board as representatives of the Near North Unitarian Universalist Fellowship. McGill said:

We hope that this Commission will arrange to compel testimony under oath from the surviving persons who were responsible for that massive assault against civil liberties, so that we can learn the real reason that it was done, before it is too late.

McGill was referring to persons such as Bendetsen and McCloy. Unfortunately, while the Commission heard such persons, their testimony was not given under oath. McGill was blessed by a rare gift in the hearings: a sense of humor. She was raised in Port Edwards, Wisconsin, and described a community event there during the war years:

> Later during the war, the baseball team of the Nisei 100th Infantry Battalion . . . training at Camp McCoy, Wisconsin . . . came to town and played our team. They were very popular and well-liked there, but we did not know they were Japanese Americans. They were presented to us as Hawaiians, and many people said they looked just like the Japanese.

McGill then recommended $40,000 as an amount for individual reparations and added other recommendations:

> We ask that this Commission recommend individual payments without delay. If Congress will not take responsibility for voting to compensate these victims, it should pass legislation enabling them to sue for reparations, to have their day in court.

> While the time for legal action was running, they were still under psychological duress from having been abused by their own government. A combination of alternating intimidation and flattery kept them from legal action until the statutory time had expired. That combination appears to be still at work.

> We hope that you will recommend legislation enabling the victims who wish to sue to do so and this without regard to any other recommendations that you may make.

> An apology has also been suggested. It would be nice for a copy of a resolution of Congress apologizing to the victims to accompany each individual check. Also, that resolution of apology should be carved in stone or cast in bronze and prominently and permanently displayed in the nation's capitol.

The Commission ignored this and other requests for legislation to enable legal action. We may never know why, because the Commission failed to record minutes of its meetings and deliberations.

Peter Suzuki

Peter Suzuki was one of the few persons officially invited to testify at a hearing by the Commission. He was an anthropologist in the Urban Studies Department of the University of Nebraska. His testimony was a startling criticism of unethical behavior by social scientists:

> Within the War Relocation Authority was a Community Analysis Section with headquarters in Washington, D.C. By late summer of 1943, each of the ten camps had a branch of the Community Analysis Section headed by a person called a Community Analyst.

> The entire Community Analysis Section operation both in Washington and the camps was an anthropological undertaking inasmuch as twenty of the twenty-seven in the Community Analysis Section were anthropologists. Ostensibly, these social scientists were hired to study the culture patterns of the internees.

> As it turned out, a significant number carried out such activities as informing, spying, and the gathering of intelligence data. Because of the intelligence gathering activities

of the community analyst at Jerome, Arkansas, Edgar McVoy, at least three internees were removed to Leupp, Arizona, the isolation camp.

It was perhaps this naming of names that made Suzuki's testimony such a difficult problem for the Commission. A diffuse and general acknowledgement of wrongdoing was probably permissible. But concrete and specific allegations of wrongdoing by individuals were not what the Commission wanted. Nevertheless, Suzuki continued naming names:

The community analyst at Topaz, Weston LaBarre, worked closely with the camp's attorney regarding its inmates.

E. Adamson Hoebel, the community analyst at Granada, Colorado, gathered intelligence data on draft evaders.

G. Gordon Brown of Gila, Arizona, and John Rademaker of Granada were members of the camp review boards which judged cases of loyalty. Rademaker reported regularly to the FBI and to the Office of Naval Intelligence at Granada as he gathered intelligence information on the internees. He also spied on "suspicious visitors" and on his fellow white co-workers, with reports to the intelligence agencies at Granada.

John Provinse, the anthropologist who headed the Community Management Division, one of the largest units within the WRA, made arrangements to furnish the Washington office of the FBI with cards on the internees leaving camp on a permanent basis so that wherever they "relocated" the FBI could monitor them.

John de Young, the Minidoka, Idaho community analyst, informed on the dissidents of that camp when they complained about camp conditions to the Spanish Consul.

Edward H. Spicer, the head of the Community Analyst Section in Washington, D.C., passed on information to the Tule Lake director about some internees who had moved from Topaz to Tule Lake because he had suspected them of having taken part in a protest movement at Tule Lake.

The first head of the Washington Office of the Community Analysis Section clearly saw the Section as intelligence gathering channel, as brought out in John F. Embree's report to the FBI, declassified in 1975.

Although not with WRA because she was with the research project entitled, "Japanese Evacuation and Resettlement Study," the anthropologist Rosalie Hankey Wax turned informer while doing research at Tule Lake from 1944 to 1945. A direct result of her informing to the FBI was that the person whom she informed on ended up in Japan. Parenthetically, Wax was expelled by WRA from Tule for her intelligence work. Other cases of improprieties and unethical behavior by the social scientists in the camps can be cited. They are fully documented in several recent articles of mine.

Suzuki supported his testimony with documentation from the National Archives. He summarized his thesis and presented recommendations:

The camp experience was a corrupting one for those social scientists who, under the pretext of scientific research, undertook the questionable practices referred to in the previous paragraphs. To be sure, there were some who did not indulge in such unethical practices. But the fact remains that the internees had to suffer yet another indignity in addition to those which are already known, but perhaps more painful than those because this added indignity came from scientists whose ethics should have obviated the intolerable behavior that went under the guise of "scientific research."

Recommendations: investigate the following:

1. Who authorized the community analysts to spy, inform, and gather intelligence data?

2. What was the relationship between the government intelligence agencies in the camps and the Community Analysis Section in Washington, D.C. and its field officers?

3. Whatever happened to the known victims of the spying and informing by the community analysts? How can they now be helped?

4. Although a government employee, why were materials by Alexander Leighton, an anthropologist at Poston, Arizona, sent to the Bancroft Library of the University of California instead of to the National Archives?

5. Were social experiments on the inmates carried out by community analysts? For example, did certain community analysts "float" rumors in order to test the reactions of the internees? Were there any other kinds of social experiments in which the internees were used as the social scientists' guinea pigs?

Given the fact that a number of unanswered questions remain solely on the issue of the anthropologists in the camp, finally, I recommend that the life of this Commission be extended to look into these and many other issues which still remain to be investigated.

Rachel Sady

Suzuki was followed by Rachel Sady, who had worked in the Community Analysis Section that Suzuki had just so roundly indicted. Sady was visibly surprised and displeased by Suzuki's testimony. Sady provided another, official view of the role of community analysis:

The [WRA] saw its job as restoring human rights and providing for the welfare of evacuees. In doing so, it was compelled to counteract the image of them that resulted from their expulsion. WRA opted not for "concentration camps" as so often and understandably is charged but for abolishing the relocation centers, getting the people back in the mainstream of national life, and lifting the ban against them on the West Coast. [This was] not easy in a country at war and extremely hard on the victims, buffeted by the series of programs that resulted from that decision.

To help achieve its aim, WRA turned to social scientists as staff advisors. Before the liquidation of WRA in June 1946, thirteen anthropologists and eight sociologists had become employed over time as Community Analysts. . . .

The Community Analyst's role was a new one with little or no precedent. It was to study and report on evacuees' attitudes and behavior in the situation in which they were caught. It is a mistaken, but again understandable, idea that these social scientists were preoccupied with explaining to the administration enough about the evacuees so that they could be manipulated. Particularly, I want to emphasize that analysts did not transmit covert information about individuals to anyone at all. We studied the attitudes and behavior of the administration, too, seeking ways to make them understand the very real fears, anxieties, and concerns of the center populations.

Much of this was done through oral reports and discussion. Most importantly, the head of the section was in constant contact with WRA's top echelon. Beyond talk, we wrote a wide variety of Community Analysis reports on our research. They were reproduced and distributed in Washington and the centers. Each analyst had a small staff of evacuee assistants that helped in gathering data and preparing reports. Some of these Japanese Americans, with that start, are distinguished social scientists today.

Unfortunately, there was little questioning following the presentations of Suzuki and Sady. Suzuki had the support of his documents. Without having seen them, Sady was ill-equipped to counter his charges. Moreover, Sady's following of the official "party line" of the WRA raised questions about her credibility. The facts simply do not support her contention that the WRA's primary objective was "abolishing the relocation centers." The WRA Solicitor, Philip M. Glick, fought hard against the court challenges which would have forced the camps to close much earlier. The "permanent leave" program of the WRA released only small numbers in 1942 and 1943. The WRA's insistence on the maintenance of euphemisms such as "relocation center" and "evacuee," which Sady herself continued to use and defend almost forty years later, demonstrated the WRA's desire for public acceptance of the camps rather than their elimination. The public certainly did not want the camps to be abolished. The WRA's record of not resisting public pressure was hardly an example of courage.

Shirley Castelnuovo

The final panel of witnesses at the Chicago hearings included Professors Shirley Castelnuovo and Victor Rosenblum. Castelnuovo's recommendations included adopting the German Federal Government's approach to compensating Jewish survivors of the Holocaust:

The United States Government did breach the basic moral value of our political system and in the process violated basic constitutional rights. It is with this in mind that I recommend the following to the Commission on Wartime Relocation and Internment of Civilians:

1. That the Commission on Wartime Relocation and Internment of Civilians recommend to Congress an individual compensation model based on the West German Federal Compensation Law, developing categories of damage based on testimony of individuals and government officials, archival records, and other documentation;

2. That the Commission . . . recommend to Congress a simplified administrative approach rather than a judicial adversary approach for determining claims;

3. That the West German approach establishing minimum and maximum sums within each category as a way of fine tuning individual differences and damages be recommended;

4. That the appeal cases involving the West German Federal Compensation Law of administrative settlements to German Courts of Claim be examined so that areas potentially troublesome to the claimants can be identified and avoided if relevant to the Japanese American circumstances;

5. That the Commission fully explore the legal and moral culpability of officials who formulated and implemented the policy decisions of exclusion and internment with the apparent knowledge that these policies raised serious constitutional questions, including the violation of *habeas corpus* rights;

6. [That] the role of Congress in so readily acquiescing to executive military action in time of war also needs to be examined by the Commission. Major General Kramer makes it clear in his previously cited memo that Congress could have mandated that administrative hearings be held prior to detainment;

7. [That] in the light of these last two recommendations, the Commission should explore whether enabling legislation shall be passed to allow charges to be brought against these

officials and/or whether specific legislation be recommended to prevent a future occurence of 1942.

As she began to explain the rationale for using the German approach to reparations, Chairperson Bernstein told her that her time had elapsed. Accordingly, she summarized:

I have recommended the Federal German Law as a model for individual compensation knowing full well the differences between the Holocaust and what happened to Japanese Americans in the United States. I think the crucial similarities are that both groups of people were selected out as a class on the basis of ancestry; that selection was rooted in a history of racism; and that the selection and internment took place with little or no outcry of protest from their fellow countrymen. Citizenship and legal residency provided no protective rights. In short, both of these people experienced betrayal and abandonment by their government and fellow citizens. I think that that model is the most appropriate in terms of dealing with the damages suffered.

Professor Castelnuovo's recommendations were as ambitious as they were appropriate. Few persons would be willing to draw the parallel that she did between the Holocaust and the mass exclusion and detention of Japanese-Americans. America's war against the Axis Powers was a popular war. Like a morality play, it was a war of good against evil. The Nazis were evil, and the Holocaust proved that. The Japanese were evil, and Japanese atrocities proved that. Democracy and America were good. But while Nazism was an ideology, Japaneseness was racial. Democracy would overcome Nazism. Americans would overcome the Japanese. How could "good" America commit evil? The few Germans I've met who were in Germany during the war protest their innocence; they were unaware of the death camps. Most Americans I've met in the Midwest protest their innocence; they were unaware of the ten detention camps. By making the parallel, Professor Castelnuovo forces Americans to reconsider their version of the Second World War as a morality play. Americans, too, by our practice of anti-Semitism, share in the responsibility for the Holocaust. And by our treatment of Japanese-Americans, we have demonstrated our capacity for concentration camps and perhaps far worse evils.

It was also encouraging that Castelnuovo recommended the enabling of legal action against the wrongdoers. Of course, that was probably the furthest thing from the commissioners' minds. The wrongdoers testified next, in November.

19. HEARINGS
SECOND WASHINGTON HEARINGS

The staff of the Commission on Wartime Relocation and Internment of Civilians had warned me that the Senate Caucus Room would be crowded, so that I should arrive early, but the warning was a false alarm. These hearings were the most sparsely attended of all, with only fifty to sixty in the audience section with room for two hundred. The small audience was disappointing, considering the impressive witness list. Bendetsen, Ennis, and Hewes for the first day. Eisenhower was ill and did not attend. McCloy, Dedrick, Glick, James and Mari Michener, and Masaoka for the second day. Except for the Micheners, these were the movers and shakers of mass exclusion and detention. Apparently more people were interested in listening to stories from victims than explanations from decision-makers.

Karl R. Bendetsen

Karl R. Bendetsen was first pointed out to me while he was engaged in conversation with Mike Masaoka and John J. McCloy. He appeared to be a friendly waiter, or maybe a properly solicitous butler, a cross between Edward Everett Horton and Douglas MacArthur. He had a ready smile with crinkled eyes and was in good physical shape. He had been the chief architect of the internment program.

Commission Chairperson Joan Bernstein set the tone by announcing that the hearings were not an inquisition. The commissioners were there to gather information. The witnesses were not subpoened; they were invited. They were not testifying under oath; they were simply reporting their recollections. Nice, if you tell the truth. Nicer still, if you don't.

Instead of being asked to summarize his eighteen-page statement, Bendetsen was asked to read it. This would have taken about forty-five minutes. Instead of reading it, however, he spoke extemporaneously for sixty-seven minutes. Finally, Chairperson Bernstein interrupted him so the commissioners would have time to ask questions. His testimony and the questions and answers that followed took four hours.

Retired Colonel Karl R. Bendetsen used body language. As he began by discussing reports of atrocities committed by Japanese troops in the Philippines, he was flipping his silver pen. John J. McCloy, on the next day, would exhibit the same mannerism. According to Bendetsen, the reports created a climate of public hostility and required that Japanese-Americans—he consistently said "Japanese"—be moved into the protective custody of relocation centers. The troops who guarded the centers, he explained, were guarding the inmates from the hostile public. Later, when asked about the policy of protecting the inmates' property with the Federal Reserve Bank, he played with his glasses until one of the lenses fell out; then he busily tried to place the lens back into its frame. He was hard to comprehend because he constantly moved away from the microphones and would push them away, as though he did not want to be heard. A staff member came forward and moved the microphones closer to him. His words were often slurred. This may have been due to his age. But to make matters worse, he often spoke with his hand to his mouth and muffled his voice.

Bendetsen used both the Philippines atrocities and the history of anti-Japanese racism on the West Coast as justifications for the program of mass exclusion and detention. He deplored such racism. He also said that he had only followed orders from higher authority. When confronted by Arthur Goldberg with his *Who's Who in America* entry in which he described himself as the chief architect of the program, he explained that he was only responsible for methods, not policy. When asked why he had dropped this description in following editions of *Who's Who in America*, he smiled his best crinkly-eyed smile and said that probably his secretary had changed it.

He aggressively rejected the term "internment" when used by Commissioner Brooke. He stated categorically that there were never any troops inside a camp—ever. (In Manzanar, a contingent of troops entered the camp, positioned themselves in front of the police station, and fired tear gas and bullets, wounding eight unarmed inmates and killing two unarmed youths. Then troops patrolled the streets of the camp in their Jeeps for two weeks.) When asked about racism, Bendetsen stoutly defended all his associates as untainted. He remained completely unrepentant.

Bendetsen's written statement included these false assertions:

I did not recommend [mass exclusion and detention] . . .

We harvested all crops; we sold them; we deposited all money to their respective accounts . . .

Under my direction, the relocation centers were built and furnished with residential equipment, bedding, beds, dressers, tables, chairs . . .

[Japanese-Americans] were not to be restricted so long as they did not seek to remain or seek to return to the war "frontier" of the West Coast.

Persons of Japanese ancestry along the western sea frontier were not interned.[1]

He concluded his written statement, with his initials written on each of its pages, by describing Franklin Delano Roosevelt as "a man of compassion and integrity" and Attorney General Francis Biddle as "a man of compassion." Of Henry Stimson, he wrote, "His place in history bespeaks his humane qualities." Of John J. McCloy, he wrote, "a man of towering stature, tolerance, compassion and discretion."

If Bendetsen were one's only source of information on this event, one might wonder what all the fuss was about. Why should there be hearings, if people were never interned but only temporarily discomforted? Lillian Baker and S. I. Hayakawa would seem reasonable in their criticism of the redress movement. According to Bendetsen's account, desolate, barbed wire enclaves with armed soldiers standing guard against dangerous inmates had never existed. There never had been racism in the Army command; the word "Japs" was never used by Franklin Delano Roosevelt, Francis Biddle, or John J. McCloy. There never had been the degradations of detention, tarpapered shacks, unpalatable food, loose bowels, boredom, and suspect loyalty.

Bendetsen failed to understand the banality of his own evil. He had lived an American life and had climbed the ladder to success. His rise through the military ranks had been meteoric: in December 1939, he had entered the Army as captain; in April 1941, he became major; ten months later he was Lieutenant Colonel; and within two more weeks he was a full Colonel. The U.S. Army had rewarded his willingness to design and implement the program of mass exclusion and detention. He had been the beneficiary of racism rather than its victim. He had played by the rules. He had been loyal to his leader. He had taken the oaths of allegiance and had agreed to defend the Constitution, so help him God. In civilian life he had risen to the top of the corporate ladder as head of Champion International. How could he have possibly been involved in an evil so monstrous, requiring reparations totaling billions of dollars? He was no criminal. The 125,000 voices had to be wrong. They simply did not understand. Not at all.

The commissioners followed Ms. Bernstein's cue and asked Bendetsen few hard questions. Commissioner Marutani was probably the toughest of the lot. He forced Bendetsen to correct a few of his obvious flaws. But Bendetsen's sweeping revision of history remained largely uncontradicted.

Bendetsen was a good soldier, faithful and loyal to the very end. Surprisingly, former Assistant Secretary of War John J. McCloy remained at the hearings throughout Bendetsen's four hours on the stand. McCloy was scheduled for the next day. Given his power and influence, his extended presence was all the more remarkable. Perhaps Karl R. and John J. were a team. Perhaps John J. was a thorough, careful man.

It had been a long morning, without a break. Finally, Bendetsen was through, and the hearings adjourned for lunch.

Edward Ennis

At 2:30, Edward Ennis began the afternoon session by announcing the position of the American Civil Liberties Union. During World War II, Ennis was Director of the Enemy Alien Control Unit of the War Division of the Department of Justice. For the past several decades he had been active with the ACLU; he was currently on the national board of directors of ACLU. According to him, the Union, as he called it, opposed the evacuation as unconstitutional then and now. While supporting monetary damages for the violation of constitutional rights, the Union does not feel it appropriate to suggest what form such compensation should take, such as whether the amount should be fixed or vary according to length of detention or whether the awards should be granted to heirs of the deceased.

Ennis's claim that the Union opposed evacuation was inaccurate. In his book, *Justice at War*, Peter Irons reveals that the ACLU was badly divided on the question of exclusion and detention. According to Irons, "personal and partisan loyalty to Franklin Roosevelt, who signed [the exclusion] order, led the ACLU's national board to bar . . . constitutional challenges [to the exclusion order.]"

Nor had the Union taken forceful positions in support of Japanese-American redress. The ACLU declined to support the Lowry Redress Bill. However, it did support the concept of monetary redress.

Like other witnesses, he had gaps in his knowledge. He seemed uninformed about the loyalty oaths. When pressed on the matter of enemy aliens in Latin America, he talked about the Germans there but seemed unaware of the Japanese.

Then he talked about the 1942 release of Italians from enemy alien status:

> [Attorney General] Biddle went to the President and said, "Ennis said—he's in charge of this—he suggests releasing the Italians." The President remarked, "My God! That's a great idea! I wish I'd thought of it. Do it." So we went to New York and had a big show with [Mayor] LaGuardia and a big party at Carnegie Hall and issued an order for the release on October 12th, Columbus Day, releasing all Italians from enemy alien status . . . right before the elections.

Father Drinan pushed Ennis on a legislative remedy:

> On the question of compensation, do you feel that some existing statute could be the model for a statute we could propose to the Congress, so that individual plaintiffs or class action suits could be brought and the Japanese that were interned could get at least nominal damages, just like the damages that were awarded by the Federal Court in the District of Columbia when 2,000 demonstrators were illegally confined? Would you give us your thoughts on the matter?
>
> I really want to follow the great legal genius of the ACLU to help frame a statute. They have been involved in cases like that. In fact, they were the prime movers in this case of the 2,000 demonstrators. . . . I would think that that frankly would be more likely to pass than a lump sum for all the people. Would you feel there would be any constitutional difficulties?

Ennis:

> Well, if Congress wants to provide a way for persons to go to court . . . I don't see any constitutional—perhaps the Justice Department would have a problem with this, that this would not be a justiciable controversy within the Constitution. We can't make the courts do administrative chores. It has to be a claims court.[2]

If, as Drinan suggested, the ACLU has legal genius, Ennis was not its best exponent of the constitutionality of a lawsuit. As our lawsuit would later demonstrate, the redress of Japanese-American grievances is "a justiciable controversy within the Constitution."

Laurence Hewes

The first day seemed very long. The last witness that day was Laurence Hewes, formerly of the Farm Security Administration. He looked like a tall farmer well-advanced in years. He described the opposition of the FSA to the evacuation. He confirmed the support and cooperation that the FSA received from the military. The FSA's task was to locate operators to run the farms that were abandoned by Japanese-American farmers as they were shipped off to assembly centers. Most farms, he reported, were under lease. He thought that Japanese-Americans were superior farmers, that many of the new operators would learn the hard way that the quality and abundance of produce was not in the land but in the farmer's skill. The task began in early 1942 and ended in August 1942, when he was glad to wash his hands of the entire matter. Despite his sympathies, he was not able to provide much information in response to questions such as how many farmers returned and similar information.

The Morning of the Second Day

John J. McCloy

On the second day of the second Washington hearings, former Supreme Court Justice Arthur Goldberg took the time to explore the many honors bestowed on John J. McCloy—"Jack" to his friends—and from among them to select and confer on McCloy the title "High Commissioner." But this was lengthy and pretentious. Except for Goldberg, the commissioners used "Mr. McCloy."[3]

Nevertheless, John J., unlike comedian Rodney Dangerfield, doesn't get no respect; he commands a lot. He was president of the World Bank; he served as U.S. High Commissioner for occupied Germany; he chaired the Chase Manhattan Bank, the Ford Foundation, and the Council on Foreign Relations. At the time of his testimony, he continued to be regarded by some as one of the ten most powerful men in the United States. He had joined David Rockefeller and Henry Kissinger in getting the Shah of Iran into a New York hospital for treatment, an event which led to the Iranian hostage crisis. He was called to testify before the Commission about his role as Assistant Secretary of War during World War II.

There was little in his behavior to give away his eighty-seven years. His movements were sure. His mind was quick. His memory was reliable. He spoke articulately. He appeared at the hearings with Adrian Fisher, an attorney and an associate from his War Department days whom he just happened to see the night before, as he explained it, and who might be able to offer additional recollections germane to the Commission's inquiry. This seemed a happy coincidence. Chairperson Bernstein invited Fisher to join McCloy at the witness table. But at one point while he was talking to the commissioners, Fisher referred to McCloy as his client. McCloy, on the previous day, had privately complained to the commissioners that the hearings were adversarial; McCloy had come prepared.

Ironically, the former U.S. High Commissioner for occupied Germany defended America's benign and humane concentration camps. McCloy protested the use of the term "incarceration," when used by Commissioner Marutani. He disputed the existence of racism in any officials. He argued that an apology was inappropriate. He rejected compensatory redress out of hand. He argued that many suffered during the war. The camps were simply one of many occurrences of the war. One wondered if McCloy had not learned from the many German war criminals whose sentences he had shortened during his tenure as High Commissioner.

When Commissioner Marutani raised the question about the possibility of racism, McCloy responded:

> I didn't see the slightest suggestion. Mr. Stimson was a man of great integrity, you know who—he's the man who saved the town of Kyoto from bombing. He was as compassionate, as thorough a statesman I know. He couldn't possibly decide this thing on racial grounds.

Marutani wasn't buying and persisted:

> What other Americans, Mr. McCloy, shared in the war by having their mothers, fathers, grandfathers, younger brothers and sisters incarcerated during the war?

Without hesitation McCloy replied:

> Lots of Americans. I saw what was done, the solicitude extended. I don't think the Japanese population was unduly subjected, considering all the exigencies to which—the amount it did share in the way of retribution for the attack that was made on Pearl Harbor.

What was that word? Dead silence in the room. "Retribution." The word hung in the air. Marutani quickly asked the stenotypist to read back the words just recorded. The stenotypist may have had a sense of the dramatic moment. Or perhaps he was not certain of his transcription. He decided to playback the audio recording he was making of the entire hearing. It took a little jockeying of the recorder to find the exact spot. Then we heard it again:

> I don't think the Japanese population was unduly subjected, considering the exigencies to which—the amount it did share in the way of retribution for the attack . . .

McCloy quickly interjected:

> I think "retribution" is wrong.

The tape continued:

> . . . that was made on Pearl Harbor.

Marutani closed in warily:

> Do I understand your statement that because of what the Japanese did at Pearl Harbor, what happened to the Japanese-Americans here was fair or it was not retribution?

McCloy amended the record:

> I don't think I like to use the word "retribution" in connection with it. I say "consequences."

Perhaps McCloy had made a Freudian slip and Marutani properly had allowed McCloy to correct this intrusion of his subconscious. But later, when answering a question by the CWRIC special counsel, Angus MacBeth, McCloy made himself quite clear:

> Within ninety miles of our shores [there are] a hundred, roughly a hundred thousand people, thoroughly trained, thoroughly equipped, well trained in modern warfare, that are being set up to serve as proxies for the Soviet Union in the various strategic parts of the world. Suppose there was a raid some ten, twenty, thirty years hence on [Florida], wouldn't you be apt to think about moving [Cuban-Americans] if there was a raid there? You can't tell.

McCloy was the best witness for the government. He had the credentials. In addition to his chairmanships, he had "befriended and advised nine Presidents, from Franklin Roosevelt to Ronald Reagan."[4] He was no kook. He showed no partiality against Japanese-Americans; he'd just as easily have it done to Cuban-Americans. He made it clear that the mass exclusion and detention of Japanese-Americans was a military decision. He'd do it again regardless of news media sensationalism, popular racism, panicky members of Congress, or an especially racist Lieutenant General.

Even as McCloy confirmed the rationale for the government's action, he revealed the racism that infected the leaders of government. His suspicions of "Jap" disloyalty continued into 1981. Angus MacBeth asked:

> Wouldn't it be fair to say, looking at the 442nd and general history of the war, it was the overwhelming history of loyalty to this country on behalf of Japanese aliens and citizens?

McCloy replied:

> I think some of them—if [the Battle of] Midway had been lost—ah, there might have been some who were pledging allegiance to the other side.

Later Mike Masaoka would object to this veiled attack on the loyalty of the 442nd. He would be interrupted by Commissioner Brooke, who seemed to remember that MacBeth's question, while specifying the 442nd, also included Japanese aliens. But McCloy, in speaking, never made the distinction between "Japanese," which he preferred, and "Japanese-American," which he did not trouble himself to use. He hadn't bothered to exclude members of the 442nd from his expressed suspicion.

McCloy's testimony lasted four hours, extending from morning into afternoon. McCloy had had the good sense to ask for a break at midmorning. Otherwise, his testimony would have been a test of endurance. Even so, it was one o'clock before the hearings adjourned for lunch. When Jack Herzig and I arrived at the cafeteria, there was still half an hour before nonemployees of the Senate were supposed to be allowed to use the cafeteria, but we entered without challenge.

The Afternoon of the Second Day

The Washington hearings had gone through the important testimony of Karl R. Bendetsen and John J. McCloy, chief architect and primary decision-maker, respectively. The two men of power had stood against the tide of 700 victims who had testified to the injustices suffered, the deprivation inflicted, the shame and heartbreak endured. Bendetsen and McCloy proclaimed that their program was comprised of humane treatment, compassion, solicitude, and the absence of racism. The two stood firmly against the victims' demand for compensatory redress. The two opposed even an apology. It was truly unfortunate that the large audiences of earlier hearings had dwindled. The few victims who did attend were disabused of any hope for a Confucian sense of moral obligation among the perpetrators; the War Department in its momentary reincarnation possessed no heavenly mandate. On Tuesday afternoon, lesser characters testified, providing no denouement, only a reverberation of subplots from the WRA, Census Bureau, and JACL.

Philip M. Glick

The final session was to have begun with Calvert L. Dedrick, but he could not be found. So Philip M. Glick, Solicitor for the War Relocation Authority, began. As Solicitor, Glick was the chief legal authority for the WRA. We had met earlier during the luncheon break. Jack Herzig had found him in line and invited him to join us at our table. He was a friendly man. He was without pretentions and had an orderly manner of thought and speech. He spoke in grammatically correct sentences—a quality lacking in most persons, especially noticed when one is transcribing the spoken to the written word. As we shared our recollections, Glick spoke of the desire of the WRA to close the camps and of the internees' opposition. He explained that the internees had become institutionalized. I disagreed. He seemed genuinely surprised when I told him of the difficulty of starting a new life with just twenty-five dollars, especially if one had a family to shelter and feed. Hadn't he known about this pittance? He also reported that the WRA was dismayed by the loyalty oaths, a term he cautioned me against. He did not know where the oaths came from. So I related my reading of the Earl Warren Oral History Project's two-volume segment entitled, "Japanese-American Relocation Revisited," and of WRA director Dillon Myer's interview in which Myer said that while he was opposed to segregation of "disloyals," he was outvoted by the project directors of the ten camps. "Didn't this suggest that segregation and the loyalty oath came from within the WRA?" I explained. In his testimony, the same sort of question was put to Glick, and he responded:

> I have never been able to find out who in the Federal government prepared the questionnaire containing questions 27 and 28 . . . I don't know. I asked Mr. Myer. I've asked Rex Lee, who was in charge of our relocation office. . . . None of them knows. . . . My recollection was that the Justice Department had distributed it, and that I was angry at the Justice Department for not having cleared this with us in advance. But I have been told since that the Justice Department denies that they prepared the questionnaire.

After the hearings, I learned that the loyalty oath had been drafted by the U.S. Army.

Glick's testimony seemed straightforward and sympathetic. He described the goals of the WRA as:

(1) bringing work to the relocation centers;

(2) persuading the military to reestablish the military draft for Japanese-Americans;

(3) persuading the military to "reopen the excluded areas and allow evacuees to return to their homes"; and

(4) closing the relocation centers.

But these policies were not as benign as he said they were. When he described the leave clearance program, for example, he suggested that all that was required was a place to live and a job. He omitted reference to the Japanese American Joint Board, comprised of representatives from the WRA, the Provost Marshal General's Office, and Army and Naval Intelligence. The Board's purpose was to run security checks on all U.S. citizens requesting leave. He also omitted reference to the lengthy leave clearance questionnaire with more than eighty questions, requiring disclosure of personal, political, religious and ethical preferences and beliefs.

Glick's account of constitutional challenges to exclusion and detention is at odds with historic facts. He spoke sympathetically about the constitutional test case of Mitsuye Endo:

> [Mitsuye Endo] and her lawyers were operating with calm intelligence. They had decided she was the perfect plaintiff in a suit to challenge the constitutionality of detention.
>
> So I issued written instructions to the Project Attorney that they were to take no step whatever to interfere with the prosecution of the Mitsuye Endo case.

Emphasizing this point, Glick continued:

> You see, we were very much concerned that even our efforts in persuading her to leave, to give her a permit after she filed suit, could be misinterpreted as a move to checkmate or check the evacuees at every step, if they tried to short-circuit the detention process.

Peter Irons, in his book *Justice at War* reports a different version of Glick's efforts. He describes attorney James Purcell's first and only meeting with his client Mitsuye Endo:

> Purcell met his client only once during the entire course of her case, during an interrogation conducted by WRA solicitor Philip Glick, who offered to release her from internment in return for an agreement that she would not return to the "restricted area" of the West Coast, which included all of California. Despite this offer to escape from internment, made as part of the government's effort to avoid a Supreme Court test of its powers to detain Japanese Americans, Endo refused to abandon her legal challenge and remained behind barbed wire for another two years.

Had Glick, in fact, tried to make moot Endo's legal challenge to her illegal internment? Was Glick now attempting to rewrite history and place himself in a sympathetic role?

Calvert Dedrick

Calvert Dedrick was next. He had been waiting since the day before. He had been present during the Bendetsen and McCloy testimonies. I saw him nodding in agreement with their statements. His testimony made vocal his silent assents. He had been a statistician for the Census Bureau. During an early phase of exclusion and detention, he had been temporarily transferred from the Census Bureau to the military's Western Defense Command. He arrived on the West Coast on February 27, 1942. He proceeded to create what he described as a war room, with maps showing where the Japanese—he never used "Japanese-Americans"—lived. His basic source of information, which he brought with him, was a duplicate set of punched cards which contained Census Bureau data for about 130,000 persons of Japanese ancestry.

(The mechanical processing of these cards took a long time. Just sorting 100 million cards took many machine-years. By the end of 1941, the Census Bureau had managed to sort the cards by race, but not by national origin. To the Census Bureau, Japanese-Americans were the "Japanese race.")

He consistently mentioned that these duplicate cards were never turned over to the War Department. When the Wartime Civil Control Agency (WCCA) was formed in March, he was placed there under the command of Colonel Karl R. Bendetsen. The commissioners questioned Dedrick closely, but they failed to penetrate his defenses. He remained an employee of the Census Bureau after his transfer. In this way his access to the duplicate cards during his temporary assignment with the WCCA would not violate the letter of the law. According to Dedrick, only tabulations from the cards were released to the WCCA.

This subterfuge is like handing over to an enemy a scientist who knows how to make an atomic bomb with the claim that atomic secrets were not being disclosed to the enemy. That scientist would never release the secret of the bomb; he would merely provide instructions for processes and assemblies, resulting in the construction of an atomic bomb.

This was a delicate matter. The law forbids the Census Bureau from releasing its information on individuals and families to other government agencies. The issue was made particularly delicate by the 1980 census, in which the Census Bureau's television advertisements had assured Americans of the confidentiality of census information by referring to the Bureau's staunch refusal to hand over the records of Japanese-Americans in 1942. This assurance of census confidentiality was challenged by Raymond Okamura in the press and by John Toland in his book, *Infamy*.

Marutani clarified the legal restrictions by quoting the law:

> ". . . in no case shall information furnished under authority of this chapter be used to the detriment of the person or persons to whom such information relates."

But Dedrick had a response:

> That, sir, has special reference. Our attorneys at the Bureau of Census have since informed me that [that] relates to age search and other special tabulations which are purchased [from] the Bureau of Census by, say, J. Walter Thompson or an attorney. Many attorneys seek to get information for a client about that client's brother, when the client is suing a brother. And that provision of the law that you are now quoting says that we may not furnish that information which would be detrimental to that person.

Dedrick's obfuscation of "special reference" didn't fool Marutani. The commissioner tried reducing Dedrick's reasoning to an absurdity:

> Well, as I understand it, then, your solicitors have advised you that this language [of the law] means . . . that [if] A wishes to sue B you can't get information, but, on the other hand, if X wishes to incarcerate 112,000 people, you can get the information. Is that the advice that your solicitors gave you?

Dedrick rejected the absurdity by feigning ignorance:

> This matter did not come up before our solicitors at that time, I'm sure.

But, of course, Dedrick did admit to having in his possession one card for each individual of the Japanese race. He did admit to identifying where Japanese-Americans lived down to a city block. His tabulations were performed for the WCCA, whose specific purpose and intent was to exclude and detain all persons of Japanese ancestry. Though legally employed by the Census Bureau, he did his tabulations while ensconced in the WCCA, under the command of Colonel Bendetsen. It would be too much to expect confession from Dedrick. What remains inexplicable is the Census Bureau's 1980 use of this gross violation of the law as a public example of census confidentiality.

Mike Masaoka

Since the other witnesses of these hearings were persons who shaped the wartime events, the testimony of Mari and James Michener seemed out of place. Their words were not unlike those of the 700 who had spoken in other cities. Perhaps their presence was meant as prologue to the final witness, Mike Masaoka. However, there had already been a prologue of sorts at the beginning of the day with the distribution of a document submitted by NCJAR. The document consisted of an NCJAR cover letter, an 18-page letter written on April 6, 1942, by JACL National Secretary Masaoka to WRA Director Milton Eisenhower, and Frank Chin's 11-page CWRIC testimony of September 9, 1981.

Mike Masaoka began his testimony by waving this document in the air and saying:

> Some of you may have received a document as you came inside the door. I would like to have the privilege of commenting on this—not only for the record but for the information of the Commission. This purports to be a message from the NCJAR. And it says that it is public knowledge that the Commission was conceived by me. This is not true.

Masaoka credited the commission idea to one of the five Japanese-American members of Congress. He was partly correct. In January 1979, the JACL's National Committee for Redress met with the four Democratic Japanese-American members. Senator Inouye proposed a commission. But at that time, the commission was viewed as a device for determining the method of payment. The idea of a commission as a fact-finding body came later, at a March 1979 meeting of the National Committee for Redress, from Masaoka and Kaz Oshiki.

In the October 1981 issue of *Borderline,* a newsletter of the San Diego Chapter of the JACL, Kaz Oshiki wrote "A Response to Bill Hohri," which stated:

> Bill is correct, however, in stating that Mike Masaoka and I originated the Commission approach to the redress issue.

I had written the statement, to which Oshiki responded, based upon audio tapes of the March 1979 meeting.

Masaoka continued with an attack on NCJAR:

> [The] point is this: if the public knowledge which this Council purports to have is as unreliable and [inaccurate] as what they say about the conception of this Commission, I would suggest that the Commission take another look at it.

Unfortunately no one was allowed to challenge Masaoka. He was there in response to a specific request that Dr. James Tsujimura, president of the JACL, made during the Seattle hearings. Tsujimura and the JACL wanted Masaoka to rebut the statement of Frank Chin at the Seattle hearings. I thought this favoring by the CWRIC of one group over others was unfair and misleading. Without the debate essential to the democratic process, Masaoka's accusation of dishonesty against NCJAR remained valid in the minds of the commissioners.

Instead of responding to Frank Chin's charges, Masaoka criticized the Lowry Redress Bill in a manner similiar to the attack he made before the House Committee in June 1980. When he did respond to Chin, Masaoka's defense was ad hominem and functional, not substantive:

> Let me say also that the accusations made against me personally and against the JACL organization read like a fantastic movie scenario that some playwright decided to write. And he selected and chose some words out of context, if you will, in certain places to create his fantasy. He certainly didn't produce all the facts that are available in order to create the imaginative climax that he wanted for his drama.

I say for the record, and I repeat, not once has this Mr. Chin, who testified in Seattle, talked to me about any of the events to which he refers, nor have any of the officers of these various organizations who are now questioning what the JACL did. We in JACL point to the status of Japanese Americans today as vindication of our wartime leadership, emphasizing then and now [that] none have come up, even today, with more viable alternatives.

This again is an abuse, not the practice, of democratic debate. Chin's charges could have been criticized point by point. And had Chin been invited to rebut, the commissioners might have been enlightened. Instead, Masaoka rambled on and on. And as he did, his credibility seemed to ebb. It was getting late, almost six o'clock. But there was merciful intervention. The stenotypist announced that he was using his last audio tape. The hearings were forced to a close. Just before they did, Commissioner Brooke entered a document for the record—a memorandum dated May 13, 1944, from the Chief of Staff George C. Marshall to John J. McCloy:

I have gone over your memorandum of May 8th concerning the return of persons of Japanese ancestry to the West Coast and related papers. In my opinion the only valid military objection to this move is the one presented by G-1 that the return of these people to the West Coast will result in actions of violence that will react to the disadvantage of American prisoners in the hands of the Japanese. There are, of course, strong political reasons why the Japanese should not be returned to the West Coast before next November, but these do not concern the Army except to the degree that consequent reactions might cause embarrassing incidents.

The introduction of the memorandum is the work of two adventurous staff persons, Aiko Herzig and Donna Komure. As a result of their pluck, "failed political leadership" became one of three causes cited by the Commission for the wartime events.

20. HEARINGS
NEW YORK HEARINGS

The hearings in New York were held in response to pressures from Japanese-Americans there. They were the final field hearings of testimony from victims. There were two subsequent hearings: one on legal issues, and the other on socio-psychological effects. The New York hearings were held at the Hotel Roosevelt on a single day, Monday, November 23, 1984. In the absence of both the chairperson and vice-chairperson Arthur Flemming served as chairperson. Again, this was a hearing that I could not attend, so my description is based on my reading of the transcripts. The pace of this hearing seemed far less hurried and pressured than any of the other field hearings. Testimony in New York described the arrests of Japanese-Americans there, an organized resistance to the military draft, the individual exclusion of an American not of Japanese descent, and the treatment of American civilians in Japan.

John Coventry Smith

John Coventry Smith had been president of the World Council of Churches and vice president of the National Council of Churches. He had also been a civilian internee in Japan, one of the 10,000 American civilians who were in Japanese hands early in the war. His account of his treatment was illuminating:

> I think I have great sympathy also for the Issei, the first generation that came to the United States. They were enemy aliens as I was an enemy alien in Japan. We were each covered by the Geneva Convention. Japan had said at the last minute that she would abide by the Geneva Convention. [The Issei] had people from the Spanish Embassy; we had people from the Swiss Embassy in Japan.
>
> We were hungry, and we were cold, but so were the Japanese police. We had the same food and the same shelter and the same lack of heat that the Japanese police had. But we didn't have property taken away from us. Some of the people, later, after they had left Japan and were exchanged, [had] their property...taken over by the Alien Enemy Property Commission. But while we were in the camp and could have access to our homes to get things, all of our property belonged to us. In fact—you will be surprised—at the end of the winter, I was able to sell the furniture in our house in Tokyo through a cook and a lawyer to a secondhand dealer. I got three times as much as I had expected I would get for this secondhand property. I had enough to pay my cook and her expenses and to share some of the funds with people, who did not have enough in the camp, and to bring some of it home in American dollars when I finally got here. Much different from the way these people on the West Coast were treated.[1]

The experiences of Americans in Japanese hands must be heard in order to judge the quality of care received by Japanese-Americans. Japanese-Americans who were in Japan—even though they, too, were enemy aliens— were not interned.

Howard Spragg

Howard Spragg was instrumental in obtaining $7,500 from the United Church Board for Homeland Ministries (UCBHM) to help NCJAR pay for the cost of mounting a class action lawsuit. This was the only institutional grant we sought and received. Aiko Herzig had asked Spragg to act on our behalf; she had once worked for Spragg on the UCBHM. (Also Spragg had been pastor at the South Congregational Church on Chicago's South Side from 1943 to 1948. That was one of the few churches that welcomed Japanese-Americans during resettlement.) Spragg made this comment about liberals and progressives:

> I might say that in those days many of the liberals and many of the progressives to whom we as churchmen looked for support—[we] were surprised that it was not forthcoming. Along with the churches, there were very few voices raised against this disaster. As a churchman—if I may be permitted some expression of pride for my own church and the other Protestant groups particularly—I take this opportunity to say that, at least in that instance, there was some measure not only of confession but of active and alive testimony dealing with a great injustice to these people.

Jack Tono

Jack Tono was part of the Heart Mountain draft resistance movement which culminated in the trial of sixty-three young men in the Cheyenne federal court. Although several hundred men refused induction while they were interned, the Heart Mountain group was unique because it was organized. I first met Tono at a meeting in Chicago following the second Washington CWRIC hearings, a meeting where Frank Chin discussed his views of the redress movement. Chin was particularly welcomed because of his critical report on the Los Angeles hearings, which he had characterized as "A Circus of Freaks." Just as the meeting was closing, Tono got up and said he had some words to say. He told of his experience as a draft resister and about the problems the resisters had with the JACL. Following his statement, he was applauded and warmly greeted by those present. He, too, was officially invited to testify by the CWRIC. The only remaining hearing was New York. He said:

> I am one of the handful which I consider of a different breed of men. We are that group of guys who refused the Selective Service Draft in 1944 from Heart Mountain, Wyoming. Going back to our faithful [sic], or shall I say unfaithful [sic] days, of April third and fourth of 1944: it was roundup day for the FBI. The whole haul netted sixty-three of us. After the usual routine procedure, we were separated to various county jails, namely, Cheyenne, Laramie, and Casper, Wyoming. The [last] was my temporary quarters until the trial. We spent two-plus months at the county jail. In the meantime, the families obtained the services of the American Civil Liberties Union, and the "man of the hour" was Mr. Wirin, attorney, who represented us at the trial.

> Today, when everything in life is back to normal, the atmosphere is relaxed and ordinary. But back in 1944, this was the dark hour of our country, more so for us Niseis. Every turn of our head was of a suspicious nature. . . . to tackle the task such as ours, I shall never forget the Union for their gutsy services. My admiration and esteem for the organization is beyond what I can relate in words. Others have left us high and dry: mainly the Japanese American Citizens League. We were expecting this group to give us their full support, but instead [they] turned their back on us. To this day, I still feel the knife in the back.

> A day or so before the trial, the Japanese American Citizens League surprised us with a visit from their VIPs. Their main purpose was to get us to change our minds about resisting the draft. Some of the comments made to us were:

We were doing an injustice to the men in uniform.

In time of war, we have to do our part in supporting the Government.

If you go to prison, you'll get beat up with a two-by-four.

[They were] just scare tactics.

The two men who visited the resisters were Joe Grant Masaoka and Minoru Yasui of the JACL. Following their visit, Masaoka and Yasui wrote a report for the FBI. Tono jumped to the future for a moment to continue his discussion of the difficulties that the JACL made for the draft resisters after they had gone to prison, served time, and became eligible for parole:

> The parole officer at the prison received a letter stating that there was an organization against our release for parole. They felt that if we were let off easy, many others would follow. So, our parole was denied.

> One of the boys worked as a clerk in the office, so the information wasn't just rumor. Our great war hero, Kuroki, labeled us "fascist" in the Wyoming newspaper. For all of these two-faced coins we have the appropriate phrase: "the yellow Uncle Toms." We were a thorn in their sides.

Tono then switched back to trial:

> Finally, after spending two-plus months in the county jail, our trial date came about. The exact date has escaped me, but I believe the trial started after the 15th of June 1944 in Cheyenne, Wyoming. Looking back to the first day of our trial, we were men of many emotions. This was the first time in our lives we were being tried as felons, not knowing what to expect because of the conditions of that time. We expected the book to be thrown at us.

> The trial started by the prosecuting attorney stating that this group has violated the law by not going for our physical examinations. Then and there we knew our goose was cooked. But we were determined to pursue our righteous principles and let the nation know of our feelings. The trial lasted about a week. All we wanted was our natural-born rights returned, not the arm and leg of the Government—simply the restoration of our livelihood . . . to the prewar days and our families leading the normal lives they once had. Then and only then will we bear arms for our country to preserve democracy as President Roosevelt has often stated.

At this point, one should remember Elmer Davis's words to President Roosevelt when he recommended an all-volunteer combat unit of Japanese-Americans:

It would hardly be fair to evacuate people and then impose normal draft procedures, but voluntary enlistment would help a lot[2] (emphasis added).

Unfortunately, the U.S. Attorney in charge of prosecuting this case, Carl L. Sackett, had a considerably different view of conscription of concentration camp inmates. The report of Masaoka and Yasui includes this description of Sackett's opinions:

> Mr. Sackett was firm in declaring that the Nisei draft violators had full opportunity to discuss their decision beforehand, and to be prepared to accept the full consequences

of their act. To his way of thinking, Mr. Sackett averred that by refusing to comply with the draft, these boys were a detriment to the war effort and are sabotaging this country in the present war. He stated that he had more respect for the man who would declare his loyalty to another country openly. He believed that these boys were merely exploiting the matter of this "protest refusal" as a cover, pretext, and excuse; that the Nisei had been claiming unqualified loyalty and allegiance to the United States of America, but that when they were given an opportunity to demonstrate their loyalty, they had come out into the open regarding their real loyalties.[3]

From the U.S. Attorney's perspective, what was at issue here was not constitutional or civil rights; what was at issue was the loyalty of Japanese-Americans. Without blind allegiance to the United States, Japanese-Americans must be loyal to Japan. One-third of the eligible male population of Hawaiian Japanese-Americans had volunteered for combat. By an extension of Sackett's reckoning, the remaining two-thirds were disloyal to the United States and loyal to Japan. One was not even permitted to share Elmer Davis's doubt about the propriety of drafting men from detention camps. To doubt was to be disloyal. The resisters never knew how stacked against them the deck was. The JACL strongly opposed draft resistance. In their memo to the FBI, Masaoka and Yasui went so far as to recommend solitary confinement:

> It seems too that the incarceration of these boys in one group bolsters and inspirits each other. Anyone of the group who might be inclined to doubt the wisdom of their conduct would be quashed by the arguments expressed to us: "We're in this far; we might as well see this through." Those who might want to change their minds, convinced of the error of their ways, would probably not be tolerated. *For these reasons, separate and individual cells would allow considerable introspection and self-analysis*. It would supplant individual decision for group pressure[4] (emphasis added).

What really undercut the U.S. Attorney's statements and those of the JACL was the price that the resisters willingly paid. Tono explained:

> We had men with bleeding ulcers, high blood pressure, and other ailments, which were all 4-F material. So, to them, medical deferment was the easy road out. But we were all in the belief of our righteous principles taught in our history classes, and we stuck together. The main purpose of our protest in time of war was to right the wrong which has been done to us Japanese Americans.

> After the trial, we were sentenced to three years in the federal penitentiary, on or about the 25th of July 1944. A total of 33 men under the age of 25 were sent to McNeil Island Federal Penitentiary, and the remaining 30 were sent to Fort Leavenworth, Kansas.

Tono ended his testimony on a note of pride:

> Looking back at those 37 years, we were really ahead of our time. The society of the sixties protested; modern day society is proclaiming their civil rights; but we, the "silent majority," contested with honor. Our homework from elementary school days was not done in vain; we didn't forget. And I must honestly say the 112 men truly treasured their citizenship and being men of the different breed.

Commissioner Marutani asked Tono a question which seemed to reveal Marutani's ignorance of the role of Minoru Yasui as one of the JACL representatives who tried to change the minds of the resisters in the Cheyenne jail:

Would [the act of resistance] be somewhat similar or akin to what Yasui and Hirabayashi did? They violated the law as well.

Tono seemed taken aback by the reference to Yasui:

Well, Yasui—I mean—I am very familiar with Gordon [Hirabayashi] because we were at the same joint and—well, this is our con language.

It was another instance of the JACL's past obstructing a sincere effort today to heal the differences and wounds of the past.

Karl Akiya

Karl Akiya testified on behalf of the Kibei as a class of persons who were unfairly treated and stigmatized:

I was born in San Francisco in 1909, and I am Nisei but was sent to Japan, when I was a child, to be educated and then to return to the United States. And we call that Kibei. To define that name "Kibei," it is that "Ki" means return and "bei" means the United States.

He then talked about returning to the U.S. in 1931 to escape the Japanese military draft and his organizing of Kibei for furthering their Americanization, at first independently, then within the JACL. Then he discussed the aftermath of Pearl Harbor:

Right after Pearl Harbor, I remember receiving a visit from a certain person in Navy Intelligence. The reason was for me to cooperate with them. I do not know how they were able to contact me. Of course, I replied that I would cooperate.

First of all, I was shown a list of Issei people, of which I recognized some—whom I knew personally. I couldn't believe my eyes. One of the listed was a member of the Japanese Association, another, a member of the prefecture association, and another a member of another organization. However, I had never known of any action that these people had taken which could be considered as being anti-American.

At this point, following Pearl Harbor, I had been informed that all the leaders of the Japanese community had been arrested by the FBI and had been taken away some place. The Government was probably trying to find some subversive elements in the general Japanese Issei group. I felt somewhat uncomfortable. My idea of loyalty to America did not mean that I should conduct my activities of this nature. I realized that because of the war there was increased suspicion against the Japanese. I saw that I should protect the Japanese as a whole, that this is not just a matter of the individuals; therefore, I made up my mind to sever all connections with this.

Then, after expressing his surprise at the mass exclusion and detention of citizens and aliens alike, he proceeded to describe the discriminatory treatment accorded Issei and Kibei in the camps:

Today I will speak of the particular treatment of Kibei and Issei. Throughout, the camp administration was exceptionally prejudiced toward the Issei and Kibei. The Kibei were looked upon as the center of the camp violence. They were considered dangerous and

175

un-American, loyal only to the Japanese government, not to the U.S. government. Many were isolated as dangerous elements. It is my contention that the bitterness of the Kibei toward the United States was rooted not in the Kibei being un-American but the forced, illegal evacuation and incarceration of the Japanese American citizen.

The Issei and Kibei were not allowed to take a leadership position within the camp's self-government, which was only allowed to the Americanized Nisei. At both Tanforan and Topaz . . . I insisted upon the necessity of the leaders of the Nisei and Kibei participation. But this was not realized at all.

As I read Akiya's statement, I wondered whether he was familiar with the position the JACL's Anti-Axis Committee had taken respecting Kibei. According to an FBI memorandum dated January 20, 1942, the JACL's Anti-Axis Committee came to the Los Angeles Field Division Office and discussed, among other things, the Kibei:

According to several individual members of the J. A. C. L., the most dangerous group in the Japanese Colony in this country is the Kibei, those American-born Japanese who, at an early age, were sent to Japan for their education. In Los Angeles there has been established in the J. A. C. L. a group known as the Kibei Division. This division has about 200 members, holds its own meetings, and publishes a monthly magazine known as "SHINNIN NO TOMO." Issues of this magazine for the past two years have been obtained and are being examined by translators of this office. The articles appearing therein are written by Kibei in Japanese and appear to be strongly pro-Japan.

According to officials of the Japanese American Citizens League, there are also Kibei Divisions located at San Francisco, California, and Seattle, Washington, that in San Francisco being known as Dai Nippon Seinen Kai (The Greater Japanese Youth Association.) A complete list of the members of the Kibei Division of the Los Angeles Japanese American Citizens League was obtained by this office, and a similar list is being secured from the San Pedro Chapter.

William Kochiyama

William Kochiyama was virtually a native New Yorker. He was born in Washington, D.C., but moved to New York as an infant with his father and had lived there ever since. As he said, "Not surprisingly, I grew up believing I was a white, Anglo-Saxon Protestant." He was caught on the West Coast while trying to work his way into college there. He described his entrance into his first detention camp:

On May 6, 1942—four days before my twenty-first birthday—I entered Tanforan Assembly Center in San Bruno, where most of the Japanese in the San Francisco Bay area were incarcerated. At the entrance of the converted race track stood two long lines of troops with rifles and fixed bayonets pointed at the evacuees as they walked between the soldiers to the prison compound. Overwhelmed with bitterness and blind with rage, I screamed every obscenity I knew at the armed guards, daring them to shoot me.

This exceptional behavior, this act of brassy defiance which sharply contrasted with typical West Coast Nisei behavior, may be attributed to his growing up thinking of himself as white, as a first-class rather than a second-class citizen. Similarly, several leaders of resistance in the camps, Harry Ueno, Joe Kurihara, and Kiyoshi Okamoto, came from Hawaii, where there was far less racism directed against Japanese-Americans. Kochiyama also benefited from attending the two Washington hearings and said:

According to Colonel Karl R. Bendetsen, the chief architect of the evacuation scam, the soldiers, the weapons, the barbed wire, and the watchtowers were there to protect us.

Hogwash!

Kochiyama, like others, demolished the notion of protective detention. He continued:

At Tanforan I lived in a horse stall with two other young men who had no family ties. There we lingered until September 16, 1942. On that day we boarded ancient trains for parts unknown. Several days later, we arrived in central Utah. Situated in a desert, the stalag-looking camp was named Topaz, an obscene misnomer.

Kochiyama was refreshingly candid about one reason he volunteered for combat:

On January 7, 1943, I volunteered for the 442nd Regimental Combat Team. Next day, I was riding a freedom train to New York.

He then described his return to New York:

In New York I was reunited with my father after two and one-half years of separation. He told me that soon after the outbreak of the war, every Issei in the metropolitan area had been visited and investigated by the FBI. I also learned that some permanent resident Japanese were taken into custody by Federal agents and police and whisked off to Ellis Island. A number of them were subsequently sent to Justice Department internment camps located in isolated parts of the United States. To this day, few of these victims will speak of their experiences of wartime captivity.

Although most New Yorkers of Japanese ancestry did not suffer overt prejudice during the war years, the city and its surrounding regions were not spared the cancer of racism. For example, New York City's liberal Mayor Fiorello H. LaGuardia and New Jersey's Governor Walter E. Edge strongly opposed the resettlement of Japanese evacuees on the eastern seaboard—be they American citizens or not.

Kochiyama then made a much needed response to the incredible charge made by John J. McCloy at the second Washington hearings:

Returning to my personal experiences, from June 16, 1943 to December 30, 1945, I served as a rifleman with Company K, 442nd Infantry Regiment. In France in one action alone while we were effecting the rescue of the "Lost Battalion," my company suffered 90% casualties. Only 23 men remain unscathed, and I was among the traumatized survivors.

I had not intended to dwell on the exploits of the 442nd, but when I heard John J. McCloy, the former Assistant Secretary of War, allege that if the Battle of Midway had been lost, some of us Nisei might have pledged our allegiance to the other side—McCloy's opposition tore through me like a dum-dum bullet. For the record, I bitterly resent his assumption and categorically deny that some of us would have become turncoats.

After Kochiyama had completed his testimony, Commissioner Marutani asked, "Mr. Kochiyama, I wonder if there's a distinction between recognizing past wrongs and dwelling on past wrongs?" It was an oblique question. Did Marutani think Kochiyama's testimony ascerbic, angry, too un-Nisei-like? Was there a subtle conflict here between a West Coast and East Coast Nisei? Kochiyama replied, "I don't think I dwell on past wrongs." Marutani countered, "I'm not suggesting you are." To which Kochiyama, probably confused by this switch, said, "I see." Then to really confuse matters, Marutani confessed, "All of us may to some degree, including myself." Marutani failed to provide a verb: to some degree what?

Colonel De Guttadauro

Colonel De Guttadauro began the afternoon's testimonies. His testimony is unique because it described the individual exclusion order given to his father, a naturalized Italian-American citizen:

> In 1942 he received an order dated 1 September 1942 to appear before an Individual Exclusion Board [hearing], which was to be held on 8 September 1942[. It was issued] by Headquarters, Western Defense Command and Fourth Army. The order stated, . . . "Material in the hands of the Board will not be made available for your inspection," and further that my father's counsel, if he had one, would "not be heard by the Board nor be permitted to examine witnesses."

> The result of the Board was that an Individual Exclusion Order was signed by Lieutenant General DeWitt on 23 September 1942 and gave my father two days to remove himself from various parts of the territory of the continental United States, which was 20 states and prohibited zones in another nine states. So, in fact, it excluded an American citizen from living in over half of the United States.

> The result was that my father had to immediately leave California. He went as far as Cheyenne, Salt Lake City. He was 44 at the time, trying to find work. He was an accountant, and because of the Exclusion Order, he was unable to find work in his profession.

> The Exclusion Order was finally cancelled on 13 March 1944. At that time, my father returned to San Francisco in an attempt to take up his profession again.

In response to a question, the Colonel further explained:

> We stayed behind. We could stay behind in California. We were not excluded; it was only my father.

De Guttadauro's testimony reveals several differences between the treatment accorded individual excludees and the mass excludees and detainees. Both types of exclusion were the result of EO9066. His father had a hearing, however limited it may have been. He was not detained. He remained free in the interior states. His family was not required to move. Of course, even this form of exclusion was unconstitutional. The Department of Justice thought that individual exclusion was unconstitutional and thus refused to arrest and prosecute violators of individual exclusion orders. As Attorney General Francis Biddle said in his letter to President Roosevelt:

> I shall not institute criminal proceedings on exclusion orders which seem to me unconstitutional.

Biddle refers here to two specific cases of individual exclusion. He presses home his point:

> You signed the original Executive Order permitting exclusions so the Army could handle the Japs. It was never intended to apply to Italians and Germans.[5]

In late 1943, after 254 individual exclusion orders had been issued, the issuance of such orders ceased because of legal action. According to De Guttadauro, the orders were cancelled on March 13, 1944. Had military necessity ceased to exist by then? In January 1945, immediately after the rescission of mass exclusion and when the cessation of military necessity in the Western Defense Command was officially announced, thousands of individual exclusion orders were issued for Japanese-Americans in Tule Lake and elsewhere, but without even the minimal legal procedures De Guttadauro's father received. The revived exclusion orders demonstrated the government's double standard on constitutional rights.

Kinichi Iwamoto

The New York hearings provided the additional perspective of the experiences of Japanese-Americans on the East Coast during World War II. Kinichi Iwamoto was an Issei doctor who was rounded up in the hours following Japan's attack at Pearl Harbor:

Shortly before midnight on December 7, 1941, FBI, led by local detectives, took me to the local police station. There were a dozen or more Japanese gathered there, and the FBI took us to the Federal Court at Foley Square in his Buick limousine. We were arraigned, fingerprinted, and photographed with a number hanging from our neck. I was one of the first 20 Japanese who were shipped to Ellis Island on a small government boat. Outside of the cabin door I saw a soldier standing. I could see his rifle and bayonet through the darkness.

At Ellis Island, I felt the food was adequate, rooms were comfortably heated, but the living quarters were overcrowded. Hundreds of bunks of Army/Navy type were squeezed into an immensely large hall where 150 to 200 people were confined. The hall had a high ceiling with glass windows on one side, and little sunlight came through the windows. We had a separate mess hall and large-sized toilet and bathroom.

We played cards, chess, or whatever was available to us. We had to play on the bunk bed, as we did not have enough space. We slept on the same bunk bed. We were able to get certain everyday necessities, such as toothbrush and paste, laundry, etc. There was an American lady volunteer who did errands for us. I heard that as a token of appreciation, this lady was invited to Japan after the war by the Ellis Club of Tokyo, which was organized by the repatriates of Ellis Island. Families and friends visited us on alternate Wednesdays. We were given the privilege of going outside to the adjoining grounds for two or three hours every week for fresh air and exercise.

The FBI visited me in February to get my consent to have my office and home searched.

My hearing was held in March at the Federal night court at Foley Square. At the hearing, my family background in Japan and my whole life history in Japan and the U.S.A. was thoroughly scrutinized.

I had two character witnesses, both of them First World War veterans. One was a doctor, the other was a Major in the U.S. Air Force. Besides, I had about 20 letters from the staffs of the hospital I attended. All those who signed the letters were of non-German and non-Italian descent. A postcard from Japan, a cancelled check for $10 and a telegram I received in Los Angeles on the way to Japan in 1939 were brought into court for my explanation.

I was released from the island March 27, 1942. Some of the fellow internees were released as early as February. The first group of 20 were sent to Upton Camp [on Long Island] in February.

I was permitted to resume medical practice in New York City. An FBI agent visited my office every two weeks until I was finally freed from his vigilance in the summer of 1942, perhaps in August. During my absence from home, my wife was allowed to draw $100 monthly from my frozen assets. At the time, my daughter was eight years of age, my son, six years.

When the second exchange boat arrived at New York, I was called from my duty at Lutheran Hospital, where I was a substitute intern, to Ellis Island. There I was told that I could be repatriated if I wanted to. I decided not to do it. The reasons were obvious. I had an office to practice in New York City. I had a duty to support my wife and two children.

That's all.

Iwamoto's "That's all," was as matter-of-fact as his testimony. I was struck with the difference between his treatment as an enemy alien and treatment of West Coast Issei. West Coast Issei were immediately moved to Department of Justice internment camps in places such as Montana, North Dakota, and New Mexico, far removed from their homes. At these remote camps, they received hearings under conditions which made fairness impossible. The hearings were conducted in English, which required translation for most, and often no translation was available. There was no possibility of summoning character witnesses. The FBI did not ask for permission to search businesses or homes of Issei on the West Coast.

Kinnosuke Hashimoto

Kinnosuke Hashimoto was, as he said, ninety-four and one-half years old. He must have been the oldest person to testify before the Commission. He later became one of the named plaintiffs in the NCJAR class action lawsuit against the United States. His testimony was typical. He was a store owner who, when ordered to leave the West Coast, stored his inventory in the local church. He went first to Tanforan, then to Topaz. When he was released and returned, his inventory had been stolen. He moved to New York. His wife suffered from high blood pressure. Her condition was aggravated by the high altitude of Topaz. She also had a hysterectomy, one week before the camp was closed. She was forced to leave camp in her weakened condition and endure a long trip to New York, where she died four years later. His testimony concluded:

I realize that no amount of money can repay us for the hardships we endured before, during, and after internment. Those disorienting years were spent behind barbed wire fences and where the losses were both concrete and intangible must be visibly compensated by the U.S. Government. I feel this can be done by substantial monetary grant given to each individual who was interned, the deceased as well as the living.

As time passes, I see more and more of my Issei friends passing away. I sincerely hope I will be able to benefit from the Government's long overdue acknowledgement of those tragic years.

Setsuko Nishi

Setsuko Nishi, Professor of Sociology at Brooklyn College and the Graduate Center of the City University of New York, used her "numbing blow experience" of internment to fuel her scholarly development through her doctorate and beyond. She offered both remedies and advice on prevention. On remedies, she said:

I believe that there are a number of major issues confronting the Commission. Foremost, in my view, is the constitutional question of the violation of rights, including due process and equal protection, of citizens and other law-abiding persons in the mass evacuation based solely on race/ethnicity.

I understand the Commission has gathered much expert testimony in this regard, and here we would only urge that, despite the statute of limitations, a way be established for a court test of the legal basis of mass evacuation and incarceration of Japanese Americans based solely on race/ethnicity in contrast to the differential treatment of German and Italian aliens in World War II.

She also made this pointed observation:

For many, the Commission hearings have been the occasion to open and examine old wounds, as if it were necessary and expected that old and still ugly and painful scars be displayed personally in public as proof of damage.

Had she known that the record into which all the accumulated testimony was being poured was never to be published, she might have put more bite into this observation.

Dr. Nishi then enunciated several conditions under which the event of racially based exclusion and detention might recur:

The first condition is the availability of stereotypic beliefs regarding the racial/ethnic group. These might be latent or dormant, not necessarily currently active, and could be a vestigial residue of the past. In the case of the Japanese Americans, there was a large reservoir of racial beliefs that had been fomented in west coast campaigns against the so-called "Yellow Peril."

The second condition is the existence of interest groups who view the population in question as a competitive economic/political threat. Organized labor from an earlier period and agricultural interests were among the most vociferous advocates of mass removal of Japanese Americans.

Third, a crisis that disrupts society's normal functioning or is perceived as threatening national security. In our case, it was Pearl Harbor, the beginning of World War II.

Fourthly, the spread of rumors which are consistent with group stereotypes, that the racial/ethnic group is to blame for the crisis or endangers national security—that is, the identification of the so-called "enemy within." Rumors regarding Japanese American espionage, signalling, and fifth-column activity in Hawaii were not dealt with forthrightly and authoritatively, though their falsity was known almost immediately.

The fifth condition is the mobilization of public opinion through the press by interest groups and their political representatives for the removal of the population believed to be a threat to the national security or endangering the response to the crisis. In January 1942, a west coast press campaign for mass evacuation was launched.

Finally, sixth, transfer of authority to the military for dealing with the so-called "dangerous" population. President Roosevelt's Executive Order 9066 authorized the War Department to designate military areas and to exclude any or all persons from these areas. General DeWitt's subsequent proclamations designated the west coast states as military areas and ordered the evacuation of all persons of Japanese ancestry.

She then summarized these conditions:

> Given these conditions and processes, it is not at all difficult to conceive of the possibility that what happened to west coast Japanese Americans during World War II could happen to other groups.

Nishi's analysis is a good summation of accepted academic scholarship on the event. I think it omits several other critical factors. The victims and their leaders failed to protest and resist in an organized fashion. This was due partly to their victimization, their feelings of inferiority created by patterns of harsh, overt discrimination; and due partly to the educational system which failed to inform students of the rights, privileges, and protections of a democratic society. Also, there was racism at the highest levels of governmental leadership, including the President and his cabinet. The legal community failed utterly. And almost all the institutional champions of human rights, including the American Civil Liberties Union, National Association for the Advancement of Colored Peoples, and Protestant and Catholic churches, failed to speak out.

Tadashi Tsufura

Tadashi Tsufura described the exploitation at Seabrook Farms:

> My family was recruited from the relocation camp with the promise of a good life in a place called Seabrook Farms, in southern New Jersey, to work in a factory. At this factory, it was not unusual for a worker to work 16 hours a day. I would like to clear something up. The testimony given by other witnesses stated 12 hours. This company, Seabrook Farms, used workers in an 8-hour shift and a 12-hour shift at the same time, and they allowed you to work another 8 hours if you were willing. Obviously, many of the Japanese who were on the 8-hour shift were willing to work another 8 hours to earn enough to get by or save something, to eventually leave this place of poverty.

> I can also tell you from my personal experience that while working in cold storage, a 24-hour shift was an accepted thing. That's right. So a worker could work 16 hours a day, seven days a week during the peak harvest season. Overtime pay was determined at the whim of the company, and it was not unusual to consider overtime payable only after 60 hours or more.

> Living quarters with coal stoves for cooking, heating, and hot water were initially free but were soon assessed a rental fee, which forced every member of the family to work or live without basic necessities. Other families arriving later in the year were housed in temporary barracks, sharing community water faucets and outhouses because of the lack of a sewage system.

I remember visiting a friend of mine at Seabrook Farms a few years after the war, when life was no longer a struggle for survival. I was appalled. The place seemed just like camp. It was winter, the off-season. Instead of twelve-hour work days, there was absolutely no work at all, except for the fortunate few whose livelihood was not geared to farmwork. My friend's family was large and found moving to a normal community an intimidating prospect. Nevertheless, I urged my friend to get out of the place as soon as possible. It was a continuation of camp life.

The hearings of the Commission on Wartime Relocation and Internment of Civilians were inconclusive. There were hundreds of stories, dozens of theories, moments of enlightment or illumination, rare moments of laughter, much irony, continued betrayal, a few challenges, many pleas and tentative hopes. The hearings were undeniably part of the movement for redress. Japanese-Americans confronted the official representatives of their government and the general American public and expressed their grievances; but there was little dialogue. The powerlessness of the commissioners, who lacked legislative or judicial powers, abused the trust placed in them by many witnesses; yet, redress legislation, based upon the Commission's recommendations, would be introduced into the U.S. Congress. The Commission's failure to publish both the transcripts of the hearings and witnesses' written submissions was irresponsible; but these may eventually be published by private efforts. It remains for history to judge how effective these hearings were in reaching the goal of redressing Japanese-American grievances.

21. COURTS

PREPARATIONS

NCJAR's Interactions with the Commission

The activities of the Commission on Wartime Relocation and Internment of Civilians intersected with those of NCJAR and the NCJAR class action lawsuit. Aiko Herzig, our Washington representative, joined the staff of the CWRIC. The NCJAR board and I interacted with the CWRIC hearings. And our attorneys used the CWRIC and its report to bolster our legal arguments.

On June 5, 1981, Aiko Herzig joined the staff of the CWRIC as a research associate, and became one of its most permanent members, staying two years to the CWRIC's last day, June 30, 1983. She was an indefatigable worker, extending her long days at the office with homework into late evening hours and through weekends. She made a major contribution to the Commission's research into primary documents, starting with the research she had earlier produced for NCJAR and building on this. The writers of the Commission's report, *Personal Justice Denied*, relied on three major sources: published works, testimony given before the Commission, and the primary documents Herzig retrieved. It was also through Aiko Herzig that I was able to get a copy of the transcripts of the Commission's hearings. All of the printed materials, including the transcripts, were turned over to the National Archives. As the Commission was closing shop, Herzig had the presence of mind to ask whether she could keep the word processor's disks. The National Archives was interested only in printed results, not intermediate media. She was given the disks, which were then used to produce an additional set of printed transcripts, from which I was able to select testimony for this book. The slack in NCJAR research created by Aiko's joining the Commission's staff was picked up by Jack Herzig, who continued to make trips to the National Archives and to enlarge the files of documents.

NCJAR's board decided to participate in the CWRIC hearings. I attended three of these hearings, and wrote articles about two of them for the *New York Nichibei*. I testified at the first hearing, and other NCJAR board members testified at other hearings. In the backwash of the Chicago hearings and the conference sponsored by Northeastern Illinois University, the board of NCJAR was expanded by persons who wished to follow through on the excitement and hopes stimulated by these events. The board grew from six to twenty members, resulting in increased distribution of responsibilities and deeper roots in the local Japanese-American community.

The NCJAR lawsuit also benefited from the Commission's activities. NCJAR attorneys decided to rely upon the findings of this official, governmental body to support some of the factual allegations of NCJAR's court complaint. One of the things we in NCJAR learned in the course of our research was that, as late as 1963, the Department of Justice still referred to DeWitt's *Final Report* as an authoritative account of the War

Department's program of mass exclusion and detention, even though historians by then recognized how biased and distorted many of its judgments are. We felt that a new governmental report was needed which would incorporate the scholarship and findings of the intervening decades. In the first Washington hearings, I asked the Commission to include enabling legislation for the lawsuit among its recommendations. Such a recommendation would make it easier for us to find sponsors for such legislation. And the legislation would cut through the formidable procedural barriers we faced in our court challenge. Also, some of the testimony by former U.S. officials was used in NCJAR's legal preparation. Since our Complaint used some of the conclusions and findings of the Commission's report, we timed the filing of our Complaint to follow the publication of CWRIC's report.

Ellen Godbey Carson

One important event during the Commission's hearings had little to do with the Commission itself. Ellen Godbey Carson joined the law firm of Landis, Cohen, Singman and Rauh on November 2, 1981, the first day of the second Washington hearings of the CWRIC. She became the young attorney who would work full-time preparing our lawsuit. We had been waiting for our law firm to hire this attorney. It had been six months since we agreed to retain the firm. The legal preparation was supposed to take one year, but it was delayed until an attorney could be hired. Our impatience was moderated by our own delay in making our monthly payments to the law firm: raising the second half of the $75,000 took considerably longer than the first half. (We could not maintain the pace of $5,000 a month to complete our payments by mid-1982; we made our final payment six months late, on January 6, 1983.) Benjamin Zelenko had demurred because he wanted to find the right person. His persistence was amply rewarded. Carson was eminently qualified. She had graduated from the University of Tennessee with highest honors with a bachelor of arts degree in constitutional law, and from Harvard Law School with honors. Her main interest at Harvard Law School had been in constitutional and civil rights law. Zelenko was also impressed with her commitment to the issue of Japanese-American redress. She arrived in the Senate Caucus Room with Zelenko, who introduced us. They were there to witness the hearings. Ellen Godbey Carson was joining the lawsuit with a baptism of fire. These hearings helped us to understand the role of government in the wartime events and introduced us to the cast of characters involved. Carson's university and law school lessons on constitutional law became gritty reality. She saw Colonel Karl R. Bendetsen smile his crinkly-eyed best as he faked high-toned moralism and fabricated benign intentions to clothe the grimly naked truths of the government's program of mass exclusion and detention. She heard one of America's most influential men, John J. McCloy, spout the racism of America's realpolitik with respect to Cuban-Americans as well as Japanese-Americans.

Ellen is married to Robert Carson Godbey, who is also an attorney. "Godbey," I learned is an old Methodist name, contracted from the benediction, "God be with you." For a Christian, the symbolism of that name in this struggle was powerful. I had difficulty placing her accent. It wasn't Harvard. It wasn't Tennessee. It turned out to be Tennessee reconstructed for a lawyerly presence in the courtroom. The only trace I could still detect of Tennessee was a tendency to say "tin" as in "Tinnessee." She was young and enthusiastic. I thought of her as just graduating from Harvard Law School, although she had been employed for a year in the Civil Rights Division of the Department of Health and Human Services. It may have been her youth. Or it may have been her *summa cum laude* and *cum laude* achievements, which focuses one's attention on her academic credentials. I was impressed that she had decided to join Landis, Cohen, Singman and Rauh; the firm could attract talent. The firm's choice of her and her choice of the firm were fortuitous. The Reagan administration had greatly diminished the federal government's activities in civil rights and affirmative action, bringing her work to a standstill. When she began looking for a more challenging job, our law firm was looking for someone interested in an important constitutional case. Our interests joined.

Our first task was to educate Ellen through her immersion in the literature and the mountain of documents we had accumulated. Aiko and Jack Herzig had already been passing to the firm documents which they thought were relevant to our lawsuit. Ellen went through these documents, law journals, and a few books, such as Morton Grodzins's *Americans Betrayed*, Jacobus tenBroek's *Prejudice, War and the Constitution*, Roger Daniels's *The Decision to Relocate the Japanese Americans*, Frank Chuman's *Bamboo People*, and Michi Weglyn's *Years of Infamy*. Her main task would be the preparation of our court complaint.

We sooned learned that the academic honors she had earned indicated her capacity to read, absorb, and digest facts at an intensive pace. In addition to the vast, factual history that Aiko and Jack Herzig were uncovering, Ellen had to review, select, and study legal decisions upon which to build the best possible case, a case which would not only describe the injuries sustained by the large class of victims but withstand the scrutiny of adversarial criticism and judicial review. We were aware of the legal barriers which barred our entrance to a trial. In order to overcome these barriers, our complaint would push the existing body of case law and attempt to break new ground. Within six months, a preliminary version of the complaint was written.

NCJAR Tries to Grow

In the meanwhile, NCJAR continued to try to extend its organization into other regions of the United States. In mid-1981, Rev. Lloyd Wake established an NCJAR Bay Area Group in San Francisco. But it failed to take root, even though Wake continues to serve as an NCJAR spokesperson in that area. A dispute broke out between the Bay Area Group and the Chicago board on the selection of attorneys and the Group's lack of influence on legal considerations affecting the lawsuit. The upshot was that the Bay Area Group declined to help with fund-raising while continuing to represent NCJAR.

NCJAR had many supporters in Los Angeles. But we had no one who could sponsor a meeting. Finally, Nelson Kitsuse prevailed upon his brother Richard to obtain space for a November 1981 meeting at Sage United Methodist Church in Monterey Park. Playwright Frank Chin, Professor Mitsuye Yamada, and I put together a program for NCJAR supporters. I had a chance to meet some of our supporters for the first time. Yamada read some of the poetry she had written while interned. I spoke about the need to accept the risks contained in NCJAR's legal challenge. After all, I argued, those who had the courage to challenge the government in the dark days of our exile had little to hope for except to keep us believing in the injustice of our treatment. Frank Chin had become controversial through his "Circus of Freaks" article in the *Rafu Shimpo*, a widely read Japanese-American newspaper in Los Angeles. I introduced Chin by stating my personal debt to him for urging me to take a leadership role in the redress movement. Chin began by asking if there were any questions—presumably to his controversial article. Hearing none, he discussed and attacked the collaborationist role of the JACL during the wartime years, especially its emphasis on cultural assimilation. We made an impression on Rev. Wes Yamaka, pastor of Sage United Methodist Church who became an NCJAR supporter.

It was during this trip that I met Hannah and Dwight Holmes, a deaf couple. Hannah had been interned in Manzanar with me. She would become a staunch supporter of NCJAR, even to the extent of becoming a *ronin* supporter, in spite of her disability and disability level of income. I asked her if she would introduce me at the meeting at Sage, and she did.

A year later, Hannah Holmes almost singlehandedly organized a dinner in honor of Harry Ueno. This dinner, honoring a dissident, was memorable. Many of Ueno's friends attended. We also honored Joe Kurihara with a scroll, presenting it to two of his cousins, Albert and Mary Kurihara. It was Ueno's evening. He talked for about an hour about his wartime experiences, at times with humor, at times with tears. I found great beauty in this celebration organized by a disabled person to honor two men of courage of Japanese-American history. Hannah was a great source of strength for the redress movement.

But we failed to establish an organizational base in Los Angeles. Nor was NCJAR able to develop organizational roots in other areas where support existed, such as Seattle and New York.

Despite these failures in organizational extensions, NCJAR and the NCJAR lawsuit succeeded in becoming an integral part of the movement for Japanese-American redress. What we lacked in organization was more than offset by the substance of our activities, the quality of our friends, and, of course, the impact of our lawsuit. Undoubtedly, the redress movement's most successful organizational effort was the establishment of the Commission on Wartime Relocation and Internment of Civilians, thanks largely to the Japanese American Citizens League. Although many in the JACL view the

Commission's success as primarily political or in public relations, it accomplished much more. It elicited words, both descriptive and reflective, from many victims, conducted new research, and produced a drastically revised official explanation of the mass exclusion and detention of Japanese-Americans. Still, it was a tremendous public relations success. Its hearings attracted news media attention, both nationally and locally, as the hearings moved from city to city. In contrast, NCJAR attracted little attention from the news media, but its court complaint would describe and provide documented evidence of the injuries suffered and the remedies required; the Complaint would require the courts to listen and adjudicate.

22. COURTS
THE COMPLAINT

NCJAR's lawsuit was filed on March 16, 1983. For the first time in the history of the mass exclusion and detention of Japanese-Americans and their aftermath, the defendant is identified and the plaintiffs defined. For the first time in this history, we, the plaintiffs, spell out our injuries from our perspective, as the injured parties. There is no muting of our grievances as occurred with the WHEREAS statements written by Shosuke Sasaki for the 1979-80 Lowry Redress Bill. Our Complaint delineates allegation of fact upon allegation of fact in sharp, compelling language. We shed official euphemisms such as "evacuation" and "relocation centers" and replace them with "forced exclusion" and "prison camps." Our causes of action, the formal statement of charges, specify each constitutional and legal right that was violated. Nor are the remedies gratuitous as they were in the Evacuation Claims Act. We seek the maximum compensation allowed for our causes of action. We reject Congressman Jim Wright's proposed apology: "The best we can do, therefore, is to take official notice that what we did under the severe pressure of that wrenching emergency was completely out of character for us—to apologize to those on whom we inflicted the insulting assumption of their disloyalty and to avow that never again will any group of Americans be subjected to such humiliation on grounds no more valid than the blood that runs in their veins." Nor do we accept the words of Congressman George Danielson who merged the victims with victimizer: "The Government is the people." We move beyond the seemingly endless media and academic discussions on the nature and extent of the wrong and the many theories propounded which, while seeming to provide insight and enlightenment, often only promoted the propounder as the source of arcane knowledge. Instead of repressing our outrage for want of focus, we victims now have a lawsuit against the United States; we now have the proper means by which to channel our grievances and our demands for redress.[1]

Twenty-Seven Billion

We are suing the United States of America for an unambiguously adversarial sum of twenty-seven billion dollars. The ante has been raised since 1979. The first Lowry Redress Bill had a projected cost of around three billion dollars. The ninefold increase of our action came not from a motive to sensationalize, but from the cumulative effect of the detailed allegations of facts and injuries embedded in our Complaint. These allegations coalesce into twenty-two causes of action. The magnitude of our prayer for relief, to use the legal expression, results from the multiplication of the class of 125,000 victims by twenty-two causes of action. We seek compensation of at least $10,000 for each cause of action.[2] Twenty-two of them yield $220,000 per victim. Given the nature of the injuries, the individual claim is modest. This claim multiplied by 125,000 victims yields 27.5 billion dollars. Our Complaint is not addressing merely property losses. We are addressing injuries we sustained through the government's violation of our constitutional and civil rights. Client NCJAR had never given its law firm instruction on a bottom-line figure for monetary redress. The figure flows naturally from the compilation of historical facts which supported causes of actions. The figure is not a measure of lost property; it is a valuation of violated constitutional and civil rights.

This is a point which many Americans fail to understand. We Americans have forgotten the hard lessons learned by the founders of our nation and the framers of the United States Constitution. Many of us think of the Constitution as the rules of self-governance, much like the bylaws of a corporation or organization. While it does specify the requirements for being president and the manner of popular representation in the two houses of Congress, the Constitution is much more than bylaws: it guarantees our individual freedoms by placing limitations on government. It mandates, for example, that the privilege of the writ of *habeas corpus* shall not be suspended "unless when in cases of rebellion or invasion the public safety may require it." Such suspension, moreover, requires an explicit act of government, such as an act of Congress. There is no constitutional provision for *ignoring* the writ as was done with Japanese-Americans. Since the writ requires that persons be tried before they are imprisoned, many other rights depend upon the faithful observation of the writ. The protection of the writ of *habeas corpus* is precious. It should be an inviolable right. Its violation withdraws the protection of the courts. The establishment of an exception to this rule of protection may easily enable the exception to overtake the rule, especially when the protection of the courts blocks the misguided will of citizens' inflamed passions or a government's will to abuse its power. There, of course, must be fiscal limitations on the cost of redressing a constitutional violation; it cannot be infinite. If the price for repairing the violation of the writ of *habeas corpus* cannot be infinite, then surely the repair itself should be infinitely secured. And so it should be with the constitutional and legal protections against the unjust taking of private property by government for public use, unreasonable search and seizure, involuntary servitude, false arrest and imprisonment, and the rest of our causes of action. Too many of us too quickly reduce all monetary issues to commerce. We fail to realize that our lives and our livelihoods are undergirded by a system of rights and privileges which were written into our Constitution from lessons learned through hard experience. When those rights and privileges are breached by the government, the government must be held accountable. And the victims have the responsibility to demand the accounting.

Defendant United States of America

The Complaint names as adversary and defendant the United States of America. The naming of defendant United States of America is disturbing for most Americans, as it is enlightening and liberating for the Americans who were the victims. Many Americans resist being held accountable for their sins, or those of their parents, of forty years ago, even though the Ten Commandments warn us of the long-term effects of our failure to obey God's ethical laws. Many of us would deny knowledge of the events; we would deny malicious intent. Why should we have to pay for someone else's mistakes? The questioners are not mollified when they are told that even the victims themselves will have to pay their share of the redress. Nor will the questioners' resistance lessen when informed that the United States Court of Claims regularly accepts judgments against the United States for which we all must pay.

The distress, I suspect, is really an averted look, an unwillingness to look at the enormity of the charges delineated. The victims charge that the rights guaranteed within the Constitution of the United States were violated by the government of the United States. Many Americans avoid looking at this. They would avoid the implication that the violation of constitutional rights of Japanese-Americans could be inflicted on any other group of Americans or to all Americans. They try to hide behind the fact that they are not of Japanese ancestry, as if one's ancestry circumscribed susceptibility. They do not see the violation as a violation of *their* rights. And they resist the blemish to their cherished heritage. They raise defenses against this criticism of the purity, nobility, and greatness of American democracy, especially as they had so wholeheartedly committed themselves to America's war of freedom against the forces of tyranny. They resist the confusion of their all-white-all-American self-images becoming colored by alien, Asian characteristics. Could Jack Armstrong be called Jack Sakamoto? Could the all-kinetic American boy sit still in Eastern meditation? Could Miss America smile at us with epicanthic eyes?

Just as many Americans fail to recognize the preciousness of our constitutionally guaranteed freedoms, many lack any strong sense of identity with Americans of Japanese ancestry. They want to identify Japanese-Americans as Japanese from Japan. They ask with revealing indignation, "What about Pearl Harbor? What about the Bataan Death March?" Japanese-Americans remain "those people" and "they," not "we." Many Americans fail to realize that the movement for Japanese-American redress is a gift to America: the repairing of damages to the constitutional foundations of America's freedoms.

For us, the victims, the naming of defendant United States of America is enlightenment and liberation. We never knew quite what had hit us. Of course, we had grown up with racism. We had heard about Lieutenant General DeWitt's outlandish remark, "A Jap's a Jap." We knew the term "Jap" as one that was particularly hostile and hate-filled as well as demeaning. To us in that time, the term was an obscenity like "fuck," differing only as an obscenity accepted in polite and public language by leaders of government and teachers of our children, in newspaper editorials and comic strips, by radio commentators and standup comedians. We victims were mired in our "Japness." And we have been overwhelmed with a variety of theories of why mass exclusion and detention happened to us, and of who the culprits were. We were told of public racism, commercial greed, political opportunism, media excesses, military paranoia, and stupidity. This diversity of explanations tends to diffuse and confuse the source of our injuries. The naming of the defendant as the United States of America clarifies reality and brings it into focus.

We Japanese-Americans confront our lifelong nemesis which once barred our parents and older sisters and brothers from citizenship and ownership of land, which once sanctioned restrictive housing covenants and job discrimination, which swooped down on our homes and seized our fathers on the "date that will live in infamy" and in the days following, which issued curfew orders, ordered mass exclusion, forced us into buses and trains for the long ride to prison camps in unknown places, which marked us as enemies of the state and forced us to prove our loyalty by giving our lives in combat and turning informant on our neighbors. We gradually lift the cloak of self-doubt that caused us to be forever prepared to defend our loyalty to America and to construct airtight proofs of our innocence. The Complaint becomes our liberation. Instead of bowing and yielding to a government which deprived us of our liberties, instead of taking an oath of unqualified allegiance and subscribing to a creed of sycophantic obedience, we are identifying the government as our adversary in our effort to remedy the injuries we had sustained from the government's abuse of privilege and power. The defendant United States of America becomes as singular and identifiable as a single gray rock in a garden of white pebbles.

Plaintiffs: Japanese America

NCJAR selected twenty-five persons, living and dead, to represent the class of 125,000 victims and plaintiffs. These twenty-five represent Issei who had been interned in Department of Justice camps; Issei, Nisei, and Sansei who had been excluded and detained in one of the ten prison camps; a Buddhist priest for the special religious discrimination applied to leaders of Eastern religious faiths; veterans of the 442nd Regimental Combat Team, volunteers and draftees; a deaf person for those disabled; a dissident who doubly suffered in the isolation camps of Moab and Leupp; a draft resister who resisted because he was denied entrance to branches of the armed forces other than the U.S. Army; mothers and fathers, sons and daughters, children, adults, and the elderly. The representation is geographical as well. Several were selected from the District of Columbia because we filed our lawsuit in that federal district court. The rest came from New York, Chicago, Seattle, San Jose, and Los Angeles. The twenty-five named plaintiffs are a rich and varied cross-section of the class of 125,000 plaintiffs on whose behalf the lawsuit was filed.

The Complaint brings together elements of Japanese America that were separated through the stresses engendered by the government's abuse of their rights: the government's demand for unquestioned obedience; its repression of dissent; its sanctioning of racial stereotypes that induced self-hatred within its victims. Of course, these deep wounds of separation would take more than a lawsuit to repair. But the lawsuit is a step in the right direction. We victims are asserting ourselves as an inclusive, whole body of people: Issei, Nisei, and Sansei; volunteers for combat duty, dissidents, and draft resisters; Christians, Buddhists, and others; patriots, renunciants, and ordinary folk; physically disabled and healthy, but all Japanese-Americans.

Allegations

The *Factual Allegations* of the Complaint open with numbered paragraph 43:

43. Following the outbreak of World War II, defendant maliciously and unlawfully conspired to and did deprive plaintiffs of their constitutional rights by subjecting them to forcible segregation, arrest, exclusion, and imprisonment solely on the basis of their Japanese ancestry. Defendant intentionally concealed and misrepresented the illegal nature of its actions by fabricating claims of "military necessity."[3]

The allegations extend for sixty-eight paragraphs through paragraph 110, establishing the character of the defendant. They then describe in chronological order the events and actions preceding Pearl Harbor, the exclusion order, expulsion and detention, life in the camps, the constitutional test cases, release and relocation—all implicating defendant United States in twenty-two causes of action.

Establishing the Character of the Defendant

The allegations covering the years before Pearl Harbor establish the character of the defendant United States by describing them as "years of racial hostility and invidious discrimination" towards the plaintiffs. They refer to anti-Japanese laws which forbade immigration of all persons of Japanese ancestry, regardless of nationality, and prohibited permanent resident aliens of Japanese ancestry from applying for naturalized citizenship. They describe the secondary effect of alien land laws passed by state governments prohibiting land ownership by persons ineligible for naturalized citizenship. Government-sanctioned racism led to other forms of racism, such as discrimination in housing, employment, business practices, and public schools.

The Complaint points to a specific interest of defendant United States in establishing concentration camps. On October 9, 1940, Secretary of Navy Frank Knox sent a memorandum to President Roosevelt which recommended building concentration camps in order to impress Japan with the seriousness of U.S. preparations for war. The Complaint's allegations describe the monitoring and investigations conducted by the government of a suspect Japanese-American population, including a secret break-in at the Japanese Consulate in Los Angeles in March 1941. The result of these intelligence activities refuted the foregone conclusion of mass internment. Official intelligence reports recommended that only a limited number of persons were suspect and that Japanese-Americans as a whole were "loyal to the United States or, at worst, hope that by remaining quiet they can avoid concentration camps . . ."

Moving Toward Exclusion

The allegations describe the defendant's actions on Pearl Harbor day and in the days following: the arrest and incarceration of Japanese nationals, Issei, "without issuance of warrants according to law, without notice of any charges against them, and without provision of a trial to determine their guilt or innocence of any criminal acts." The plaintiff class is thereby broadened. So much emphasis in earlier pleas for redress had been placed upon U.S. citizenship that they tended to consign interned Issei to their fate as though what happened to them was perfectly legal. But these Issei were often arrested on nothing more than the word of informants—who were pressured into informing as proof of patriotism—or because of general criteria such as being community leaders or teachers of the Japanese language.

During the early weeks of the war, the government did conspire and concoct a devious plan to exclude and imprison Japanese-Americans, paying special attention to avoid violation of the Constitution. The government planned to designate military areas from which "any and all persons" would be excluded, thereby not discriminating racially, and then, through a system of permits, to allow "everyone but the Japs" to return.

Also during this period, the case for military necessity was fabricated. Reports of illegal signals and radio transmissions had occurred. These had been investigated by the FBI and the Federal Communications Commission and found to be without substance. Nevertheless, these reports, plus the patently racist notion of a Japanese affinity for espionage and sabotage, were used to establish the existence of military necessity, setting the stage for mass exclusion and imprisonment.

Toward Expulsion and Imprisonment

The allegations continue with the issuance of Executive Order 9066 (EO9066) by President Roosevelt on February 19, 1942. True to the plan, EO9066 specified no racial criterion and stated "any and all persons may be excluded." The order continued, "and with respect to which, the right of any person to enter, remain in, or leave shall be subject to whatever restrictions the Secretary of War or the appropriate Military Commander may impose in his discretion." On the following day, Secretary of War Henry Stimson designated Lieutenant General John L. DeWitt as an "appropriate Military Commander." DeWitt made quite clear his predilection:

> In the war in which we are now engaged, racial affinities are not severed by migration. The Japanese race is an enemy race, and while many second and third generation Japanese born on United States soil, possessed of United States citizenship, have become "Americanized," the racial strains are undiluted . . .

Then DeWitt invoked the fabricated rationale for military necessity:

> It, therefore, follows that along the vital Pacific Coast over 112,000 potential enemies of Japanese extraction are at large today. There are indications that these are organized and ready for concerted action at a favorable opportunity. The very fact that no sabotage has taken place to date is a disturbing and confirming indication that such action will be taken.

The logic of "no sabotage has taken place to date is a disturbing and confirming indication that such action will be taken" is the precursor to the Vietnam era illogic: "We destroyed the village in order to save it."

DeWitt quickly satisfied his predilection. He imposed "stringent curfews, reporting requirements, travel and contraband restrictions, and other losses of liberty" on Japanese-Americans, including declaring a broad, roughly 100-mile swath along the coast and into Arizona as military areas of exclusion. During this period, the War Relocation Authority (WRA) was established and Public Law 503 was enacted to provide mechanisms for implementing mass exclusion and detention. Here, the allegations are trenchant:

69. Using military troops with drawn guns and bayonets, defendant forced plaintiffs from their homes, crowded them onto buses, trucks, and railroad cars, and took them to prison camps, surrounded by barbed wire, sentry towers, and armed guards. Defendant subjected plaintiffs to threats and acts of physical violence, arrest, fine, and imprisonment for any non-compliance with the orders excluding plaintiffs from their homes and confining them to prison camps.

70. Defendant made only rare exceptions from the exclusion orders; even the sick, disabled, and hospitalized were arrested and imprisoned. Orphanages and mental and medical institutions were raided, with defendant demanding custody of anyone with even the slightest Japanese ancestry. Proof of longstanding loyalty to the United States was ignored; decorated veterans of the U.S. armed forces and leaders of American civic organizations were arbitrarily arrested and imprisoned solely because of their Japanese ancestry. Over 70,000 of these Americans were women, children, elderly and disabled persons against whom the defendant did not even attempt to advance claims that they had any access or ability to carry out illicit activities. Further, approximately 72,000 of those imprisoned were United States citizens, second and third generation Americans due the full rights of citizenship.

Life in the Prison Camps

If one was blessed with a healthy body and mind, life in the prison camps was spartan but tolerable. "The housing construction," the Complaint alleges, "was designed according to specifications . . . for temporary housing for seasoned combat units." Unfortunately, we were hardly "seasoned combat units." Even the healthy suffered from the severe deprivations of privacy through the communalization of sleeping, eating, bathing, and toileting. If one could tolerate this for three uninterrupted years, there remained other obstacles to survival. We had to withstand a diet which "fell below the standards required for prisoners of war by international convention." We had to cope with "deprivations of liberty" made real by barbed wire. We were forced to work at jobs prohibited by international convention for prisoners of war, and were compensated at six to eight cents an hour, approximating involuntary servitude. (As a teenage gardener in 1941, I earned sixty cents an hour.) The Complaint alleges further restrictions on liberty by the prohibition on speaking Japanese in public meetings, censorship of mail, warrantless searches and seizures of person and property, limitations of religious freedom, substandard education, and inadequate medical services.

Continued Exclusion and Segregation

The allegations take defendant United States to task for its failure to release inmates for the cowardly reason of "unfavorable community sentiment" and for continuing the prison camps long after the War Department itself had determined that military necessity no longer required the exclusion of Japanese-Americans from their homes on the West Coast. The War Department made its determination as early as April 8, 1943, twenty-one months before mass exclusion was lifted on January 2, 1945; it continued exclusion and detention "for the sole purpose of facilitating the President's reelection in November 1944."

The Complaint brings up the "loyalty questionnaires" and their pernicious effect of causing "plaintiffs great anxiety, confusion, and stress, due to the unlawful actions defendant had taken thus far against them, and defendant's threats and authority to take further punitive measures against plaintiffs.'' The Complaint further alleges:

> The non-citizen permanent resident members of the plaintiffs class were caused extreme anxiety by the questionnaires, which in effect asked them to renounce the only citizenship they had and were permitted to hold, while at the same time defendant continued to treat them as "enemy aliens" subject to arbitrary deportation, and to deny them any citizenship or liberty rights as Americans.

(I questioned Ellen Carson about this use of "Americans" to designate Issei. I had thought that "American" was to be reserved for U.S. citizens. She explained that the Issei had made their homes in America and had lived most of their lives here, and so they deserved to be called "Americans." It was another step of enlightenment I achieved through the court action.) The loyalty oath was more a test of obedience than loyalty. The Complaint points out that the defendant imprisoned draft resisters who "sought their reinstatement of [constitutional and civil] rights before being subjected to combat service." The defendant judged as disloyal all persons whose responses to the loyalty question were qualified, regardless of their reasoning. In a constitutional democracy, one would expect that appeals to constitutional principle or misgivings about the meaning of a poorly worded question would produce dialogue, not imprisonment and punishment. Again, the plaintiff class is broadened to include draft resisters, other dissidents, and the so-called "disloyals."

The Complaint also alleges that Public Law 405 was passed to enable imprisoned American citizens of Japanese ancestry to renounce their citizenship. As Wayne Collins, wartime attorney for renunciants, said, "You can no more resign citizenship in time of war than you can resign from the human race."[4] The Complaint characterizes this law as "forcible deportation" of over 4,700 plaintiffs. These renunciants are another group of Japanese-Americans who in the past were relegated to the scrap heap of history for their "disloyalty." Michi Weglyn has written a wrenching account of their treatment in *Years of Infamy*. Their inclusion again broadens the plaintiff class.

Illegalities in the Judicial Process

The Complaint points to recently declassified documents as demonstrating affirmative misrepresentations and suppression of evidence by the government in the legal battles of the period. It alleges that the government was "shielding its illegal acts from judicial scrutiny, and denying plaintiffs access to a fair trial and to any form of fair judicial redress for the injuries inflicted on them." It cites Justice Department attorney Edward Ennis's memorandum of April 30, 1943 relating to the first Supreme Court test case of Gordon Hirabayashi:

> Thus, in one of the crucial points of the case, the Government is forced to argue that individual selective evacuation would have been impractical and insufficient when we have positive knowledge that the only Intelligence agency responsible for advising Gen. DeWitt gave him advice directly to the contrary.
>
> In view of this fact, I think we should consider very carefully whether we do not have a duty to advise the Court of the existence of the Ringle memorandum and of the fact

that this represents the view of the Office of Naval Intelligence. It occurs to me that any other course of conduct might approximate the suppresssion of evidence.

Of course the government failed to listen to Ennis's warning and failed to advise the Court of the Ringle memorandum.

In addition, the Complaint alleges that the Court was not advised of the fabrication of military necessity in a "battle of the footnote" between the War Department and the Justice Department in the Korematsu test case. The Justice Department wanted to include a footnote to the government's brief that would warn the Court of the lack of factual support for military necessity. The War Department opposed this warning and the warning was not included.

The Complaint alleges that the defendant conspired "to prevent plaintiffs from adjudicating their legal claims against defendant's actions . . . [and] sought numerous delays, raised frivolous procedural disputes, claimed in bad faith that plaintiffs failed to exhaust nonexistent administrative remedies, removed plaintiffs from the jurisdiction of the courts, and released selected individual litigants from its custody in order to avoid an adjudication of defendant's illegal conduct." The Complaint highlights the seriousness of this conspiracy by citing the defendant United States' response to Mitsuye Endo's appeal for her freedom under the writ of *habeas corpus*. The defendant threatened to suspend the writ of *habeas corpus* and to revoke citizenship and residency status.

Ending Exclusion and the Aftermath

Although the mass exclusion order was rescinded at midnight, January 2, 1945, thousands of plaintiffs continued to be excluded from their homes by means of individual exclusion orders. The Complaint alleges:

These orders were issued by defendant . . . without hearing, probable cause, or recourse by plaintiffs.

(The absence of probable cause in its application led to its capricious use. I recall my being served with an individual exclusion order which banned me from the state of California when I tried to visit my parents in Manzanar. In March 1945, I traveled to Manzanar from Madison, Wisconsin in an attempt to dissuade my father from relocating to Madison, where jobs were practically impossible for an Issei to find and the resources of our makeshift family stretched thin. Upon my arrival at the camp's entrance gate—the camp was still surrounded by barbed wire fencing—I learned that I required permission to enter the camp. Upon learning the reason for my visit, I was denied permission. The administrators did not want me to discourage my father from leaving. But mass exclusion had been rescinded, so they could not keep me from visiting. A Manzanar High School teacher, who recognized my plight, offered to invite me into camp as his guest. But the Western Defense Command issued an individual exclusion order for me, and forced me, at gunpoint, to board the next bus to Reno. What aggravated this abuse of governmental authority was the fact that I was otherwise a free citizen, undetained and uncharged with any wrongdoing and going about my own business. Although I attempted to complain, I was, of course, completely unaware of the larger constitutional issues implicit in the declared absence of military necessity and in the individual exclusion order itself.)

Twenty-Two Causes of Action

Our lawsuit is impelled by twenty-two causes of action or counts. Like punch lines, they are the distillate of the dozens of allegations. Most are quite straightforward and easily understood. The first is entitled Due Process and states that what Japanese-Americans suffered they suffered "without individual hearings or the opportunity to be heard, in violation of the Fifth Amendment's guarantee that individuals shall not be deprived of life, liberty, or property without due process of law." The second, Equal Protection, is equally clear: Equal Protection was violated because the defendant acted "solely on the basis of race and national ancestry."

But the third, Unjust Taking, is more subtle. The Fifth Amendment states, "nor shall private property be taken for public use, without just compensation." This cause of action attempts to extend the idea of unjust taking from the destruction of our "real and personal property, commercial interests, livelihood, reputation, liberty, and other property rights," to "privileges, and entitlements secured by federal, state, and local law," charging that the defendant "failed to compensate or has provided grossly inadequate compensation for plaintiffs' losses of property rights." Our attorneys were anticipating the legal defense of sovereign immunity, whereby one may sue the government, the "sovereign," for monetary damages, only when the government consents to be sued. This Fifth Amendment clause mandates compensation. By this attempt to extend its meaning to encompass constitutional rights, our attorneys hoped to find a way around sovereign immunity.

The fourth count is based upon the Fourth Amendment's protection against unreasonable arrest, search, and seizure, an obvious violation. The fifth is based upon the privileges and immunities clause of Article 4, Section 2 of the Constitution:

> The citizens of each state shall be entitled to all privileges and immunities of citizens in the several states . . .

This little-used clause is much like equal protection, and was plainly violated.

The sixth through the thirteenth counts are again quite direct. The sixth, based on the Sixth Amendment, is Right to Fair Trial and Representation by Counsel. It is difficult to believe that this failed to occur 125,000 times. The seventh states that the Eighth Amendment's protection from cruel and unusual punishment was violated, in that our treatment was "grossly disproportionate to any security risk . . . and, in light of the absence of the commission of any crime."

The eighth through eleventh counts are based upon the First Amendment. In the eighth count, we state that our First Amendment right to freedom of religion was violated with respect to the practice of Eastern religious beliefs. In the ninth, we state our denial of the Amendment's guarantee of freedom of speech and press. This refers to the prohibition of using the Japanese language in public meetings and censorship of camp newspapers. In the tenth, we state that we were not free to associate, again in violation of the First Amendment. In the eleventh, it is the Amendment's guarantee of Freedom of Petition for Redress of Grievances that is violated. When the WRA deemed inmates to be "troublemakers" and sent them to the Moab or Leupp isolation camps, these "troublemakers" were often no more than American citizens who demanded the redress of grievances.

The twelfth count, Privacy, Travel, and other Constitutional Rights, summarizes the absence of privacy and the reality of confinement. The thirteenth count, Protection from Involuntary Servitude is based upon the Thirteenth Amendment and refers to the inadequate compensation received for labor.

I was at first confused by the fourteenth count. It cites Presidential Proclamation 2525, Presidential Orders 9066 and 9102 and Public Laws 503 and 405 as Bills of Attainder and Ex Post Facto Laws. Bills of Attainder and Ex Post Facto laws are enactments of the legislative branch of government. The count includes presidential proclamation and executive order. Why are these executive branch acts included as laws? When we examine Executive Order 9066 and Public Law 503, we see that 503 "gave teeth" to 9066 by providing penalties for violations of 9066. Taken together, the two constitute a Bill of Attainder as "a legislative enactment against a person pronouncing him guilty without trial," to cite the term's dictionary definition.

The fifteenth count is the final constitutional one: denial of *habeas corpus*, the right of a detained person to challenge the legality of his or her imprisonment. Not only was this right violated, but the government made a serious attempt to suspend *habeas corpus* through legislation in response to Mitsuye Endo's petition for freedom under *habeas corpus*.

The sixteenth through nineteenth counts are again straightforward: conspiracy to deprive plaintiffs of their civil rights, assault and battery, false arrest and imprisonment, and abuse of process and malicious prosecution.

The twentieth, Negligence, needs elaboration. The Complaint states that the defendant "failed to exercise reasonable care to protect plaintiffs' property from loss, destruction, and vandalism during plaintiffs' exclusion and imprisonment. Defendant negligently failed to feed, house, and otherwise care for plaintiffs adequately during their incarceration in the prison camps."

The twenty-first count, Contract, is explained by the Complaint:

133. Defendant secured plaintiffs' cooperation in peacefully leaving their homes, businesses, and property, on the basis of defendant's promises (1) that plaintiffs would

be free to relocate to inland communities, and there pursue normal life, work, and schooling; (2) that defendant would protect plaintiffs and their property during relocation; (3) that plaintiffs would be permitted to return to their homes as soon as the alleged temporary military emergency subsided; (4) and that plaintiffs would not be deprived of their constitutional rights.

The twenty-second and final count, Breach of Fiduciary Duty, was added on August 8, 1983 in order to take advantage of a Supreme Court decision, *United States v. Mitchell*, rendered in June 1983. This count states that since defendant United States assumed "comprehensive and pervasive control, management, and supervision of every aspect of plaintiffs' daily lives during the period of detention," fiduciary duties were assumed as well. Given this, the "defendant breached its fiduciary duties to plaintiffs and is accountable for damages resulting therefrom."

The Complaint was a solid achievement. It was a product of heart, mind, and soul. The monetary contributions from hundreds of supporters, including *ronin* supporters, made it possible. Many of these checks were as much from the heart as from checking accounts. Aiko and Jack Herzig had left to their posterity and ours the allegations resting on documents they had retrieved. Ellen Godbey Carson, the "young attorney," and Benjamin Zelenko, together with their colleagues at Landis, Cohen, Singman and Rauh, had forged a powerful, compelling document, making the case for Japanese-American redress unmistakably clear, comprehensive, and specific. But it had to undergo the twisting and tearing of adversarial challenge and judicial scrutiny. What would survive? Would anything?

23. COURTS
FILING AND THE MOTION TO DISMISS

March 16, 1983 was a big day for the National Council for Japanese American Redress. It was the date on which NCJAR filed its class action lawsuit. The filing was a culmination of more than two years of legal preparation, historical research, fund-raising, and struggle. It was a day to celebrate this act towards redressing the grievances of Japanese America. Yuriko and I went to Washington to join our friends, Aiko and Jack Herzig, named plaintiffs, Kaz Oshiki and Kumao Toda, and attorneys, Benjamin Zelenko and Ellen Godbey Carson to participate in the filing and in one of three press conferences— the other two were held in Chicago and Los Angeles—to mark the occasion.

The day began with Yuriko and I, David Field, and Ellen Godbey Carson finding our separate ways to the front of the U.S. District Courthouse for the District of Columbia at shortly before nine o'clock. A two-man television crew from Bonneville Broadcasting was there to record the occasion. Carson had two copies of the NCJAR Complaint which were to be filed. David Field, a law clerk for Landis, Cohen, Singman and Rauh, was acting as the disinterested—but definitely not uninterested—third party who was to serve these Complaints to the U.S. Attorney for the District of Columbia, Stanley S. Harris, and to the Attorney General of the United States, William French Smith. But first we had to have the Complaints processed by a clerk of the court: a number issued, a judge assigned, and rubber stampings made to identify these actions. Yuriko and I took some photographs outside with my ancient, but trusty, Nikon S-2. Cameras and tape recorders are not permitted inside; as we entered, we turned ours over to the guard at the entrance. The door to the clerk's office opened at precisely nine o'clock. In addition to the two official copies to be delivered by David Field, Carson submitted several additional copies to be stamped as mementos. The number given was 83-0750. The judge's name was stamped, "OBERDORFER, J." Later I learned that the Judge's first name is not John or Joseph, but Louis, Louis F. Oberdorfer. The "J." stands for "judge." We then paid the fee for filing: ten dollars. The estimate of the redress sought was twenty-five billion dollars.[1]

United States' Motion to Dismiss

Two months later, on May 16, 1983, the Department of Justice, represented by Jeffrey Axelrad, filed a Motion to Dismiss our lawsuit. This, of course, had been anticipated. We knew that the defendant's best arguments would be procedural ones to bar our access to trial. Their brief contained three basic defenses: statutes of limitations, the Japanese-American Evacuation Claims Act of 1948 as the sole remedy for losses suffered by the victims, and sovereign immunity. As I read the motion's arguments, I became depressed. The Motion's adversarial tone was disputatious, even unpleasant. Axelrad characterized the Complaint as, "lengthy, if not prolix." I had to look up "prolix." It means, "so wordy as to be tiresome; verbose; . . . long-winded." Was this derision necessary? He argued that many of the Complaint's causes of action "consist solely of legal conclusions," without specifying which. Could it be that he simply tired of reading the near-prolix allegations of fact? He misspelled NCJAR's name as "National Counsel for American-Japanese Redress," as though we were the national attorney for a group of Americans in Japan. He wasn't even "giving the devil his due."

Within the Motion to Dismiss, Axelrad recognized that "the factual allegations of the Complaint may be assumed . . . to be accurate." Since these allegations support claims for monetary damages, the question becomes whether the United States, "as sovereign," consents to be sued under the legal principle of sovereign immunity. NCJAR's Complaint invokes statutes which include waivers of sovereign immunity. Axelrad dismissed sovereign immunity by arguing that each of these statutes contains a time limitation that has expired. In addition, the general statute of limitations of six years has also expired. The Complaint's filing date, four decades beyond the events, obviously exceeds all limitations periods. Hence, he argued, since the limitations periods of the statutes waiving sovereign immunity have expired, neither these statutes nor their waiver of sovereign immunity applies.

Axelrad's arguments seemed overwhelming to me. And yet, the experience of applying the axiom of time limitations has produced case law theorems, to use the analogy of Euclidean geometry, that allow for "tolling" of limitations. "Tolling," an archaism ensconced in legal language, means the postponing of the initiation of the limitations clock. The period of limitations is not affected, but its initiation is. Tolling statutes of limitations will become crucial to this legal battle.

Axelrad's central argument was that the American-Japanese Evacuation Claims Act "is the exclusive remedy for plaintiffs' claims because Congress intended it to be the statutory means of redressing any and all claims arising from the exclusions." Axelrad argued forcefully that the 1948 Claims Act was the only remedy available to the victims of the government's program of mass exclusion and detention. He offered the expert and official opinion that once the Claims Act became law, no recourse was available other than those provided by the Act, and no claims were redressable except those claims defined within the Act.

I took small comfort in Axelrad's scoffs, his compelling arguments on limitations and the Claims Act, and my ignorance of legal history and theory. I simply had to wait and wonder what salvation our attorneys would provide for the uncertainty and anxiety caused by reading the Motion to Dismiss.

NCJAR's Motion for Class Certification

But before NCJAR's attorneys filed their opposition to the Motion to Dismiss, they were required to file for class certification. They did this on June 14, 1983. This was to certify that the plaintiffs fulfilled the requirements of a class action. They used several criteria to argue the obvious point that a single, joint action was preferable to thousands of individual lawsuits. They also attempted to make the class as inclusive as possible: they included not only survivors but representatives of deceased victims; not only those imprisoned in WRA camps but those imprisoned in Department of Justice camps; and not only those affected within the Western Defense Command but those taken from the Hawaiian, Alaskan, and other Defense Commands. They also wanted to avoid the requirement of notifying all the members of the class to allow those who did not want to join in a class action to "opt out."[2]

NCJAR Opposition to Motion to Dismiss

On July 15, 1983, NCJAR attorneys filed an opposition to the government's motion to dismiss. They first argued against the toughest defense: the expiration of statutes of limitations. Then they argued against the protection of sovereign immunity. Finally, they argued against American-Japanese Evacuation Claims Act of 1948 as the exclusive remedy.

Against Statutes of Limitations

Our attorneys argued that statutes of limitations should have tolled (postponed their initiation) while the government was engaged in "affirmative acts of concealment and fraud . . . which concealed the nature of defendant's actions." In other words, how was it possible for us, the plaintiffs, to know our causes of action when the supporting evidence for them was concealed from us? One needs more than a hunch to file a lawsuit and define causes of action; one needs evidence. They pointed out that "for purposes of the motion to dismiss," the "plaintiffs' allegations of fraud, concealment, misrepresentation, and suppression of evidence by the defendant must be assumed." Since our allegations of fraudulent concealment are part of the lawsuit, they must be assumed to be true until tested in a trial.

They also argued that the government should be "estopped" (stopped by the doctrine of equitable estoppel) from raising the defense of statutes of limitations. ("Equitable Estoppel" is one of those principles needed to keep a system from becoming contradictory, like the rule prohibiting division by zero to avoid contradiction in mathematics. To estop, the verbal form of estoppel, is to plug up, stop, or bar. Equitable estoppel is a rule to bar a party from first asserting one state of things as true, and later to assert a different state was true. You can't have it both ways.) During the war, the government described its action as evacuation and relocation for the reason of military necessity; it cannot now state that its action was exclusion and detention for reasons of racism and political expediency in order to argue that Japanese-Americans should have known their causes of action, and could have filed a lawsuit during the war years. Equitable estoppel should bar the government from this revision of its statement of wartime reality in order to prevent tolling of statutes of limitations. NCJAR attorneys explained:

United States wrongdoing, including massive deprivations of constitutional rights, denial of access to judicial relief, and fraud and misrepresentation, have caused serious injustice, so that the United States should be estopped from raising the defense of statutes of limitations.

Against Sovereign Immunity

Legal arguments are heavily dependent upon the experience of the courts in deciding prior applications of legal principles. There is, of course, a marked tendency to conform to prior decisions, so that meanings tend to remain the same. But, as new paths are tried, changes do occur. The meaning of the "Takings Clause" of the Fifth Amendment is an example of such change:

. . . nor shall private property be taken for public use, without just compensation.

As NCJAR attorneys argued, this clause "constitutes a waiver of sovereign immunity," inasmuch as its language "*mandates* compensation for governmental takings of private property." The mandate is clear enough, but what is meant by "private property?" The meaning of "private property" has been expanded by earlier applications to mean more than transferable private property; it now includes barring "plaintiffs from residing in their homes, working at their businesses, or otherwise remaining on their property." Here NCJAR attorneys argue to extend its meaning even further to encompass constitutional rights:

These United States actions also caused takings of plaintiffs' vested constitutional rights, in violation of the Fifth Amendment. These deprivations are compensable under the Fifth Amendment because they are analogous to property rights, which the government may not deprive without affording effective remedy.

If the courts accept this extension, the "Takings Clause" will circumvent the protection of sovereign immunity for constitutional violations as well as property losses. The effort is venturesome and risky.

Other points of law are also raised to circumvent sovereign immunity, such as the Federal Tort Claims Act and the Tucker Act. I only note these without discussion, since I am already dangerously far afield in legal issues which I only partially understand.

Against the American-Japanese Claims Act

NCJAR attorneys list the following as losses which remain uncompensated by "exclusive remedy" of the Claims Act:

1. Interest from the date of taking;

2. Losses from confiscation of personal property;

3. Losses by "enemy aliens";

4. Lost rent, earnings, and profits;

5. Damages to rights to use property—the right to enjoy, exploit, and use property for its natural purposes;

6. Losses of vested public benefits, employment contracts, and educational programs;

7. Expenses incurred in preparation for exclusion, and in resettlement following imprisonment; and

8. Losses from imprisonment (as distinguished from those of exclusion).

In addition to these uncompensated losses, they point to numerous violations of constitutional and other rights embedded in the Claims Act. The Claims Act cannot be the exclusive remedy or the sole waiver of sovereign immunity because it is plainly constitutionally deficient.

On August 8, 1983, NCJAR attorneys filed an Amended Complaint, which added a twenty-second cause of action, Breach of Fiduciary Duty, and some other points. The addition incorporated a June 1983 finding by the Supreme Court in the *United States v. Mitchell* case of ". . . a fiduciary relationship arising from the Interior Department's daily supervision and control of the affairs of the Quinault Indian Tribe." In other words, since the government had responsibility for the day-to-day needs of this tribe, the Court found that the government also assumed a fiduciary responsibility for the tribe's property. By extension, since the War Relocation Authority assumed responsibility for the day-to-day needs of 120,000 persons, it also assumed fiduciary responsibility for their property and rights. This responsibility was breached by the government's failure to act in our best interest, including its failure to inform us of what legal actions we should take to protect our interests.

(I remember the luncheon conversation Jack Herzig and I had with former WRA solicitor, Philip M. Glick, in which Glick stated with great emphasis how much WRA attorneys wanted "evacuees" to file suit against the government. But instead of acting in the fiduciary relationship as our advocate and advising us to file suit to protect our rights, he could only lament that his position with the WRA, presumably as our adversary, precluded such advice.)

In the months that followed, the Department of Justice filed its reply to the opposition to the motion to dismiss, oral argument was held before Judge Oberdorfer, and the Judge requested and obtained supplemental memoranda from both sides to discuss the question of tolling statutes of limitations. These activities of the court extended into 1984. The final act of this account was Judge Oberdorfer's decision of May 17, 1984.

24. COURTS
DISMISSAL

I had a premonition. Around midday I wondered aloud to Yuriko whether there was anything special about May 17. Was I forgetting an anniversary? There wasn't anything we could think of. A few hours later the date began to burn indelibly into our memories. Benjamin Zelenko called to say that Judge Oberdorfer had issued an order granting the government's Motion to Dismiss. He had only just received the Judge's fifty-nine-page memorandum explaining the order, so Benjamin could only say that he would express-mail a copy to me. I wrote a short press release for the Japanese-American press. It contained little more than an announcement of the decision. Gradually, the calls came in from the news media. I expressed my disappointment, and explained that I had not seen the memorandum and that it would be for the NCJAR board to decide whether we would appeal. But then I began to get intimations from reporters about wire services reports. The decisive point was the statute of limitations, and the Judge was referring us to congressional action.

The Judge's Memorandum

As promised, I received the Judge's memorandum on the following day. It was not easy for me to read. I did find Oberdorfer's evenhandedness helpful; his words had none of the sting of the Department of Justice's pleadings. But I found his recounting of the history of the wartime events, the first third of the memorandum, filled with governmental euphemisms such as "voluntary relocation" for movement following a military exclusion order, "relocation center" for permanent detention camps, "evacuees" for detainees, prisoners, or internees, and "evacuation" for mass exclusion and detention. It is, of course, deeply ironic that while he said that we should have known our causes of action in the late 1940s, he, himself, falls prey in 1984 to terminology carefully crafted to obscure those same causes of action. He is only the latest of victims who include most historians and the CWRIC. He also included disputed history as accepted history when he said, for example, "After Pearl Harbor, there had been insufficient time to [separate loyal from disloyal.]" This "fact" is at odds with the official military intelligence report by Lt. Commander Ringle issued before mass exclusion was decided and initiated by the military. Oberdorfer used the phrase "repatriation was slow" to refer to the process of release and relocation from the detention camps to "free" America. It is unintentionally ironic and inaccurate. One cannot return to a place one has not left.

After these preliminaries, he launched into the legal issues. The defendant United States' Motion to Dismiss raised three objections to the NCJAR complaint: 1) the protection of sovereign immunity whereby the government can be sued only "in situations where it has consented to be sued;" 2) the exclusive remedy of the Japanese-American Evacuation Claims Act of 1948 which would preclude any other claims for monetary damages; and 3) the "running of the statutes of limitations."

The Judge accepted defendant United States' contention that plaintiffs had not received the consent of the government to be sued on the fifteen constitutional issues contained in the twenty-two-count complaint—except for Unjust Takings. The Fifth Amendment states, "nor shall private property be taken for public use, without just compensation." Here the Constitution stipulates "just compensation" when private property is taken. But while accepting Unjust Takings, he rebuffed NCJAR's attempt to extend private property to constitutional rights. The Judge also accepted the potential validity of NCJAR's claims under the Federal Tort Claims Act, if separate problems of statute of limitations and agency filing procedures could be overcome.

We lost a lot on the first point. The fifteen constitutional counts were reduced to one. But we did much better on the 1948 Claims Act. The Judge rejected defendant United States' contention that the Act was the exclusive remedy for all plaintiffs' injuries arising from the wartime program. He stated, "The Act does not bar this Court from jurisdiction over all plaintiffs' claims."

So Unjust Takings remained. But only until the third point, statutes of limitations, was reached:

> . . . every civil action commenced against the United States shall be barred unless the complaint is filed within six years after the right of action first accrues.

The defendant United States argued that Unjust Takings occurred during the war and the six-year period should have started then. NCJAR argued that "defendant fraudulently concealed information essential to their cause of action." We referred to the concealment of the Munson report, the reports of the Federal Communications Commission and the FBI which contradicted key "facts" supporting the doctrine of military necessity, and the official Naval Intelligence report of Lt. Commander Ringle. The Judge accepted NCJAR's fraudulent concealment argument, but not NCJAR's timing.

Oberdorfer stated, "The FCC, FBI, and Naval Intelligence reports and others have been available, and publicized, since soon after the war's conclusion." In a closely reasoned section of his memorandum, the Judge cited NCJAR attorneys' argument:

> . . . documents previously available did not disclose the government's conspiracy or other evidence obviously different from that which had been presented to the courts in the 1940's. To the contrary, this published information merely tended to support the same arguments advanced against the government and rejected in the wartime cases—that the plaintiff class was loyal to the United States and there was no military necessity for the wartime actions. It was not until the [Commission's] work and related archival findings uncovered and published evidence of intentional government concealment and misrepresentation, that plaintiffs had evidence obviously different from that earlier ruled on by the Supreme Court.

Oberdorfer demurred, "However, it is the [Naval Intelligence, FCC, and FBI] documents, not the [recently uncovered] memoranda, which contain the direct evidence requisite to challenging the finding of military necessity." He acknowledged the assertions of concealment in the recent, Judge Patel opinion in the Korematsu *coram nobis* decision, but rejected their application to this case, "That concealment, whether intentional or not, is not a basis for tolling a statute of limitations beyond the time the information concealed by that conduct was published." He then set the time for beginning the running of the statute of limitations as "the publication in the late 1940's of the previously concealed . . . documents." He ended his reasoning, "In summary, the standard by which fraudulent concealment must be judged is not one of full disclosure but rather one of sufficient disclosure to allow the plaintiffs, through due diligence, to state a claim."

The expiration of time and the protection of sovereign immunity are used to deny the remaining causes of action. With the Complaint now stripped bare, he rejected NCJAR's request for the Court's declaration that the alleged acts of defendant United States stand "in violation of plaintiffs' constitutional, statutory, and civil rights." He stated with necessary but nonetheless painful redundancy, "There is no justiciable controversy here."

He signed his memorandum in fluid, well-formed script, "May 17, 1984 Louis F. Oberdorfer."

A Response

I remember becoming entranced as a small child by the multitude of people and events in a public park and then, to my dismay, realizing I was lost. So it is with this legal writing, which invokes precedents and alludes to concepts, sometimes in Latin, which seem ripe with meaning but beyond one's understanding. It took me a little while to assess the Judge's determination. He sets the time when we could have filed a lawsuit into the late 1940s. I had to lift my nose from the memorandum and remember the times.

Japanese-Americans were released from the camps, given a one-way ticket to the destination of their choice, and a grant of twenty-five dollars with which to begin life anew. We did not get a new suit of clothes, however. We were more like parolees than ex-convicts. We were extensively cautioned by the War Relocation Authority to be on our best behavior. Nisei GIs returned from the war, having once again proved their loyalty under combat. World War I veterans, Kinzo Wakayama and Joe Kurihara, expatriated to Japan with the certain knowledge that their battle-proved loyalty did not keep them from internment. The Heart Mountain draft resisters, who attempted to assert their constitutional rights through nonviolent protest, languished in prison. James Omura, editor of the *Rocky Shimpo*, was charged with conspiracy by the government for publishing editorial opinion in support of the resisters' constitutional rights. Law enforcement officials defined loyalty to the United States as willingness to inform on friends and neighbors, thereby cutting deep wounds within Japanese America which remain unhealed to this day. Iva Toguri, a "Tokyo Rose," returned voluntarily to America in order to vindicate her innocence in a court of law, only to be convicted of treason and sentenced to ten years in prison. Thousands of renunciants could find only a single attorney, Wayne Collins, who was willing to represent their claims in a court of law. Not only did the Supreme Court on several occasions legitimate the government's illegal and unconstitutional actions, which was mightily intimidating, but the Evacuation Claims Act required that recipients of the government's gratuitous payments sign away their right to sue.

Even in 1983, thirty-five years later, Department of Justice attorney Jeffrey Axelrad had argued vigorously that the Claims Act was the exclusive remedy. Axelrad could not know that a year later Judge Oberdorfer would rule favorably on this Motion to Dismiss, and, in so doing, set the time at which the plaintiffs should have discovered their causes of action—toll the statutes of limitations—just after the Claims Act became law. In May 1984, the court ruled that plaintiffs should have been able to discover their causes of action at the time when expert and official legal opinion, rendered as recently as May 1983, argued that there was not any basis in law whatsoever for the victims to consider filing a lawsuit, much less searching for causes of action. Axelrad's 1983 argument may have been exaggerated by his adversarial zeal. But at the time of its enactment and implementation, who would dare challenge the Claims Act as the exclusive remedy? After waiving his or her right to sue the government, who would dare turn around and file a lawsuit?

American philosopher William James propounded the notion of a "Will to Believe," which is succinctly characterized in *The Encyclopedia of Philosophy*:

We must at least believe our hypotheses sufficiently to bestir ourselves to test them.

Why should we have searched for causes of action if we were incapable of believing in the possibility of a lawsuit? Such was the social and legal situation in which Judge Oberdorfer would have us take the United States to court.

I also found myself troubled by the Judge's assumption that we have now marshaled all the facts which fully disclose the issues. We know from the 1981 CWRIC testimonies of Bendetsen, McCloy, Dedrick, and others that falsification and coverup continue. What are they trying to hide? We know from State Department historian David Trask's testimony that the United States was concerned over reprisals by Japan against 10,000 American civilians—not soldiers—in the opening months of the war and that the United States had no offsetting reserve of hostages—except the 110,000 internees. Are not reprisals to be offset by counter-reprisals? Against whom? Our lawsuit is a long way from full disclosure.

Finally, the notion of "due diligence" seems to be stretching human capacity. After all the histories and essays had been written and published by doctors of philosophy from distinguished universities, it took a theatrical costume designer without a degree named Michi Weglyn to enunciate the hostage-reprisal theory. And it was Michi Weglyn who first grasped, then explained, the meaning of the Munson report, thirty years—not six years—after it became public. If academicians, living under the pressure of "publish or perish," could not assess the significance of the FCC, FBI, Naval Intelligence, and Munson reports, what could "due diligence" of a thoroughly intimidated and struggling group of victims hope to uncover?

But it is the Judge's order, not my misgivings, that rule the courts. There is, of course, the option, if not necessity, of appealing the order. The NCJAR board voted to appeal Oberdorfer's decision, and embarked on another fundraising effort, not as intense as the first. Other parts of the movement proceeded with legislative redress efforts. A good part of the tale has been told. It's time to tell an ending.

25. COURTS
WILL AMERICA BE REPAIRED?

In the months following Oberdorfer's decision, I had mixed feelings about the redress movement: the innocence of the movement's hope and faith in American democracy and the gritty realities of failed human institutions, blind bigotry and racism, and unthinking loyalty. Will the cause of redress triumph? Will the Constitution be repaired? The answers will take time. In 1980, the first Lowry Redress Bill did not succeed. Instead, Congress created the Commission on Wartime Relocation and Internment of Civilians. While the Commission's hearings did produce occasional insight, they were mostly a parade of victims, who spoke in five-minute compressions of pain and supplication, before packed audiences and a Commission with frequent absentees. The victims, predictably, had few new insights to offer concerning the root causes of their victimization. When the Commission finally held hearings for those in government who created and implemented the program of mass exclusion and detention, their testimony was not given under oath, and their accounts contradicted victims' accounts, official government photographs, and their own written record retrieved from the National Archives. The commissioners tried to coax rather than require these victimizers to speak truthfully. The Commission's report and recommendations were modest, more a gesture of sympathy to powerless victims from the Commission's sponsor, the United States Congress, than act of contrition by the government. A few of the victims expressed their disappointment and dissatisfaction. Most praised the Commission for its accomplishments. But none recognized the eventual import of the mere fact of the Commission's creation. On March 16, 1983, NCJAR filed a class action lawsuit against the United States on behalf of 125,000 victims. The government moved to dismiss the lawsuit. In the same year, a second wave of redress legislation was introduced, including the second Lowry Redress Bill. On May 17, 1984, the U.S. District Court dismissed the lawsuit of NCJAR. And the 98th Congress adjourned without taking action on the redress proposals. The court's decision was appealed, and there was a 99th Congress. The prospects for redress waned.

But after many months of waiting, we felt hope stirring anew. On September 24, 1985, I was in Washington to attend the oral argument before the three-judge panel of the U.S. Court of Appeals for the District of Columbia Circuit. Mike Rauh's initial question—why had no one filed this lawsuit earlier?—returned in a new, significant form. Judge Ruth Ginsburg asked Jeffrey Axelrad:

> These people certainly knew back in the early forties that they were injured. Can they make a claim in court[? W]ould[n't] that depend on their ability to overcome a defense, . . . a defense that the Supreme Court accepted? With that precedent, how could they ever survive[? H]ow could they overcome that defense? That was their problem[. A]t what point in time would they have been able to overcome that defense[?][1]

I heard the question but was unable to hear the Department of Justice attorney's answer. It made no difference. The judge's question implied its own answer. We could see the way one judge was leaning, and we felt a touch of hope. Mike Rauh was optimistic. Nelson Kitsuse, elated. Ellen Carson and Benjamin Zelenko felt good. But when I tried to express my budding of hope, Zelenko cautioned me to maintain my dispassioned view.

Four months later, on January 21, 1986, hope burst into jubilation. We'd won! Again, we received our initial intimations of victory from the press. Soon, it was clear enough. In a two-to-one decision, Judge Skelly Wright wrote the majority opinion for the U.S. Court of Appeals. As part of his explanation, he gave this answer to Rauh's question:

> Given the constitutional underpinnings of the presumption of deference articulated by the Court, however, nothing less than an authoritative statement by one of the political branches, purporting to review the evidence when taken as a whole, could rebut the presumption articulated in *Korematsu*.[2]

He was referring to the Court's deference to military necessity. (The Supreme Court may be called simply "the Court.") We could not file a lawsuit earlier because the Court had ruled mass exclusion and detention constitutionally acceptable under the doctrine of military necessity. We could not consider filing until the government itself raised doubts about this deference. With this argument, the statute of limitations was tolled until the establishment of the Commission on Wartime Relocation and Internment of Civilians in July 1980. The Commission's establishment was, in effect, taken as "an authoritative statement by one of the political branches, purporting to review the evidence when taken as a whole." The appeals court reversed Oberdorfer's decision and remanded our lawsuit to trial. It was a tremendous victory.

The lawsuit was transformed from a high-risk venture into a probable trial. We were suddenly confronted with the prospect of having our day in court. For the survivors of the class of 125,000—about half were still living—our lawsuit now became part of their future. Redress was no longer simply hypothetical; it was becoming real. The time to test and verify it in a court of law was at hand.

We still faced struggle and risk. The victory, though intensely gratifying, was partial. As the opinion concluded, the decision "affirmed in part and reversed and remanded in part."[3] While the statute of limitations portion of Oberdorfer's decision was reversed, the cloak of sovereign immunity remained affirmed, so that our case was remanded to trial with our twenty-two causes of action reduced to one. We were left with the Takings Clause. This was clearly unacceptable. Mass exclusion and detention involved much more than the taking of property. The other constitutional issues were vital to our Complaint. Though we had won a major victory at this level of appeal, we needed to take our case to the Supreme Court. The courts had to examine the government's massive violation of *habeas corpus*, due process, equal protection, and other constitutional guarantees. Moreover, the Court had to be given the opportunity to review and reconsider its wartime decisions. Only the Supreme Court can overturn Supreme Court decisions. The Court needs a vehicle, a case by which to make its reconsideration. Ours was opportune.

Even as we welcomed this opportunity for lifting our appeal to the Court, we were aware of the risks. The courts provide no certitude. We would first have to withstand appeals by the Department of Justice in representing defendant United States. The U.S. requested a rehearing by an *en banc* panel of judges—all eleven of them—of the U.S. Court of Appeals to review the three-judge panel decision. On May 30, 1986, their request was denied by a six-five vote, clearing the way for appeals to the Supreme Court. In an unusual move, a strongly-worded dissent from this denial was written by Judge Bork. Bork's dissent evoked rebuttal from Judge Wright and Judge Ginsburg.

The *en banc* decision had two effects. Judge Antonin Scalia voted for a rehearing as a member of the *en banc* panel. Four months later, he was appointed as an Associate Justice of the Supreme Court. Having participated in our case, he would recuse (or excuse) himself from participating as a Justice in its appeals, leaving an eight-Justice Court to make the ultimate judgment. The vigor of Bork's dissent made more likely our opportunity to be heard by the Court. We had ninety days to file our appeal.

On August 26, 1986 we filed our petition for a writ of certiorari, the formal designation for a request for review by the Supreme Court. We were joined as friends of the court by the American Friends Service Committee, the Board of Church and Society of the United Methodist Church, the United Church Board for Homeland Ministries of the United Church of Christ, the Asian American Legal Defense and Education Fund, the Anti-Defamation League of B'nai B'rith, the Japanese American Citizens League, and the JACL's Legislative and Education Committee. The Office of the Solicitor General represents the government in the Supreme Court and now became the government's advocate. Charles Fried, the Solicitor General, in filing the government's appeal, requested and received an extension to September 1986. Both sides filed responses toward the end of October 1986. Fried filed a rebuttal to our response in November 1986.

Following this ninety-day wait and the monthly alternations of filing, extension, and response, we settled down to wait for the Supreme Court to act, expecting to wait two or three more months. But in just three weeks, on November 17, the Court granted the government's petition and left ours pending. If our appeal was left pending in order to be heard, we had first to prevail over the barriers raised by the government. But an equally reasonable argument was that our appeal had been rejected, and its rejection was left pending to avoid coloring the Court's hearing of the government's appeal.

At around this time, Ellen Carson telephoned me to say that she and her husband, Bob Godbey, had decided to move to Hawaii within a few months. She would be leaving the law firm after she had written our brief for the Supreme Court. I felt lost and disappointed. Ellen had become a dear friend to many of us, and Hawaii seemed distant. She had been our explainer of legal matters. She had served as our advocate not only as an attorney but as one of NCJAR's chief representatives in public gatherings in New York, Chicago, Seattle, San Francisco, and Los Angeles. She was a brilliant attorney. She was personally committed to the redress movement. And she was a feisty, enthusiastic, and compassionate person. As her good friend, Joyce Okinaka, said, "She's one in a million." The multi-ethnic population of Hawaii appealed to her. She and Bob had always considered their stay in the Washington area transitional; they had planned to move on before they arrived.

The Solicitor General had thirty days to file his brief. He again requested and received an extension to January 16, 1987. We responded on February 15. We received friend-of-the-court support from those who filed with our appeal, plus the American Civil Liberties Union, the ACLU of Southern California, the National Capital Area ACLU, the American Jewish Congress, the American Jewish Committee, Fred Korematsu, Gordon Hirabayashi, Minoru Yasui, and their attorneys, and the states of Hawaii and California.

General Fried, as the Solicitor General may be called, raised two issues. First, he raised a question of jurisdiction: had we been heard in the wrong appeals court? In 1982, while we were preparing our court complaint, Congress enacted the Federal Courts Improvement Act. Among other issues, the Act was intended to consolidate appellate decisions on federal, as opposed to regional or state, issues; it established a Federal Circuit appeals court. Clearly, the first fifteen causes of action in our case, those based upon the Constitution, fell within this newly established jurisdiction. But our other causes of action included Federal Tort claims (conspiracy, assault and battery, false arrest, abuse of process, and negligence); these fell within the jurisdiction of the regional appeals court. Our was a mixed case. This Act was unclear about mixed cases. In the D.C. Circuit appeals court, the government, as well as a majority of judges, agreed with us that we were in the proper circuit. But after losing, the government, in a blatant act of forum shopping, decided we had argued in the wrong circuit.

The second issue was the statute of limitations. Fried presented a novel argument. He argued that racism (coyly described as "ancestral, cultural, and ethnic considerations"), not military necessity, was the reason for the government's program of mass exclusion and detention. He was trying to make irrelevant the troubling questions surrounding the wartime government's concealment of vital evidence from the Court, evidence that contradicted the government's allegations of facts supporting military necessity. We sensed that Fried had made a fatal error. He may have neglected to obtain a copy of the transcript of the wartime Korematsu oral argument before the Court. He seemed not to have read the words of his wartime predecessor, Solicitor General Charles Fahy, who had argued that military necessity and only military necessity was the proper basis for the government's action. (This transcript was another of several important documents that were difficult to locate. After much searching, Peter Irons and Jack and Aiko Herzig were able to locate a copy in the Federal Records Center in Suitland, Maryland.)

Although I cannot discuss with any authority the jurisdictional question, I thought our position was cogent. As important as it was to consolidate the appeal of federal issues into the new Federal Circuit, it seemed to me to be equally important, as Congress stated, that regional and state issues continue to be appealed within regional circuits. I thought it more consistent with past practice that mixed cases, involving both federal and regional issues, be heard in the regional circuits. After all, the regional circuits had been hearing both issues until the new circuit had been established. Nothing would be added to their requirements. But by placing mixed cases in the Federal Circuit, this new appeals court could create inconsistencies in its rulings on regional issues, just as the regional courts had on federal issues.

On the tolling of the statute of limitations, I thought our arguments were compelling:

> With a remarkable lack of candor, the government maintains it did not mislead this Court in the wartime cases. The government fails even to acknowledge that every district court which has recently reviewed the true facts has found the government misled this [C]ourt. Forty years after the fact, plaintiffs discovered not only that the government was wrong as to "military necessity," but also that the government knowingly had gone to extraordinary lengths to keep this Court from learning the truth. This is not speculation by plaintiffs. It is the finding of the Commission and of every district court. In the light of these findings, it requires more charity than plaintiffs can muster to accept the government's contention, that it did not mislead this Court.[4]

We then rebut General Fried's interpretation of the government's reason for its wartime program of mass exclusion and detention with citations from his wartime predecessor, General Fahy. At the time, the arguments for military necessity depended heavily on the *Final Report* of General John L. DeWitt. Fried had tried to argue that a footnote in the wartime government's brief constituted an "explicit dis-incorporation" of the *Final Report*. But in 1944, Fahy had argued:

> It is even suggested that because of some footnote [sic] in our brief in this case indicating that we do not ask the Court to take judicial notice of the truth of every recitation or instance in the final report of General DeWitt, that the Government has repudiated the military necessity of the evacuation. It seems to me, if the Court please, that that is a neat piece of fancy dancing. There is nothing in the brief of the Government which is any different in this respect from the position it has always maintained since the Hirabayashi case—that not only the military judgment of the general, but the judgment of the Government of the United States, has always been in justification of the measures taken; and no person in any responsible position has ever taken a contrary position, and the Government does not do so now. Nothing in its brief can validly be used to the contrary.[5]

On Monday, April 20, 1987, the Supreme Court heard the appeal of the *U.S. v. Hohri et al.*, petitioner v. respondent. About one hundred friends and supporters gathered in Washington. Throughout this historic day, in ebb and flow, we became a memorable collection; great heroes from the past and present; Gordon Hirabayashi, Fred Korematsu, and Harry Ueno; Fred's wife, Kathryn; NCJAR attorneys: Benjamin Zelenko, Martin Shulman, Mike Rauh, and Wallace Cohen; their spouses: Barbara Zelenko, Carol Shulman, and Maggie Rauh; the Zelenkos' daughters, Laura and Carin;

former NCJAR attorney and dear friend Ellen Carson, all the way from Hawaii; attorneys from the *coram nobis* teams: Roger Shimizu, Rod Kawakami, Michael Leong, and Karen Kai; their spouses: Saki Shimizu and Kris Kawakami; the Shimizus' daughter Michelle Kumata; authors Mine Okubo (also an artist), Michi Weglyn, and Peter Irons; Michi's spouse, the courtly Walter Weglyn; named plaintiffs, many meeting each other for the first time: Chizu Omori, Harry Ueno, George Ikeda, Hannah Holmes, Ed Tokeshi, Merry Omori, Nelson Kitsuse, Sam Ozaki, Kaz Oshiki, Kumao Toda, Gladyce Sumida, and myself; my dear wife, Yuriko; two of my very old friends from Sawtelle Grammar School, Akira and Patrick Hirami; my wife's former Sunday School pupil and Hannah's expert interpreter, Janice Nishimura, who did a marvelous job of signing; supporters, friends, and relatives from around the country; Joyce Okinaka, Wes Yamaka, Sid, Kathleen, and Lisa Yamazaki, and K. T. Tanaka from California; Dorothy Takahama and her friends from Hawaii; my brother Tak and his sons Adrian and Elliot, from Long Beach; Greg Cooper, cousin to Adrian and Elliot from Philadelphia; our daughters Sasha (New York) and Sylvia (Los Angeles) and many friends of Sasha; Alice Basoms, Sally and Goji Tashiro, Mary K. and Lydia Omori, Barbara Kato, Greg Gundlach, Doris Sato, Professor Shirley Castelnuovo, Joe, Frances, and Larry Wiley from Chicago; Dr. Blanche Kimoto Baler from Ann Arbor; Katherine Chen, Tomiko Miyake, Cynthia Cajka, Tamaki Ogata, Kimiko Yamada, Jean Coolidge, Laura Akgulian from the East Coast; Arthur Wang and fellow students from Yale Law School; *New York Nichibei* editor Penny Willgerodt; Washington-based writers Kai Bird and Max Holland; the Smithsonian's Tom Crouch; attorneys and law students from the New York area: Toyo Obayashi, Tony Viero, Robert Yasui, Sam Sue, and Marc Iyeki; and others whose names I failed to retain.

Our hearing was scheduled for two o'clock p.m. We arrived at nine o'clock a.m., like customers in a deli, to obtain numbered slips of paper to secure positions for the afternoon session's line. These slips, the result of last minute negotiations by Aiko and Jack Herzig and Ellen Carson with the Marshal of the Supreme Court, were provided to avoid long hours of waiting. Once we received our numbers, we were free to leave. We had only to return before noon to form the afternoon line.

There are two one-hour hearings in the morning and two in the afternoon. It takes about thirty minutes to seat people in the courtroom because they must check their cameras, recorders, and bags into lockers, be carefully checked against a list of names if they have reserved seating, and be seated in numbered groups to insure that every available seat is used. So the courtroom is cleared for seating only after the morning session. We had to sit through the one o'clock hearing to hear ours at two o'clock.

All this waiting, this anticipation, like courtship, allowed us to become familiar with ourselves and the setting: the difference between the plaza (yes) and the steps (no) for picture-taking; the birds nesting and chirping at the top of the Court's imposing double columns; the courtroom itself with marble columns; its arrangement for nine persons not to be diminished by the attorneys seated at tables and chairs, members of the Court behind them, members of the press in the wings, and about 120 visitors.

The nine Justices are located above the assembly in high-backed chairs behind a high and wide bench that traverses much of the room, allowing desks for the Court's Clerk and Marshal at either end. The nine chairs have backs that vary in height as if to emphasize the individuality of their occupants.

It operated like clockwork. At one o'clock we all rose as the Justices entered through their curtained backdrop. Chief Justice Rehnquist began the first hearing immediately. The Justices interrupted frequently to ask questions. The exchanges were direct, without the flourishes used in the legislature just a block away. No the honorable this or the distinguished that. With only thirty minutes to a side, time was of the essence.

The first hearing was over just before two o'clock. The attorneys and a small group of visitors for the first hearing exited. Also, Justice Antonin Scalia exited. Ours was to be heard by eight Justices, requiring the government, whose appeal was being heard, to extract a five-three majority to win. At 1:59 p.m., Rehnquist said, "General Fried, you may proceed whenever you're ready."[6] Fried took the podium. Tall, he was striking in his morning coat. Reading from his text, he spoke with an eloquence befitting his high office.

Fried emphasized the jurisdictional issue. He argued that our appeal should have been heard in the Federal Circuit rather than the District of Columbia Circuit. He spent less time on the tolling question. In contrast to the earlier hearing, the Justices seemed subdued. Thus, it was like a bolt of lightning for the Solicitor General, when Justice Marshall asked Fried, "What is the difference between exclusion and killing?"

Fried's eloquence left him. The answer wasn't in his text. He hunted for words. "Killing is much, much worse," he replied.

"How much?"

"Well,—"

"When you pick up people and throw them out of their homes and where they live," Marshall pressed on, "what is anything between that and murder?"

"Well, murder suggests that life is taken contrary to law. Taking—"

"Well, is there any difference? What's the difference between that and taking the life?" asked Marshall.

Fried, having trouble finishing his responses, said, "Well, fortunately, large numbers—"

"What is the difference between banishment and hanging?"

Finally having time to finish, Fried replied, "Well, large numbers of those who were banished were able, after 1945, to return to their homes, and we should be grateful for that."

Curtly, Marshall requested, "Another."

And Fried obliged, "Well, there was great devastation among their property, Justice Marshall. That's quite correct. Which is why Congress, in 1948, passed the Japanese-American Evacuation Claims Act, and why some 26,000 family claims were filed under that Act."

The exchange brought tears to some eyes. Marshall's anger was anger we victims still suppress. The Court became human.

Benjamin Zelenko's turn came to speak on behalf of Japanese America and America. Zelenko is shorter and less angular than Fried, was dressed in a business suit, and has a voice that is quietly reasonable, not declamatory. He spoke from notes and maintained eye contact with the Justices. He had logic, history, and most of the audience on his side. He spent most of his time on the statute of limitations issue, only a few minutes on the jurisdictional one. He began, "Mr. Chief Justice, and may it please the Court. This is an historic case. The Executive Branch should find no repose when it systematically conceals the facts from this Court. The wartime imprisonment of plaintiffs imposed substantial losses on them. They seek their day in court and ask that the judgment of the Court of Appeals be affirmed."

He then divided the limitations issue into the question of concealment of evidence by the government as sufficient reason to toll the limitations clock and the question of when the clock should begin.

On the question of when to start limitations, Zelenko responded to the various times argued by the government: the war years, Grodzins's *Americans Betrayed,* and President Ford's 1976 Proclamation that rescinded EO9066. Obviously, with concealment during the war years, the Court's deference to military necessity precluded a lawsuit for losses. Grodzins's book revealed only "snippets" of key reports and, of course, contained nothing about concealment. Zelenko's main hurdle was the 1976 Proclamation. It was here that Chief Justice Rehnquist made his challenge.

Zelenko argued that the Proclamation lacked legal significance because President Ford had said, "We now know what we should have known then," in rescinding EO9066, whereas the government did know then what it knew in 1976. Rehnquist tried to make the Proclamation into a denial of the wartime existence of military necessity. But Zelenko pointed out that Ford had said that a mistake had been made only in hindsight, from the perspective of 1976.

Rehnquist then asked, "Isn't that the same thing as saying there was no military necessity?"

"No, your honor," Zelenko replied. "What we're saying is that in 1942, when this Court ruled, there was no military necessity then."

What Zelenko seemed to be driving at and Rehnquist avoiding was that the Korematsu decision may be directly challenged by the fact of fraudulent concealment occuring in 1944, but not by reason of a judgment made thirty-two years later.

Rehnquist attacked the July 1980 tolling date, "And you say that although the President's Proclamation revoking the order under which the Japanese Americans were interned had no legal effect, the report of a Commission created by Congress to study the matter and the report, which was never acted upon by Congress, does have a great deal of legal significance."

Zelenko parried by arguing that the facts disclosed in the Commission's report have legal significance.

Rehnquist then tried to dismiss the significance of the role of Congress in establishing the Commission, ". . . because it wasn't the imprimatur of the Commission; it was the facts. . . ."

But Zelenko did not oblige.

He used the argument made by the Court of Appeals for tolling, "that one of the war-making branches, namely the Congress, had stood up to the deference heretofore accorded to the military judgment, which this Court had ruled was due." He concluded his presentation by defending the jurisdictional decisions made by the lower courts and urged the Justices not to duck the main issue in judicially proper language, "No interests of justice will be served by not deciding the merits and transferring this case to the Federal Circuit."

Fried had reserved several minutes for rebuttal, but most were consumed in an exchange with Justice Stevens, who had read the transcript of the oral argument of the Korematsu case and was not convinced by Fried's minimizing the Court's reliance on the *Final Report*. Stevens was rebutting the rebuttal. For Fried, this was not a happy note on which to end, but end he must, "If there are no further questions, thank you."

The hour was the consummation of lifetime of hope, the achievement of years of organizing, learning, sustaining, encouraging, and enduring. The initial rush was relief that it was over. We had made it through the final uncertainties. We had been heard by the Supreme Court. I began to see friends whom I had not seen earlier. Others I saw but did not recognize until they introduced themselves. Blanche K. Baler, our *ronin* from Ann Arbor was one. I saw Benjamin. I congratulated him, and he wisecracked back. I asked Mike Rauh for his prediction. He had been right-on before. He said something about having four. As we retrieved our things from the lockers, my brother Tak rushed in from the outside and told me that Mr. Zelenko was asking for me to attend a press conference. I was a little puzzled because we had planned a press conference to take place an hour later. But Tak insisted. I followed. Once outside, I noticed a crowd gathered on a corner of the plaza and then saw Benjamin vigorously motioning me to come down. When I arrived, the crowd parted for me, and I went through to face a clump of microphones and several television cameras. It was the way press conferences are depicted by Hollywood, unlike any I had attended before. Someone asked about my life in camp, a standard question, to which I gave a standard reply. Then someone asked if I would consider a victory the Solicitor General's statement that the government's wartime program was motivated by racism. I called the statement a fabrication and began to relieve much of the frustration and tension of this day. I said, "It would be a victory if the Solicitor General were on our side and fighting our case. He is supposed to be the one who upholds the Constitution of the United States."[7]

In the early evening, NCJAR held an informal reception that became a wonderful event. The only program we had was introducing everyone. We formed a ring and asked each person introduced to step to its center. Hannah Holmes was the last to be introduced. She, in turn, had us sign "Happy Birthday, H-A-R-R-Y" to celebrate Harry Ueno's eightieth year. Then, as one coconspirator dimmed the lights, another brought in a two-layer cake with the Supreme Court iced on top and eight candles for the decades of Harry's life. We sang "Happy Birthday To You!" Hannah unfurled a birthday card that reached the floor and must have had hundreds of signatures of well-wishers. Harry talked a little about his experiences. In slow, halting words, he recalled for us the pain of our wartime abuse. He was one of eight-three men who had suffered imprisonment within imprisonment in a special, high security, isolation camp. None had received a hearing or trial. Today was his first day in court. It was our first day in court, too. Our exaltation began.

Six weeks later, on June 1, another Monday, our exaltation was tempered by the quencher of a cool, well-crafted opinion by Justice Powell. In a unanimous decision, the Court supported the government's jurisdictional argument and vacated the decision of the D.C. Circuit's appeals court and remanded our district court appeal to be reheard by the U.S. Court of Appeals for the Federal Circuit. We were back to square two, to the point following district court's dismissal. The narrow, procedural question had prevailed as some attorneys had predicted. The Court, I was told, tends to rule on the narrowest grounds possible. The Justices were silent on the issues surrounding the statute of limitations. Though we were still alive, the decision was a sharp disappointment to us. It appeared as though the Court was ducking the issue. And the Court's unanimity was puzzling. Given the admission in Powell's opinion of the ambiguity of the 1982 Federal Courts Improvement Act on the jurisdiction of a mixed-issues appeal, how could the Justices possibly agree? The decision posed two questions:

was the Court dealing with the jurisdictional issue in order to hear in a subsequent appeal the substantive issues in the statute of limitations? Or, was this remand the first step towards the Court's complete silence. In the evening of the same Monday, the NCJAR board voted to continue.

There was a third alternative, invisible to the Court and to most of the public. This struggle was between a small, voluntary group of ordinary persons and the world's mightiest institution, the U.S. government. While we were scrounging for a few dollars to sustain our movement, to publish our newsletter, cover expenses of postage, telephone, and office supplies, and pay legal fees and costs, our adversary was coping with trillions of dollars in budgets and debts. While we had, perhaps, one thousand supporters paying for the services of a small law firm, the Department of Justice had over 4,600 attorneys. How long could this unequal battle be sustained? Would our supporters continue to sustain us? If we could not raise the money for the continued legal costs, the appeals could not be carried forward. It seemed manifestly unfair of the fates to have forced the victims of such a grave injustice to have to fight and endure to have the injury to them, and the injury to the Constitution and our democratic society repaired. Was our struggle in danger of becoming quixotic?

The framers of the Constitution and the founders of the United States were wise enough to realize that the responsibility for freedom lies not with the government and institutions of our nation but with our nation's citizens. They made some mistakes about just who those citizens were, but provided the means for corrective action, so that we are now a people no longer divided into free and slave, male and female, or white and nonwhite. But the responsibility for extending and insuring human freedom continues into each generation and to each group or individual who suffers from flaws inherent in our constitutional democracy or from failures of the government to uphold our democratic guarantees of freedom. One of the threats to American democracy is the very size of its institutions. A trillion-dollar budget may exceed human comprehension and control. The very size and number of buildings housing the federal government intimidate us. We citizens hardly know where to begin in exercising our rights against such proportions.

Despite what the framers felt and what Fourth of July orators declaim, freedom is now not so easily asserted against our huge institutions. As a result, we tend to invest our institutions with the responsibility for our freedoms. The redress movement, like the Constitution, violates this conventional view of American democracy. We believe that a small group, with little more than its remembered pain and desire to have its grievances redressed, can act to repair a breach in our democratic society, despite the best efforts by our government to intimidate and silence us. Our movement has become part of our legacy to America, our contribution to American democracy.

Every year, since 1969, Japanese-American pilgrims have journeyed to the former campsite that was Manzanar. They gather at the Manzanar Cemetery monument, a squat obelisk. On one of its sides, three Japanese characters proclaim, "Soul Consoling

Tower."[8] These pilgrims clean and dress the modest graveyard, conduct a ceremony, and listen to speeches. They return each year as though their entrance to America, the land of the free, keeps being denied. It is almost as if the graves they care for are more than graves of the infants and elderly, who while living in this still desolate enclave, so terrified the rest of America. It is as though they were the graves of the pilgrims' civil and constitutional rights. At their 1987 Manzanar Pilgrimage, Richard Drinnon, author of *Keeper of Concentration Camps: Dillon Myer and American Racism*, spoke these words:

> [T]he nation state cannot abridge freedom of speech, religion, press, assembly, due process of law, and the rest, because these rights existed prior to the framing of the Constitution.[9]

This is a thought worth remembering and fitting to end this account. Our freedoms are a part of our existence, a part of our selves. They are expressed as guarantees in our institutions only because we put them there. It is up to us to protect them, improve them, and, as in our situation, repair them.

NOTES

ABBREVIATIONS

AB Morton Grodzins, *Americans Betrayed*, University of Chicago Press, 1949.

AJ *Amerasia Journal*, UCLA.

AK Christopher Thorne, *Allies of a Kind: The United States, Britain and the War Against Japan, 1941-45*, Oxford University Press, 1978.

AT Audio Tapes, property of William Hohri.

BP Frank F. Chuman, *The Bamboo People: The Law and Japanese-Americans*, Publisher's Inc., 1976.

CWRIC Commission on Wartime Relocation and Internment of Civilians documents.

DCK Tamotsu Shibutani, *The Derelicts of Company K*, University of California Press, 1978.

DRJA Roger Daniels, *The Decision to Relocate the Japanese Americans*, J. B. Lippincott Co., 1975.

EP United States Department of Interior, *The Evacuated People—A Quantitative Description*, U.S. Government Printing Office, 1946.

FO George H. Kerr, *Formosa, Licensed Revolution and the Home Rule Movement, 1895-1945*, University Press of Hawaii, 1974.

FR John L. DeWitt, *Final Report: Japanese Evacuation from the West Coast, 1942*, U.S. Government Printing Office, 1943.

GB Audrie Girdner and Anne Loftis, *The Great Betrayal: The Evacuation of the Japanese-Americans during World War II*, Macmillan Co., 1969.

HH Hearing before the Subcommittee on Administrative Law and Governmental Relations of the Committee on the Judiciary, House of Representatives, Ninety-Sixth Congress, Second Session, on H.R. 5499, June 2, 1980.

HS Hearing before the Committee on Governmental Affairs, United States Senate, Ninety-Sixth Congress, Second Session, on S. 1647, March 18, 1980.

JAW Peter Irons, *Justice at War*, Oxford University Press, 1983.

JIQJ Bill Hosokawa, *JACL In Quest of Justice*, William Morrow and Co., Inc., 1982.

NARG National Archives Record Group.

NL Newsletter of NCJAR.

NYN *New York Nichibei* newspaper.

PC *Pacific Citizen* newspaper.

PJD *Personal Justice Denied*, Report of the CWRIC, U.S. Government Printing Office, 1983.

POP Roger Daniels, *The Politics of Prejudice*, University of California Press, 1962.

PWC Jacobus tenBroek, Edward N. Barnhart, and Floyd W. Matson, *Prejudice, War and the Constitution*, University of California Press, 1954.

RS *Rafu Shimpo* newspaper.

NOTES

S Dorothy S. Thomas and Richard S. Nishimoto, *The Spoilage*, University of California Press, 1946.

YOI Michi Weglyn, *Years of Infamy: the Untold Story of America's Concentration Camps*, William Morrow and Co., Inc., 1976.

REFERENCES

The abbreviations are defined in the list above. Page numbers are included without the preceding "p."

Preface

[1]JIQJ, 41, 167.

Chapter 1

[1]These and all other quotes are from the unpublished transcripts of CWRIC hearings.

Chapter 2

[1]DCK, 85.

[2]PJD, 369.

[3]NARG 319 Office of Assistant Chief of Staff G-2. The so-called MAGIC cables were decoded intercepts of Japanese diplomatic cables.

[4]JAW, 79.

[5]DCK, 35.

[6]DCK, 80.

[7]YOI, 55-56.

[8]PWC, 135.

[9]CWRIC, 12504-12521.

[10]PJD, 108.

[11]PJD, 100.

[12]JIQJ, 152.

[13]CWRIC, 12504-12521.

[14]PWC, 118.

[15]PWC, 122.

[16]PWC, 116.

[17]PJD, Table 1, 138; PWC, 118; EP, Table 5.

[18]DRJA, 124.

[19]DRJA, 124.

[20]DRJA, 128.

[21]JAW, 81.

[22]DRJA, 128.

[23]PWC, 123.

[24]JAW, 85.

[25]PWC, 128-129.

[26]EP, Table 5.

[27]JAW, 87-88.

[28]CWRIC, 12504-12521.

[29]EP, Table 5.

[30]JAW, 93.

[31]EP, Table 5.

[32]DCK, 38.

[33]PWC, 126.

[34]JAW, 135.

[35]DCK, 49.

[36]JIQJ, 189-190.

[37]JAW, 130.

[38]PWC, 129; 7 *Federal Register*, 8346.

[39]CWRIC, 12504-12521.

[40]JAW, 144.

[41]EP, Table 5.

[42]JAW, 150.

[43]CWRIC, 12504-12521

[44]PWC, 133.

[45]EP, Table 5.

[46]EP, Table 5.

[47]7 *Federal Register*, 6593.

[48]EP, Table 5.

[49]JAW, 152.

[50]EP, Table 5.

[51]EP, Table 5.

[52]JD, 189.

[53]EP, Table 5.

[54]PWC, 120.

[55]JAW, 154.

[56]PWC, 133.

[57]S, 45-49.

[58]JIQJ, 195-200.

[59]S, 45-49.

[60]S, 45-49.

[61]AJ, vol. 2, no. 2.

[62]PWC, 359.

NOTES

[63]NARG 338; Memo from Bendetsen to DeWitt 5/3/43.

[64]JAW, 150.

[65]PWC, 169.

[66]PJD, 256.

[67]PJD, 256.

[68]PJD, 246.

[69]RS, 12/19/81.

[70]RS, 12/19/81.

[71]RS, 12/19/81.

[72]CWRIC, 8718-8722.

[73]PJD, 257.

[74]DCK, 61.

[75]PJD, 257.

[76]DCK, 61.

[77]EP, Table 5.

[78]DCK, 61; RS, 12/19/81.

[79]JAW, 309.

[80]DCK, 61.

[81]EP, Table 5.

[82]PJD, 235.

[83]JAW, 345.

[84]PWC, 173-174; CWRIC, 9611-9614.

[85]EP, Table 5.

[86]EP, Table 5.

[87]EP, Table 5.

[88]EP, Table 5.

[89]EP, Table 5.

[90]EP, Table 5.

[91]EP, Table 5.

[92]EP, Table 5.

[93]EP, Table 5.

Chapter 3

Chapter 4

[1]YOI, 73.

[2]YOI, 73-74.

[3]FO contains a good account of this history.

[4]YOI, 55-56.

[5]PJD, 223.

[6]Arnold Krammer, *Nazi Prisoners of War in America*, Stein & Day, 1979, 271.

[7]NYN, 11/19/81.

[8]NYN, 11/19/81.

[9]JIQJ, 167.

[10]*Harper's*, February 1983.

[11]Unpublished transcripts of CWRIC hearings.

Chapter 5

[1]PJD, 103.

[2]DRJA, 113.

[3]DRJA contains an excellent set of documents substantiating this thesis.

[4]Excellent accounts of this tragic event are published in YOI and in Arthur A. Hansen and David A. Hacker's essay, "The Manzanar Riot: An Ethnic Perspective," published in *Amerasia Journal*, 1974, vol. 2, no 2.

[5]YOI, 122.

[6]S, 364.

[7]EP, 90.

[8]Letter from Joseph Y. Kurihara to Yoshiko Hosoi. I obtained a copy of this letter from Kurihara's good friend, Harry Ueno.

[9]RS, 12/19/81.

[10]PJD 187.
[11]CWRIC, 20026.
[12]DCK, 61.

Chapter 6

[1]AJ, vol. 2, no. 2, 73.
[2]Raymond Okamura, who cochaired the National Ad Hoc Committee with Mr. Uno, has written an excellent essay on this subject in *Amerasia Journal*, vol. 2, no. 2.
[3]JIQJ, 279-280.

Chapter 7

[1]JAW, 78.
[2]PC, 4/6/79.
[3]PC, 4/6/79.
[4]AJ, vol. 2 no. 2, "Background and History of Repeal Campaign," Raymond Okamura.
[5]JACL Bulletin, April 7, 1942.
[6]CWRIC, 20032.
[7]Japanese term for persons of Japanese ancestry who are not citizens of Japan, including Japanese-Americans.
[8]At 3/3/79 of meeting of National Committee for Redress of the JACL.

Chapter 8

[1]Charles W. Ferguson, *Organizing to Beat the Devil*, Doubleday & Co., 1971.

NOTES

[2]NL, 11/3/79.
[3]HH, 3.
[4]NL, 5/5/80; RS, 7-81.

Chapter 9

[1]RS, 3/13/80.
[2]HS. All following quotes in this chapter are from this hearing.

Chapter 10

Chapter 11

[1]HH. All following quotes in this chapter are from this hearing.
[2]Emphasis derived from audio tape of HH.

Chapter 12

[1]BP, 323-327.

Chapter 13

[1]*Los Angeles Times*, April 2, 1981.

Chapter 14

[1]This and all other quotes are from the unpublished transcripts of the CWRIC hearings, except as noted.

Chapter 15

[1]RS, 8/21/81.
[2]This and all other quotes are from the unpublished transcripts of the CWRIC hearings, except as noted.
[3]FO, 211.
[4]CWRIC 26391, Letter from Marshall to General Emmons, October 7, 1943.
[5]Edwin O. Reischauer, *The Japanese*, Harvard University Press, 1977, 152-153.
[6]RS 8/21/81.
[7]Ibid.

Chapter 16

[1]This and all other quotes are from the unpublished transcripts of the CWRIC hearings, except as noted.
[2]It is the American Convention on Human Rights, signed during the Carter Administration on June 1, 1977, and submitted for ratification by President Carter to the U.S. Senate on February 23, 1978.
[3]Robert A. Wilson and Bill Hosokawa, *East to America*, William Morrow and Co., 1980, 168.
[4]PJD, 191.
[5]PJD, 192.

Chapter 17

[1]This and all other quotes are from the unpublished transcripts of the CWRIC hearings, except as noted.

Chapter 18

[1]This and all other quotes are from the unpublished transcripts of the CWRIC hearings, except as noted.

[2]Milton Mayer, *They Thought They Were Free*, University of Chicago Press, 1955.

Chapter 19

[1]Bendetsen's testimony is taken from the NYN 11/12/81.
[2]This and all other quotes are from the unpublished transcripts of the CWRIC hearings, except as noted.
[3]McCloy's testimony is taken from the NYN 11/19/81.
[4]Alan Brinkley, "Minister Without Portfolio," *Harper's*, February 1983.

Chapter 20

[1]This and all other quotes are from the unpublished transcripts of the CWRIC hearings, except as noted.
[2]PJD, 189.
[3]CWRIC, 20031-20036.
[4]Ibid.
[5]YOI, 73.

Chapter 21

Chapter 22

[1]A copy of the Complaint may be obtained from NCJAR, 925 West Diversey Parkway, Chicago, Illinois 60625 for a nominal fee.
[2]For causes of action not standing in tort, i.e., constitutional violations, the lawsuit specifies the maximum of $10,000. For causes of action standing in tort, the amount is left for the jury to determine.
[3]These and all other quotes are from the Complaint, except as noted.
[4]YOI, 253.

Chapter 23

[1]At the time of filing, there were only twenty-one causes of action. Thus, 25 billion dollars is the proper estimate. Later, when a twenty-second cause of action was added, the estimate became 27 billion dollars.

[2]In many class actions, there may be members of the class who would prefer to file their own claims. The courts provide for them the option to "opt out."

Chapter 24

Chapter 25

[1]Transcripts of Proceedings in the United States District Court of Appeals for the District of Columbia Circuit, William Hohri, et al., appellants v. United States of America, appellees, No. 84-5460, Washington, D.C., September 24, 1985, 29.

[2]Opinion, United States Court of Appeals for the District of Columbia Circuit, No. 84-5460, decided January 21, 1986, 46.

[3]Ibid., 56.

[4]Brief for Respondents, On Writ of Certiorari to the United States Court of Appeals for the District of Columbia Circuit, No. 86-510, 21.

[5]Ibid., 26.

[6]Official Transcript, Proceedings before the Supreme Court of the United States, Case no. 86-510, United States, Petitioner v. William Hohri, et al., Washington, D.C., April 20, 1987 (Revised Copy). This and the other quotes are from this transcript.

[7]*San Francisco Chronicle*, April 21, 1987.

[8]Sue Embry provided this translation.

[9]Richard Drinnon, unpublished speech read at the Manzanar Pilgrimage, April 25, 1987.

BIBLIOGRAPHY

Chuman, Frank F. *The Bamboo People: The Law and Japanese-Americans.* Del Mar, California: Publisher's Inc., 1976.

Commission on Wartime Relocation and Internment of Civilians. *Personal Justice Denied.* Washington, D.C.: U.S. Government Printing Office, 1982.

Daniels, Roger. *The Decision to Relocate the Japanese Americans.* New York: J. B. Lippincott, 1975.

Concentration Camps USA: Japanese Americans and World War II. New York: Holt, Rinehart and Winston, 1970.

Daniels, Roger; Sandra C. Taylor; and Harry H. L. Kitano. *Japanese Americans From Relocation to Redress.* Salt Lake City: University of Utah Press, 1986.

DeWitt, Lieutenant General J. L. *Final Report: Japanese Evacuation From the West Coast, 1942.* Washington, D.C.: Government Printing Office, 1943.

Drinnon, Richard. *Keeper of Concentration Camps: Dillon S. Myer and American Racism.* Berkeley: University of California Press, 1987.

Eisenhower, Milton S. *The President is Calling.* Garden City, New York: Doubleday & Co., 1974.

Embrey, Sue Kunitomi; Arthur A. Hansen; and Betty Kulberg Mitson. *Manzanar Martyr: An Interview with Harry Ueno.* The Oral History Program. Fullerton: California State University, 1986.

Fisher, Anne Reeploeg. *Exile of a Race.* Seattle: F. & T. Publishers, 1965.

Gardiner, C. Harvey. *Pawns in a Triangle of Hate: The Peruvian Japanese and the United States.* Seattle: University of Washington Press, 1981.

Girdner, Audrie, and Anne Loftis. *The Great Betrayal: The Evacuation of the Japanese-Americans During World War II.* New York: Macmillan, 1969.

Grodzins, Morton. *Americans Betrayed: Politics and the Japanese Evacuation.* Chicago: University of Chicago Press, 1949.

Hansen, Arthur A., and David A. Hacker. "The Manzanar Riot: An Ethnic Perspective." *Amerasia Journal*, vol. 2, no. 2, Fall 1974.

Hansen, Arthur A., and Betty E. Mitson, eds. *Voices Long Silent: An Oral Inquiry Into the Japanese American Evacuation.* Fullerton: California State University, 1974.

Hosokawa, Bill. *JACL in Quest of Justice.* New York: William Morrow and Co., Inc., 1982.

Irons, Peter. *Justice at War.* New York: Oxford University Press, 1983.

Ishigo, Estelle. *Lone Heart Mountain.* Los Angeles: Anderson, Ritchie & Simon, 1972.

Kitagawa, Daisuke. *Issei and Nisei: The Internment Years.* New York: The Seabury Press, 1967.

Kikuchi, Charles. *The Kikuchi Diary: Chronicle From an American Concentration Camp.* Edited by John Modell. Champaign, Illinois: University of Illinois Press, 1973.

Kitano, Harry H. L. *Japanese Americans: The Evolution of a Subculture.* Englewood Cliffs, New Jersey: Prentice-Hall, 1969.

Kogawa, Joy. *Obasan.* Boston: David R. Godine, Publisher, 1982.

Leighton, Alexander H. *The Governing of Men: General Principles and Recommendations Based on Experience at a Japanese Relocation Camp.* Princeton: Princeton University Press, 1945.

Mori, Taisanboku; Muin Ozaki; Keiho Soga; Sojin Takei. *Poets Behind Barbed Wire.* Edited and translated by Jiro Nakano and Kay Nakano. Honolulu: Bamboo Ridge Press, 1983.

Myer, Dillon S. *Uprooted Americans: The Japanese Americans and the War Relocation Authority During World War II.* Tucson: University of Arizona Press, 1970.

Nicholson, Herbert V. *Treasure in Earthen Vessels.* Whittier, California: Penn Lithographics Inc., 1974.

Okada, John. *No-No Boy.* Rutland, Vermont and Tokyo: Charles E. Tuttle, 1957.

Okubo, Mine. *Citizen 13660.* New York: Columbia University Press, 1946.

Rostow, Eugene V. "Our Worst Wartime Mistake." *Harper's* 191 (1945): 193-201.

BIBLIOGRAPHY

Saiki, Patsy Sumie. *Ganbare! An Example of Japanese Spirit.* Honolulu: Kisaku, Inc., 1982.

Sone, Monica. *Nisei Daughter.* Boston: Little, Brown, 1953.

Suzuki, Lester E. *Ministry in the Assembly and Relocation Centers of World War II.* Berkeley: Yardbird Publishing Co., 1979.

Tateishi, John. *And Justice for All: An Oral History of the Japanese American Detention Camps.* New York: Random House, 1984.

tenBroek, Jacobus; Edward N. Barnhart; and Floyd W. Matson. *Prejudice, War and the Constitution.* Berkeley and Los Angeles: University of California Press, 1954.

Thomas, Dorothy Swaine, and Richard S. Nishimoto. *The Spoilage.* Berkeley and Los Angeles: University of California Press, 1946.

Thorne, Christopher. *Allies of a Kind: The United States, Britain, and the War Against Japan, 1941-1945.* New York: Oxford University Press, 1978.

Weglyn, Michi. *Years of Infamy: The Untold Story of America's Concentration Camps.* New York: William Morrow and Co., Inc., 1976.

Yamada, Mitsuye. *Camp Notes and Other Poems.* San Lorenzo, California: Shameless Hussy Press, 1976.

INDEX

A

Abe, Frank, 48, 49, 98; testimony of, 136-39
ACLU. *See* American Civil Liberties Union
Agriculture Department. *See* Department of Agriculture
"A Jap's a Jap!", iv, 17, 21, 102, 193
Akgulian, Laura, 220
Akiya, Karl: testimony of, 175-76
Akutsu, Jim H.: testimony of, 131-32
Alaskan Defense Command, 205
Aleuts, 71, 73, 75
Alien Enemy Property Commission, 171
Allies of a Kind: the United States, Britain and the War Against Japan, 22, 137
Amended Complaint: filing of, 207
American-Japanese Evacuation Claims Act of 1948, 205; opposition to, 206-7. *See also* Japanese-American Evacuation Claims Act of 1948
American Baptist Churches U.S.A., 85
American Civil Liberties Union, 7, 11, 55, 65, 79, 142, 144, 159, 172, 182, 218; National Capital Area, 218; redress and, 56, 160; of southern California, 218
American Convention on Human Rights, 60
American Friends Service Committee, 134, 135, 217
American Jewish Committee, 118, 218
American Jewish Congress, 218
American Loyalty League, 6
Americans Betrayed, 187, 222
Americans for Historical Accuracy, 95-96
Americans of Japanese Ancestry, 12
Anti-Axis Committee, 7, 8, 176
Anti-Defamation League of B'nai B'rith, 217
Anti-Semitism, 136; practice of, 156. *See also* Racism
"An Appeal to Obtain Redress for the World War II Evacuation and Imprisonment of Japanese Americans": contents of, 39-40
Application for Leave Clearance. *See* Loyalty oath
Armstrong, Jack, 16, 193
Army Intelligence, 112, 165
Asian American Law Students Association, 59
Asian Legal Defense and Education Fund, 217
Asian Pacific American Federal Employees Council, 83

Assembly centers, 7, 11; terminology of, 96
Axelrad, Jeffrey, 203-4, 212, 215

B

Bainbridge Island: exclusion from, 9
Baker, Lillian, 87, 92, 106, 111, 124, 158; testimony of, 95-96, 107-9
Baldwin, Roger, 11
Baler, Blanche Kimoto, 220, 223
Bamboo People, 187
Bannai, Lorraine: testimony of, 117
Bannai, Paul: appointment of, 88
Barnett, Arthur: testimony of 124-25
Barrows, Leland, 89, 92, 108
Basoms, Alice, 220
Bataan Death March, 10, 193
Bay Area Attorneys for Redress, 117
Bendetsen, Karl R., 10, 13, 21, 24, 28, 87, 89, 97, 145-46, 148, 152, 164, 166, 177, 186, 212; appointment of, 9; duties of, 5; testimony of, 157-59
Benedict, Ruth: writing of, 111
Bernstein, Joan, 4, 88, 89, 90, 95, 96, 99, 141, 143, 144, 148, 156, 157, 159, 161; appointment of, 85; CWRIC and, 1
"Better Americans in a Greater America," 126, 129
Biddle, Francis, 8, 91, 158, 159, 160, 178
Bird, Kai, 220
Birth rates: incarceration and, 133-34
Black, Hugo, 96
Black, Lloyd D., 12
Block Managers Evacuee Food Committee, 103
Board of Church and Society, 44, 217
Bonneville Broadcasting, 203
Borderline, 168
Bork, Judge: dissent of, 217
British Museum, 51
Broadway High School, 125
Brooke, Edward, 2, 112, 119, 138-39, 148, 158, 163, 169; appointment of, 85
Brown, G. Gordon: community analysis by, 153
Buck, Pearl: warnings of, iii
Bureau of Census. *See* Census Bureau
Byrne, Jane, 148

C

Cajka, Cynthia, 220
California-Nevada Conference of the United Methodist Church (1981), 111; resolution of, 112